FRE QUENT FLY YER

BOB REISS

One plane,

One passenger,

and the spectacular feat of commercial flight

SIMON & SCHUSTER
NEW YORK LONDON SYDNEY TORONTO TOKYO SINGAPORE

SIMON & SCHUSTER
Rockefeller Center
1230 Avenue of the Americas
New York, New York 10020

Designed by Songhee Kim
Manufactured in the United States of America

10 9 8 7 6 5 4 3 2 1

Library of Congress Cataloging-in-Publication Data.
Reiss, Bob.
    Frequent flyer : one plane, one passenger, and the spectacular
feat of commercial flight / Bob Reiss.
        p   cm.
    Includes index.
    1. Aeronautics, Commerical.   I. Title.
    HE9776.R44   1994
    387.7—dc20
                                                        93-34983
                                                            CIP

ISBN: 0-671-77650-9

ACKNOWLEDGMENTS

A VERY SPECIAL THANKS TO CRAIG, KATHY, LARA AND EMILY ARONOFF, BUDDY DOLL, JOHN G. FULLER AND HIS BOOK, *The Ghost of Flight 401*, PHIL GERARD, ZIA KHAN, W. DAVID LEWIS AND WESLEY PHILLIPS NEWTON, AND THEIR BOOK, *Delta: The History of an Airline,* ALICE MAYHEW, JACK MCMAHAN, CHRIS AND LISA MERRILL, ESTHER NEWBERG, PAULETTE O'DONNELL, LES RAMIREZ, CARL SOLBERG AND HIS EXCELLENT BOOK *Conquest of the Skies*, WHICH SUPERBLY TELLS THE STORY OF AVIATION HISTORY, WILLIAM T. TURNER, AND BROOK WILLIAMS AND TERRY TEMPEST WILLIAMS.

IN A FEW INSTANCES I HAVE CHANGED A PERSON'S NAME AT HIS OR HER REQUEST.

CONTENTS

PROLOGUE

Several years before beginning work on this book about commercial airplanes, I nearly fell into the Atlantic Ocean in one.

It was winter, 1989. As my wife and I packed for a long-awaited ski vacation, the last thing on our minds was an air accident. We'd blocked out ten days of free time, found a cheap fare on Swissair to Zurich, and booked reservations in an alpine inn where we looked forward to Swiss wine, fondue, hot chocolate, and spectacular scenery.

Loading our Honda for the ride from Brooklyn to JFK Airport, we were like millions of other air travelers that day. We didn't think about the thousands of acts necessary to get our 747 from New York to Switzerland. We wondered what the movie would be. Pam had a stack of *Glamour* magazines. I'd bought a Ken Follett novel.

We figured we'd sleep on the overnight flight.

The weather was clear. No storms. As we drove along Eastern Parkway toward Queens, we could make out the markings on the big jets coming in over Brooklyn toward Flushing Bay, arriving from all parts of the world. I recognized the long white background and red lettering of TWA. The baby blue "Clipper" on a Pan Am Air Bus. Every half minute, another plane. Northwest. Eastern. United. Lufthansa.

A scant eighty years earlier, an aircraft filled with passengers would have drawn thousands of awestruck gapers. But by 1989 a flying machine able to carry 300 people from New York to California in the time it would take the driver of a car to reach Boston,

Massachusetts, from Manhattan, was as natural as television. Or taxicabs.

Still, we started talking about air travel. Pam had grown up in a small town in New England, had been captivated as a girl by photographs of stewardesses wearing stylish caps and long white gloves. Girls actually paid to fly all over the world. "I loved the gloves," she said, running one hand up her arm, as if putting them on. "They seemed so elegant."

Pam had decided to become a flight attendant. In high school she'd told her guidance counselor, and he'd laughed at her. To the counselor, straight-A students like Pam could do better than becoming what he considered glorified waitresses. Years later, when she *was* a stewardess, flying international, spending her nights in Cairo or London or Athens, she'd run into the man again, back in New England. Wistfully, he'd said, "I envy you."

I told Pam I'd grown up within thirty minutes of the biggest international airport in the United States at the time, but as far as people in my neighborhood were concerned, Idlewild Airport, soon to be renamed Kennedy, might as well have been on the other side of the planet. Nobody I knew got to fly on airplanes. Once, in a group of cub scouts, I'd visited the control tower at LaGuardia and watched, entranced, as the lumbering prop planes and early jets filled the windows, coming in.

I told Pam about the time my mother and I had driven my father, a young attorney, to the new TWA terminal at Idlewild for his first out-of-town business trip. This was in the 1960s, when commercial aviation was finally becoming affordable to millions of average Americans who had never been in a plane until World War II. My father looked proud. A business trip on an airplane was a milestone for him. I still remembered him walking out of view in the terminal, with his lawyer's briefcase. He'd come back from New Mexico tanned, wearing a cowboy hat.

Later my parents had saved enough of their own money to actually take a vacation on an airplane. In January, with snow on the ground, they'd come back from Antigua with photographs showing them standing on a long white beach, in front of aquamarine water. An impossibly magical sight.

But now it was years later, and I was a journalist, and had gotten so used to flying I never thought about those days anymore. I'd been lucky enough in my work to travel widely. I loved it but never considered the flying machines that made it possible.

We parked in the long-term lot and rode a bus to the Swissair terminal, checked our luggage, went through security, and boarded a 747 as dark was falling in New York. Pam flipped open a *Glamour*. I watched the movie screen in front of our cabin. Swissair displayed a map of the Northeast United States and Atlantic on it. There was a little cartoon jet on the ground in New York.

The screen also broadcast our altitude, 24 feet at the moment in the cabin, and our speed, zero.

As the plane began moving, so did the numbers. Fifty miles an hour. A hundred. Liftoff at 178. At 600 feet high, outside my window, New York glittered and tilted while the plane banked. The Cross Island Parkway was a ribbon of white headlights and crimson taillights. The bridges linking Manhattan to the outer boroughs were lighted in emerald green. The towers of the financial district grew smaller, and then they were gone, and I looked down at the beaches of Rockaway as the big jet crossed the border between land and ocean. In the mass of black below, a few ships broke the sense of void with red and green lights.

The cartoon jet on the video screen swerved around and faced Europe across the long Atlantic. Little dots extended back to Kennedy Airport, showing the portion of route we had traveled.

An hour later, as flight attendants served drinks and dinner, at an altitude of 33,000 feet, there was a crashing noise, and the plane seemed to lift up momentarily and jerk down. Luggage racks fell open. Someone cried out. On the screen, our speed and altitude began dropping. A stewardess talked urgently into a phone near the galley, jammed the receiver into its cradle, and rushed toward the cockpit. I asked what had happened.

"I don't know," she said, white. "I saw flames coming out of an engine."

Our altitude dropped to 31,000 feet. Thirty thousand. Twenty-nine.

The captain addressed us over the intercom.

"We've lost an engine," he said as if it were no big deal, although the numbers kept dropping. We could still make it to Switzerland, he said, but "we have a choice." We could keep going or turn around.

"Let's turn around," I told Pam. But the captain was into logistics. On one hand, if the weather held and the three remaining engines kept functioning, which they should, reaching Switzerland would be easy. And if not Switzerland, definitely France.

On the other hand, if there was a snowstorm in France, we might have a problem. But probably we wouldn't have a problem, he said.

The bottom line was, the pilot would keep heading toward Europe for twenty more minutes and then make up his mind.

"That's 150 more miles we have to make up," I said, "if he goes back."

Twenty minutes later the captain decided to head back to New York.

For the next two hours the plane limped toward the mainland, still losing altitude. We dropped to 18,000 feet, 17,500 feet, 16,000. The speed dropped to 250 miles an hour. I told Pam, "Why don't they take those stupid numbers off the screen?"

To make matters worse, I started remembering crash stories. I remembered a woman who lived in my parents' current neighborhood, who had survived a Mohawk Airlines crash. She'd been in the hospital for months. And walked around with a cane for half a year after that. "She survived because she sat in the back of the plane," my mother had told me. Pam and I were near the front.

I also remembered an art gallery in Brooklyn that sold black-and-white photographs of the worst air disaster ever to happen in New York, which had resulted in part of a United Airlines jet falling in my neighborhood, burning, killing three. In the photo, the smashed tail section lay near a church on Seventh Avenue. The jet had collided with a TWA plane.

When the pilot announced we'd be landing soon, I decided I'd never been so happy to see the lights of New York. Fire trucks lined the runway. We touched down, and the passengers burst into applause.

Then, amid the celebration, the captain's voice came over the intercom again. Swissair would try to get all of us on flights to Switzerland tonight, he said. A Pan Am jet was due to take off soon, and many of us would be on it.

But the passengers erupted. "I'm not going on Pan Am,"

snapped someone behind us. Pan Am's Flight 101 had been blown up by terrorists over Lockerbie, Scotland, a few months before. The same passengers who had sat cooperatively during the engine loss now panicked at the prospect of flying on Pan Am.

That night, on another Swissair plane, over the Atlantic again, I started thinking. What really happened tonight? Who flies these planes anyway? How do they train? Who maintains the engines? Who cleared all that airspace over New York when we had to come back?

The questions multiplied. Back home after the vacation, I kept wondering what went on behind the scenes in aviation? Then my agent called and told me Alice Mayhew, an editor at Simon & Schuster, was looking for a writer to do a book on a plane. Was I interested?

I was. Over breakfast at Rockefeller Center, and in later meetings at Simon & Schuster on Sixth Avenue, we outlined a book. It would be for average fliers, like us. People who flew regularly but had no idea what went on behind the scenes. It would be nontechnical but would include some technical detail. It would cover commercial aviation from the Wright Brothers to crashes to pilots to terrorism.

And it would do it all by focusing on one plane. One average jet I would fly everywhere with.

After all, we figured, anything affecting aviation affects every plane.

I would need an airline's permission to fly in the cockpit with the pilots. I would have to spend time with flight attendants, mechanics, company executives, and ground personnel who worked on the plane. At corporate headquarters I would learn how an airline ran. I would meet the engineers who had designed the plane. The management who'd risked millions of dollars on such a big purchase. I would try to learn what special skills were necessary to keep an airline healthy in the 1990s, as weaker companies went broke. I would visit Air Traffic Control centers to meet the controllers who held the fate of the plane in their hands each time it traveled through their airspace.

We wrote Delta and United Airlines, asking if they would be interested in participating in the project.

United responded from Chicago that the book sounded "interesting" but their rule was that writers at the company needed public relations escorts at all times. United couldn't spare the personnel, and I wasn't interested in a watchdog type of arrangement anyway.

Alabama-born Delta archivist Paulette O'Donnell called up from Atlanta headquarters. The proposal had been circulated among senior executives. "We'll do it," she said.

I explained the criteria for choosing a plane. We wanted a wide-body plane with some history to it, that flew to scattered destinations, including exotic vacation spots. She said Delta's Lockheed 1011s, or TriStars, seemed a good bet. They were Delta's biggest jet and had been carrying passengers for the company since 1974. The international models flew to Hong Kong, Frankfurt, Tokyo, Bombay. Larger TriStars with shorter range fuel tanks carried up to 302 passengers per trip to U.S. cities including New York, Los Angeles, Atlanta, Dallas, Honolulu, Miami, Chicago, Salt Lake City, San Francisco, and Seattle.

"The TriStars are the queens of our fleet," Paulette said.

And the fleet had an unusual history. Delta, originally a crop-dusting operation so tiny it was blocked from carrying the U.S. Mail by the Postmaster General, who awarded the lucrative contracts back in 1930 to competitors like United, American, Pan Am, and TWA, had risen in the intervening years to become the fourth largest carrier in the world. When I was growing up, Delta was considered a small southern airline, if Yankee fliers considered it at all. Then it merged with Northeast, then Western. Then it acquired Pan Am, staying healthy as airlines who once mocked them went out of business.

By the time I talked with Paulette, it seemed half the fliers I knew traveled on Delta. A Seattle poet told me he was giving a reading in New Mexico, flying Delta. A Brooklyn businessman was cashing in his frequent-flier miles and going to Hong Kong, on a Delta L-1011. A musician visiting his son in Israel. An Atlanta business consultant heading for Hartford. A Korean grocer visiting his birthplace in Seoul. A Moscow-born taxicab driver just emigrated into New York. In 1991 alone, Delta carried 77 million passengers.

Also, if the health of an airline is linked to its labor-management relations, Delta was the only big airline that had no unions outside of ALPA, the pilots' organization. When I started the book, at least, the company had not laid off employees since 1957, even during recessions. This was clearly a different policy from, say, TWA, where flight attendants had been furloughed, laid off, and finally fired during a stormy strike. Delta attendants, during similar times of economic hardship, had initiated a company-wide employee effort to *buy* the company a plane in gratitude. That kind of labor-management relationship didn't seem to exist at other airlines. Why?

I planned chapters on management. And labor relations.

On paper, at least, Delta looked good.

"Looks like I'll be living in Atlanta for a few months," I told Pam.

"Sounds like they must be confident in their operation if you're not going to be supervised," she said.

Four months later on a battleship-gray March morning, I ran through a cold Atlanta downpour toward a parked jet in Delta Airline's "runup area," for repair, near the corporation's maintenance hangers at Hartsfield International Airport.

Ship 714, an eighteen-year-old widebody jet, sat with one of its three engines roaring, in a far corner of the taxiway, facing a corner of a steel windbreak or "blast deflector," which looked like an avalanche fence and was designed to keep jetwash from blasting onto an airport roadway 50 feet beyond it and blowing cars over. Nestled in the corner, 714 reminded me of a student being punished. The green warning light was on. Jet wash shot back, hit the pounding drops, and formed a long tube of shimmering air that looked like minnows flashing in shallow water.

Tomorrow I would start three days of flying with 714. Wherever it went, I would go. If the schedule changed, I'd stick with the plane. If the crews changed, I'd stay with 714. Looking up at the front of the plane I was struck by the resemblance, at this angle, to a bottlenose dolphin, with its black nose cone and wide sloping forehead over cockpit windows looking like eyes. The belly was painted silver, with 714 in dark blue on the open nose gear doors. The fuselage seemed flatter on bottom and more curved at the top, and appendages, which looked like toy rudders, jutted from the plane's outer frame or "skin" at regular intervals. These were streamlined antennas.

The upper body was white, with a red TriStar spread-eagle logo on the tail, by the word "TriStar." In fact when landing, a TriStar looks like a bird of prey; nose up, wings back to slow descent, twin four-wheel rear landing gears extended like reaching talons. But on the ground the planes look plain beside larger, sleeker widebodies like the 747.

"She's a baby, she's a baby," one pilot instructor had told me, patting 714 like a favorite horse.

The engineers designing Lockheed TriStars had given them three engines. One on each wing. One on the tail above the plane. A few years back, the fortunate location of the third engine had enabled a Delta pilot named Jack McMahan to save what otherwise would have been an out-of-control TriStar one night out of San Diego. McMahan had told me the story and played the chilling flight recording for me in his Atlanta basement. I planned to put his story in a chapter about pilots.

For months I'd been learning about Delta Air Lines, aviation in general, and 714, interviewing corporate officers, pilots, mechanics, air traffic controllers, FAA inspectors and crash investigators, Washington lobbyists, engineers who had designed 714, flight attendants, historians. I'd read books and articles on aviation and airline history. I'd spent hours at the Smithsonian Air and Space Museum in Washington, gazing up at the original Wright Brothers' Flyer. I'd walked the sand dunes at Kitty Hawk, North Carolina. I'd even flown in the cockpit of other Lockheed 1011s, getting a feel for the planes and the people who flew them.

Now it was time to show how all these factors and people coalesced into a system enabling a 400,000-pound aluminum tube to fly halfway around the globe and back, avoid bad weather, thread skies filled with other flying machines, do it safely, on a time schedule, and do it so effortlessly that the people paying for a ride would spend more time considering the state of the baked chicken they were eating than the fact that they were 40,000 feet above the earth inside a machine guiding itself by autopilot.

Paulette the archivist laughed when I told her my plan. "You won't sleep," she warned. "I don't think you realize how much those planes stay in the air."

At the moment, if everything went on schedule, 714 would fly twelve legs in the next three days, to destinations including Salt Lake City, Los Angeles, Maui, Las Vegas. I'd fly to New York and Orlando and Atlanta and back.

"That's what you think," Paulette had laughed. "In aviation things change by the hour."

Now, out in the warmup area, it was time to meet my plane. No ladder led to 714's door today, so I would have to use a trapdoor. I climbed onto the hood of a small tractor which had hauled the plane to its parking spot, and hefted myself up into a narrow electronics room, or "avionics compartment," which felt like the cramped hold of a ship and lay directly beneath the cockpit.

I could hear rain outside hitting the plane. There was a faint greasy odor. Dozens of black boxes slightly smaller than automobile batteries lined steel shelves. They comprised the electrical system of 714.

There were no wall panels down here, just the shell of the plane, and behind the shelves and boxes, I made out steel cables running back toward the wings. They reminded me of frailer wires on the original Wright Flyer, in Washington's Air and Space Museum. Eighty years after Kitty Hawk, the logistics of flight control hadn't changed since Orville and Wilbur Wright figured out you could steer an airplane by adjusting the control surfaces of the wings. Accordingly, the cables were linked to the flaps on the back of 714's wings.

Inside the compartment I eased down a cramped aisle leading to a small peephole in a wall. It looked out on the landing gear. The hole was designed to let a crew member visually double-check whether the gear were down, in case cockpit warning lights indicated they were stuck. Often it's the light that malfunctions, not the gears. A peephole like this one had played a key role in the crash of an L-1011 in the Everglades in 1972. I planned to tell that story in a chapter on ghosts.

I climbed up a steel ladder and emerged into the empty cockpit. Seven-fourteen was in the runup area today after the number 2 engine had delivered less than full power during takeoff the day before. Nothing dangerous. But the captain had reported it for repair. Mechanics had adjusted the throttle linkages, the cables controlling the amount of power the engine gave out. There had never been anything wrong with the engine. Just the cables. Now mechanics were testing engine number 2 to ensure it had been adjusted properly.

I walked into the cabin. The power was off. Gray, weak light sifted in through the windows, accentuating the sense of intimacy. Rain battered the roof. I smelled polish. I sat alone in First Class and watched rain stream down the window. I walked down the aisles, and cardboard strips protecting the vacuumed carpet rustled underneath. In the Coach section, row after row of gold and aquamarine seats were empty, clean, ready for passengers. There was a polished coffeepot in the galley, an ice bucket on the floor, an unopened bottle of Charles Lefranc Cellars 1988 on one Coach seat, with a plastic bag filled with cups beside it, as if someone had been interrupted when they were about to have a party.

The galley also featured an elevator that took flight attendants down to a galley beneath the Coach section. Stories of sex-on-planes that I'd heard centered around the galley and elevator. I planned to tell those stories in a chapter about flight attendants.

Back in the empty cockpit, raindrop shadows ran down control consoles for the pilot, copilot, and engineer. Every part of the plane was controlled from here. Rain coursed down the windshield.

During March 1992, the month which was ending, 714 had flown to New York, Los Angeles, Boston, San Diego, Las Vegas, Cincinnati, Maui, Dallas, Portland, Salt Lake City. By April 1992, 714 had been flying Delta passengers for eighteen years. It had been in the air 53,769 hours. Had made 28,908 takeoffs and landings. Conservatively guessing it had flown half-full all that time, I calculated it had safely carried over 3 million people around the United States.

I left 714 for my Atlanta apartment, packed and went to dinner with friends: a Georgia Supreme Court clerk named Les Ramirez and an Emory University law school junior named Ruth Heinzmann. We ate at an Atlanta restaurant called Lettuce Souprise You. Over dinner, the conversation turned to dreams. We tried to remember the best dreams we'd ever had.

"In my favorite dream," Les said, "I was flying. Not in a plane.

Just me, soaring through the air in a time before people. I flew over forests, rivers." Les smiled. "It was beautiful."

"I used to have my favorite dream a lot when I was little," Ruth said. "I was flying too. Everyone would watch me, envy me. I even tried to fly when I was awake," she said shyly. "I used to jump off walls and think I would stay in the air. I was surprised when I didn't."

Ruth added, "I hurt my head when I jumped off a wall once, and the doctor told me if I kept trying to fly, I could do damage. So I finally stopped."

My own favorite dream had come in junior high school. I'd been walking alone in my old Queens, New York, neighborhood on a clear night, when I'd seen a flying saucer in the sky. "As soon as I saw it," I said, "I was yanked by my feet into the air. I was pulled through the sky toward the saucer. The whole neighborhood—the cars, streets, and houses—got smaller. But I wasn't scared. I was excited. I thought, This is the greatest thing that's ever happened to me. I was going to travel, to see new places. I don't think I've ever been so disappointed as I was when I woke up."

"I wonder why all our favorite dreams involve flying," Les said.

Flying, I thought. FLYING.

I drove home and the phone was ringing. A professor friend was calling to wish me luck on the trip. "What will you ask the pilots?" she said.

I said one thing I'd always wondered was just how a plane manages to stay in the air.

"I know that," she said eagerly. "It's because of fluid mechanics." She started telling me about the way air moves over a curved surface, about how a bigger bulge on the upper part of a wing creates a vacuum above it, and this gave the plane lift. I'd heard this explanation many times. I said, "You live in Hawaii. When you go home from Atlanta, and the plane touches down in Honolulu, do you start applauding with the other passengers?"

"Yes," the professor said.

"Why?" I said. "Fluid mechanics?"

The professor laughed. "No."

"In your heart," I said, "do you really believe a 400,000-pound machine stays in the air because of fluid mechanics?"

She laughed again. I imagined her sitting at home, surrounded by scientific papers and maybe even airline tickets to the cities where she regularly spoke on her specialty, biology. She wouldn't look like a professor at this moment, who gave speeches and won grants and traveled all over the world doing oceanic research. She'd be grinning like a ten-year-old.

"I guess not," she said.

"How come you really think planes fly?" I said.

There was an instant of silence over the line.

Then a giggle. "Magic," she said.

"What If?"

OJ Greene draped his arm over the back of his copilot's chair, looked at me from behind stern-looking reading glasses, and warned, "No talking below 10,000 feet."

No distracting the pilots, was what he meant. No questions. No comments. Once a commercial airliner pushes back from a gate, even a captain who says something like "Think the Braves won last night?" or "Got any gum?" can lose his license if investigators later determine his question caused the crew to miss a crucial air traffic command during takeoff or landing. He and his airline can be fined up to $10,000. That is, if he's still alive to pay.

I stuffed my blue duffel bag under the jump seat and strapped myself in. I had no desire to distract the pilots anyway. I smelled coffee brewing through the open cockpit door from the First Class galley. The flight attendants were greeting passengers trickling into the plane.

It was April 1, 1992, and in half an hour ship 714 would join Delta's 8:30 A.M. push, or fleet departure from Atlanta's Hartsfield International Airport. It would rise into the gray, drizzly morning and head for Salt Lake City, Los Angeles, Honolulu and finally, tonight, the Hawaiian island of Maui. Sunrise on the East Coast. Sunset on the far end of America, on the most isolated group of islands on earth.

"If we lose an engine during takeoff," the big man in the copilot's seat told the pilot, "you want to climb straight ahead. You want max power on the airplane."

Standard talk before any flight. Commercial aviation is the safest means of travel on earth, but the central paradox of the industry is that it stays that way because people who work in it never stop talking about what can go wrong. In 1990, for instance, according to the National Transportation Safety Board, thirty-nine people died in commercial airline accidents in the United States, compared to 24,170 in cars, 6,475 walking across streets, 642 on bicycles, 601 in train crashes, and 865 in recreational boats. It wasn't that OJ Greene was worried about engines failing. But he would be negligent in his job if he didn't cover the possibility.

What if? In stories, questions, casual conversation, pilots never stopped talking about "what if?" What if the control tower gives you the wrong instructions? What if you're heading for a thunderstorm? What if the radio goes dead at a crucial moment? What if you get wind shear? Or lose pressure at 39,000 feet? Suppose a volcano goes off nearby? What do you do if the landing gears get stuck? What if a writer in the jump seat asks questions just when the pilot needs to pay attention to another plane nearby?

I looked around. Even on the ground I had the sensation of hovering in a glass bubble. On a Lockheed 1011, the jump seat occupies a slightly raised position behind the captain and below a ceiling escape hatch for the crew *if* a quick exit is necessary. There are red fire pull handles on the ceiling *if* there's an engine fire, and an arm's length away is an oxygen mask *if* the plane loses pressure.

The pilot and copilot sat in front of me, in pressed white shirts with gold and black epaulettes. The flight engineer, on my right, did preflight checks on a instrument panel that seemed to take up his entire wall. The whole cockpit was filled with so many gauges—running across the instrument panel below the windshield, lining the ceiling above the pilot and copilot, spread over a knee-high platform between them—that it seemed impossible any person could memorize them all. But despite the gauges, the curving window from my hip to head opened the cockpit up, gave light and accentuated the feeling of floating above the runway, 15½ feet below.

OJ Greene bent toward the pilot. Although he occupied the copilot seat, he seemed to be giving the captain instructions instead of the other way around. I realized he was *teaching* the other man how to fly the plane. His student, Malcolm Simpson, was in the final stage of learning to captain an L-1011 and would be at the controls from Atlanta to Salt Lake City. OJ Greene said to him, "Okay. You know the FAA regulation that you can't move the aircraft on the ground while a passenger is out of his seat? Before we push back, the flight attendant tells passengers to sit down. If they won't, stop the plane. Because if there's an FAA man aboard or somebody writes them a letter, you'll be fined. There are so many things to remember, I've got four Ps to help, before pushback." Greene counted them on his fingers: "*People* seated. *Predeparture* clearance information entered into radios and navigation systems. *Panel* updated, meaning the weight of the airplane. *Pushback* checklist. Do the four Ps, and you won't land up pushing back with someone standing up. 'Cause it's not on the checklist."

I'd sat in on pilot training at Delta, but it hadn't occurred to me that 714 might be flown by someone still learning to captain the plane.

But OJ Greene was a "line check airman," a Delta pilot certified by the FAA to instruct and qualify other pilots.

Malcolm Simpson, the tall, boyish-looking, sandy-haired fifty-eight-year-old in the captain's seat, was an Atlanta native and veteran Delta pilot of other planes. He'd grown up loving John Wayne fighter-pilot movies. Had decided to be a fighter pilot but never thought of flying as a job. "I figured I'd go to college, join the service, fly planes, and fly the National Guard afterward."

After getting an engineering degree from Georgia Tech ("A stepping stone to a better life"), Malcolm flew for the Air Force in California. The Guard didn't take him afterward because "they flew F86s and I hadn't." He got a job at Delta's engineering department, where two other fliers, also engineers, "were always talking about becoming commercial pilots. They told me commercial pilots had the best life in the world. Best hours. Best pay. I checked it out and found it was true."

Malcolm talked his boss into arranging an interview with personnel. By the time he boarded 714 this morning, he'd been flying Delta planes for thirty-three years. He'd started on models which could only carry fourteen passengers and fly, depressurized, at 14,000 feet. He'd ended up earning roughly $180,000 a year piloting Boeing 767s to Europe. He could pick the routes he wanted because he had seniority. He lived in a big house next to a country club, with a pool in back and antique golf clubs on the wall and lots of animal statuettes and wind chimes on the patio.

"I wanted the good life. And I got it."

With only three years to go until retirement, Malcolm had gone back to ground school to learn a new plane because he liked the cities the TriStars flew to.

"They go to Copenhagen. Madrid. The 767s lay over in Frankfurt. I don't want to spend my last three years doing that."

Airman OJ Greene, fifty-one, of Snellville, Georgia ("Where everyone is someone," according to the sign at the edge of town), had grown up in a trailer park beside the Charleston, South Carolina, airport. A tall, balding, nonstop gum chewer with an amiable disposition and eyes so blue they seem to emit light, he was still so enthusiastic about flying his wife told me he never stopped talking about it. "I knew when I was a boy that I wanted to fly planes. Other kids in my neighborhood wanted to be police or firemen. But in my dreams I had a scooter, and I flew around my neighborhood on it. An American Airlines pilot who lived in the trailer camp brought me a steel model of a DC-6. I still have it in my basement. With six coats of paint on it."

Greene went to Clemson University and then flew A-4s, a small jet bomber off aircraft carriers, for the Navy. At Delta, his first choice for a job, he piloted DC-9s, 727s, 757s, 767s, and now TriStars, when he wasn't qualifying other pilots.

The reason the FAA often relies on Greene and other line check airmen to train commercial pilots is that, without them, the system would become backlogged, FAA spokesmen say. The FAA doesn't have the manpower to do the job without help.

"But if the government lets you qualify your own people," I'd asked Delta Chief Instructor Bill Gibson in Atlanta, "isn't that an incentive to go easy on them?"

"Absolutely not," he said, and so did everyone else I asked at Delta. "We have pride in our work. And our wives fly on these planes. So do our kids. Our friends. Us. Do you really think we're going to do anything to make them less safe?"

It made sense to me. Now mechanics finished refueling below. The Dobbs Food Service trucks pulled away from the fuselage. The last of the baggage disappeared into the plane. The 168 passengers entrusted to Greene and Malcolm this morning had all boarded. Tammy Mattiello sipped coffee she'd bought in the airport and strapped herself into seat 23J. She was a nurse on her way to Oakland to hook up with her boyfriend in Squaw Valley for a week's vacation. Retired carpenter B. L. Winfield, seventy, was heading to California to visit his sister. "Then to Reno for a family reunion." Eight-year-old Sharon Lane, one of a growing number of children who travel alone, would change planes for South Dakota, where she would visit her dad, divorced from her mother. She was so small her feet barely stretched over her seat. She pulled crayons from a blue-denim shoulder bag. "Usually I go in summer. On airplanes I meet a lot of people. I always wanted to be up high, and now I am."

The flight attendants checked computer-generated passenger lists posted in the galleys. Seat 13G to get a low-calorie meal. Seat 10D was elderly.

OJ told Malcolm, "Stop me if I'm talking too much. I'm a motor mouth. What if you lose *two* engines? One's not so bad. With two you're down to serious stuff. You've lost a lot of systems. Suppose this airplane weighs 379,000 pounds. That means it'll only fly at 3,800 feet above sea level, 'cause of air density. But Salt Lake City is 4,300 feet above sea level."

He was saying that an L-1011 that loses two engines over Salt Lake City will crash unless it gets rid of weight fast.

"So I have another acronym," Greene said in the same informational tone he used talking about seat-belt signs or food service. "CRAP. *C* means *cleanup*. Get the flaps and gear up. *R* is *ram air turbine*. The little air turbine to provide hydraulic pressure to run the flight control. *A* is *APU. Auxiliary power unit*. It can provide electricity to the airplane if you need it. *D* is *dump fuel*. Get the weight off the airplane. Otherwise if you're up to 430,000 pounds in Salt Lake City, and you lift off and lose two, you're not gonna fly."

"You said CRAP," I said from behind them. "CRAP is *P. Dump* is *D*."

Greene chewed gum. "Yeah, but I say it anyway. And the last letter in *dump* is *P*."

Again, it wasn't that Greene thought a two-engine-out would occur. In almost sixty years of combined flying experience, neither he nor Malcolm had ever lost two engines at the same time. They had lost one engine on five separate occasions. Each time they'd landed without problem. Planes have several engines to start with because if one fails, they can fly anyway. New models must be able to fly with an engine out or the FAA will not certify them. And all takeoff numbers are predicated on the loss of an engine.

A flight attendant stuck her head into the cockpit. "Everybody's down!" she said. The plane jerked as a tug began towing us back from the gate. The Delta agent in his red jacket waved good-bye from the boarding ramp. The faces of people pressed against the glass in the waiting area grew smaller. At a salute from a ramp agent, Malcolm fired up the TriStar's three engines, and we proceeded along the concourse ramp toward the runway.

Malcolm steered with his left hand, making small adjustments on a wheel near his hip so small it seemed more appropriate for a bumper car at Coney Island than a 372,000-pound plane.

We passed docked Delta jets, noses still in their boarding gates like animals at a feeding trough. From the glass bubble and through a morning haze, the towers of downtown Atlanta were visible beyond white fuel tanks across the runways, still decorated with the blue logo of recently defunct Eastern Airlines.

"You don't want to stop a big airplane like this in the middle of a turn," OJ said. "Plan ahead. Fully loaded, this plane can weigh as much as 435,000 pounds. You put tremendous stress on the tires, metal, everything if the plane isn't lined up straight on a turn."

On a dike taxiway, we passed the Delta maintenance hangers, where workers swarmed over jets under repair. Time on the ground means lost money. I saw the runup area where I'd first boarded 714 two days ago. OJ worked the radio. Air Traffic Control kept referring to us as a "Delta heavy." That meant we were a big jet and would leave a strong wake of turbulence behind us. Smaller aircraft, like small boats, must steer clear of disturbances caused by bigger jets. Otherwise they could end up like Russian Cosmonaut Yuri A. Gagarin, first Soviet citizen to orbit the earth, who died later when his small MIG-15 fighter plane went out of control after hitting the wake of a heavier MIG-21, north of Moscow on a clear, sunny day. The controller, making a mistake, had ordered him across the jet wash half a mile behind the bigger MIG.

We turned onto the runway.

Greene said to Malcolm, "We've got strobe lights on the back of the wing. We don't want to turn them on *before* we get on the runway, because they'll be flashing in the eyes of the guy behind us. They're so bright pilots can see them fifty miles away. And there's no mandatory rule to turn them on at all. But when you're lined up, you should, because if someone landing on this runway behind us . . . I mean what if you're lined up on the wrong runway? What if he's cleared to land, and the tower forgot they put *you* on the runway? A one in a million chance. But remember that accident in LA? A 737 landing hit a Skywest on the runway? That strobe might have prevented it."

What if. What if.

At the release from the tower, Malcolm pressed down on a foot pedal to release the brakes, and the TriStar began accelerating. The sense of speed was so profound I caught my breath. The ground-speed needle hit 100 miles an hour, 120.

At 140, it touched the first of three small orange markers OJ Greene had set on the dial. He called out "V-1!" Which meant we were now moving too fast to stop the airplane before the runway ran out. At 150 he called "V-R!" Malcolm pulled back on the yoke. The ground fell away below the glass bubble. "V-2!" That meant we were moving at minimum safe climb speed.

We rose into a blue-gray haze, which seemed part mist, part pollution. I saw traffic heading for the airport. Suburbs turning green in early spring. The altimeter spun, numbers rising. On a radar screen by Malcolm's left knee little white jets jerked around like images on a Nintendo screen. An urgent, automated voice cried, "Traffic!" False alarm. It was supposed to warn if planes were close but radar was picking up a 737 already landed on another runway.

Our flight plan called for turning northwest at 4,000 feet today, and heading toward Chattanooga, Nashville, northwest over Farmington, Missouri, over Butler, Missouri, over Salina, Kansas, then Denver, then Vail. If all went well, ship 714 would touch down in

Salt Lake City three hours and thirty-one minutes after taking off. That's less time than the Mormon pioneers who settled the region needed to pack their handcarts for the overland journey nearly 150 years ago.

A warning light flashed on, on the engineer's panel. One of the flaps on the right wing was slightly misaligned with the left. Nothing serious.

The weather looked clear across the United States. The temperature in Salt Lake City was 44 degrees at the moment. And there was a ten-mile-an-hour headwind by the airport.

At 10,000 feet I saw thin, wispy clouds. OJ swung around. "It's okay to talk now. And don't be afraid to interrupt while I speak to Malcolm." He smiled. "Like I said, I'm a motor mouth."

Delta Air Lines Instructions to Pilots If They Get Hijacked by Someone Carrying an Explosive Liquid. [From a Delta Pilot's Flight Manual]

- Turn on the NO SMOKING light and have passengers extinguish smoking materials in order to eliminate a potential source of ignition.
- Keep the cockpit door closed to protect the Flight Crew from the effects of a flash fire and reduce the chances of gasoline vapors getting into the cockpit where many sources of ignition are present.
- Institute maximum air flow in the cockpit to remove as much of the gasoline vapors as possible.
- Lower the Aircraft's temperature as much as possible to reduce the vapor emissions from the volatile liquid and reduce the chance of ignition.
- Consider the fact that the hijacker must be one of several aboard.
- Give as much information about the situation as possible on the radio.

How does a pilot become captain of a commercial airliner?

For Malcolm Simpson, OJ Greene, and 9,400 other Delta pilots, the grueling process began with an application at the personnel department, like any other employee. Then came background checks, drug screens, credit check, psychological interviews, and finally, for a lucky 5 percent, ground school.

"Almost all the pilots we take have flown jets," said Capt. Richard Colby, manager of Delta's pilot training program. "Most come from the military. And have already flown an average of 3,000 hours. We might take someone with only 1,500 hours, but that person may have been flying with the Blue Angels, or on aircraft carriers. They're the crème de la crème."

Colby was an ex-military man himself, but said coming from the military could pose special problems for a pilot. "The biggest challenge is adapting to the civilian and corporate world. The world is full of stick men who can maneuver aluminum through the skies. We need more than that."

He meant that the old fighter-pilot notions of captain as Top Gun maverick or unquestioning obedience doesn't wash at an airline. A modern commercial pilot flies a fine line between being absolute commander of his plane and coordinator of job roles in an emergency. The difference is not just words but safety. "A modern airliner," one Delta pilot told me, "is 4 million parts flying down the road." One person simply can't do everything to keep it operating smoothly. A pilot has to be able to share jobs, to make sure each member of a crew knows what to do in an emergency, but to take command when necessary. A copilot has to be confident enough to speak up if he sees something wrong, and not be afraid of military-type punishment.

"In aviation, almost 80 percent of accidents are caused by people breaking down, not equipment, and 60 percent of that has been from lack of awareness," Colby said.

Just how dangerous lack of simple communication can be was demonstrated dramatically in December 1990 when a Northwest Airlines DC-9 rolled into the path of a Northwest Boeing 727 taking off at fogbound Detroit Metropolitan Airport, killing eight. The National Transportation Safety Board report on the accident blamed "lack of proper crew coordination."

"The DC-9 first officer failed to follow repeated instructions from the captain," the report said. In the confusion, the crew failed to tell air traffic controllers their position, and so they were never warned they were entering an active runway.

The catchword in the industry for communication training is "cockpit resource management"—a boring-sounding description of a crucially important aspect of flight. Delta stressed it in every pilot training talk I attended. Cockpit resource management was instituted intensely at the airline in late 1987, when Delta suffered ten safety-related incidents in a few weeks. Delta had an excellent safety record up until then, and also since then, but within a short period that year, a Delta jetliner landed on the wrong runway in Boston. A Delta 767 plunged to within 600 feet of the ocean off Los Angeles when the pilot accidentally cut off fuel to both engines. A Delta L-1011, which was sixty miles off course over Canadian airspace, narrowly missed colliding with a Continental Airlines Boeing 747. Continental reported that the Delta crew asked them by radio not to report the incident. A few minutes after the near-miss, the Delta plane strayed into the path of a British Airways jet headed from London to Toronto.

Shortly after that, a Delta jet with 113 passengers aboard hit a van while taxiing up to the terminal at National Airport in Washington, D.C. And a Delta 737 landed at Frankfort, Kentucky, after being cleared by air traffic controllers to land at Lexington, nineteen miles away.

"Delta needed to be more disciplined in the cockpit," FAA Inspector William Dubis told me in Atlanta. Dubis had conducted the FAA investigation of the incidents. "They needed to have a better oversight of their program. They needed to look harder at the recurrent check rides in the company. They needed to develop standardized procedures. And they needed cockpit resource management, which was new to the industry at the time."

I asked Dubis what he thought of Delta today. "They do a good job," he said.

Now most airlines hammer in cockpit resource management. To drive the notion home, Delta distributed a report from an FAA safety advisory group at one seminar for new pilots I attended. The report had been written by six retired airline captains, who had flown in jump-seat rides on twenty-seven U.S. airlines.

The report was critical of cockpit dynamics in general, without mentioning specific airlines. As the airline industry and aviation governing agencies grow, as more procedures and methods of operation have been developed, and as pilots have become more strongly directed by Air Traffic Control (ATC), the report said, "company procedures have resulted in computer flight planning that gives the pilot little time, opportunity, or motivation for making the final flight plan selection. The movement toward all-weather operation generates a subconscious, but real feeling in pilots that flights are no longer canceled because of weather. Weather information is often inadequate and presented to the pilot in a form not conducive to a full judgment of conditions. Cabin attendants do not relate to the flight crews, often are part of Marketing and not part of the safety team and do not understand they are under the command of the captain.

"With all this has come a new type of pilot, sometimes from the military, who is accustomed to following orders and flight plans prescribed by military necessity. All members of the flight crew are often of similar age and, in some cases, copilots are older than the captain.

"These factors have developed pilots-in-command, who are sometimes confused as to where their command begins and ends. They tend to do what the system tells them, responding precisely to Air Traffic Control requests with little question even though a flight path may be through hazardous weather. They follow flight routes the computer calls for even though better routes are available for weather avoidance or economy. They are not commander of the cabin team, and conditions have occurred in which the cabin team, on its own, initiated emergency action that was not needed and created dangers.

"The cockpit often develops too much of a 'buddy' atmosphere with excessive kidding, and with the copilot attempting to overrule and dominate the captain, and doing it successfully."

Also, the report said, "It is almost automatic that captains and copilots alternate flight legs and in many cases, because pilots are equal in age and experience, the captain is reticent to correct any errors of the copilot and seemingly embarrassed to take over a flight leg when the weather is bad. SASAG witnessed extremes such as copilot making a landing during winds of 50 knots, or doing a poor job in flying, and touching down at reference speed plus 40 knots, with the captain making no move to correct him."

At the seminar, Delta Senior Vice President and former Chief Pilot Harry Alger told the new captains a story about a recent Delta flight that had been sent out by the company to Detroit on the night of a bad snowstorm. He was furious about it. "Gentlemen, that flight never should have gone," Harry Alger said.

The flight had arrived safely, Alger added. But he told the pilots not to go if they ever felt weather was a problem. All Delta pilots I flew with over four months told me the company never questioned any decision they made not to fly for safety reasons. And not only pilots said it; every person who worked in any aspect of flight operations—scheduling, equipment, maintenance, routing—said the same thing. No management people ever complained to them that they'd made a mistake by holding back an airplane. Nobody second-guessed them. Nobody lectured them on revenue lost if an airplane didn't go. Nobody whined about the extra cost of putting up passengers in a hotel if a plane had been held for safety reasons.

The bottom line was, during my research, nonairline friends would often ask me, "What's your basic feeling? After knowing more of what goes on behind the scenes, do you feel better or worse to be a passenger?"

"Much better," I said.

"Gentlemen, fly it, fly the hell out of it, fly it by the book, but don't compromise safety," Harry Alger said.

For Malcolm Simpson, after thirty-three years of flying, it was "grueling" to go back to school to learn the L-1011.

"Friends ask me, why do you have to go to school?" he said. "The reason is, every airplane has different technology. And in school this time I wasn't as sure of myself as in the past. It's been ten years since I was in school. I think my brain is still sharp but," he said, cracking a boyish smile, "I'm not positive. When I was twenty-five, thirty, thirty-five, I could sit in ground school and hardly crack a book."

Before school began, Malcolm got hold of the course manuals, slides, and transcripts and studied them every night. An airline pilot has to know more than just how to fly a plane. He must know how the plane works. "You have to learn every system on the airplane. All the engineering stuff. How the engines work. The hydraulics. The pneumatic system. It's a very concentrated program."

"Why do you need to know so much?" I said.

"So you don't make a mistake."

Besides technical aspects of flying, pilots in ground school and recurrent training also cover antiterrorist procedures. They learn ways, if they're ever hijacked on the ground, to let anyone watching in the tower know that a hijacking has taken place. I learned the technique but thought it better to keep it secret. But it's something like, they turn a certain light on, outside the plane.

They'll probably never be hijacked, but what if?

They learn what to look out for if they have to fly in an area affected by an erupting volcano. If that sounds farfetched, consider the L-1011 pilots heading in and out of the Pacific Northwest during the eruption of Mount St. Helens in 1985.

"OPERATIONS IN VOLCANIC ASH," said the heading in the flight operations manual all Delta pilots carry. "Volcanic ash contains both abrasive and corrosive materials. Encounters with such materials in flight or on the ground can cause damage to the Air Line engines . . . the ash will probably appear to be a fine powder, like talcum powder, light grey in color. When dampened, it has been reported to set like concrete, but with an acid corrosive nature.

"Volcanic ash may be difficult to detect at night or during flight in clouds. However, the following has been reported by flight crews. Smoke or dust appearing in the cockpit. An acrid odor similar to electrical smoke. Multiple engine malfunctions such as stalls, torching from tailpipe, flameout."

In training, pilots discussed unruly passengers. Malcolm had experience over the years with that. Like the woman in First Class who kept drinking and punching herself in the face one day, during a flight from California to New York. A flight attendant calmed the woman down, but when she started punching herself again, Malcolm went back to talk to her.

"I told her, 'the one thing I'm not going to allow you to do on my flight is hurt yourself. I don't know what your problem is, and I don't need to know, but if you don't stop hitting yourself, I'm going to restrain you all the way to New York.' [Pilots carry plastic handcuffs on board.] For a while she cooperated. I think she'd taken drugs before boarding."

Malcolm laughed. "She passed out, and the flight attendants got her purse open and found her mother's ID in New York. We got on the phone to Delta in New York, and got them to call her mother. We also found a letter from a lover. She'd been dumped. That's why she was so despondent. She was really trying to hurt herself. She woke up before we stopped in Cincinnati and tried to start again, but the flight attendant sat down next to her, talked to her, calmed her."

By now Malcolm had called ahead and asked for help taking the woman off the plane in Cincinnati. "Two big burly guys came on, we were going to remove her in a stretcher. We told her we'd called her mother."

Malcolm grinned. "Big mistake. She went berserk. That's the last thing in the world she wanted. She was beating the hell out of those two guys. Hitting. Trying to bite. I'm not sure we could have gotten restraints on her."

Ground school, Malcolm said, started on a Monday. Nine days later he sat through a company oral exam. "A guy sat down with two of us and asked us questions. Like what's the procedure for an engine fire?" said Malcolm, who had never had one, but what if?

Malcolm said, "He asked, if you get an area H overheat light coming on, what does it mean?"

"What *does* it mean?" I asked.

"It means you have a duct leak, a hot air leak near the electrical system. It boils down to hot air shooting down into the avionics [electrical] department. It could set your battery on fire. It could burn down into your electronics equipment, and you could start losing systems."

"Has that ever happened to you?"

"No. But I want to know it."

After the company oral, came the FAA oral, given either by an FAA man or a company representative designated by the FAA.

"You're more relaxed with the company guy, but he'll fail you just as easily," Malcolm said.

"I thought we'd get a couple of days off after the oral, but we didn't," Malcolm said. "We started in the simulator the next day. Started out basic. Like you've never been in an airplane before. You go up, try to get the feel of it. You're in there for hours. They do weather. Wind shear. I came out drenched in sweat."

He had to pass another test in the simulator, again from an FAA man or designee, and then Malcolm was ready for his initial operating experience in an actual TriStar, which is what he was doing at the moment. He was flying, and we were over Missouri, one minute off schedule, at 35,000 feet. I looked down at brown fields.

OJ Greene, talking about anything that came into his head at this point in the flight, told Malcolm, "You're coming from a two-man airplane. You're used to you and the copilot doing everything. But with a three-man plane you have to make yourself rely on the engineer. He's responsible for the walkaround [the visual inspection of a plane before every flight]. The fuel. The air-conditioning and pressurization. If there's any kind of abnormal condition, it's the engineer who gets the books out. You have to operate at his pace. He's reading the procedure. One guy flies the plane. And the other takes care of the abnormal, the emergency. You have to put a lot of faith in the engineer."

Greene added that if the engineer ever leaves the cockpit to go to the bathroom or talk to a passenger or help a flight attendant, "make sure all the engines are running on their individual tanks." Years ago Greene was piloting a plane where an engineer walked out just as one of the fuel tanks ran dry. OJ recognized the "fluttery" feeling when the engine began quitting, reached back, and made the fuel transfer.

As the two men talked, I remembered sitting in on pilot training back at headquarters in Atlanta. During my first week there, I'd walked into a small classroom one afternoon where nine new pilots were analyzing real incidents that had happened to Delta jets.

The trainees wore topsiders, sweaters, or leather jackets. They ranged in age from late twenties to late forties. Some were new hires, others had been in the company a long time. They were moving up to flying bigger planes, Boeing 757s and 767s, which carried more passengers for longer distances, and paid more. Pilot salaries are based on the size of the planes they fly.

"A 767 was landing in Salt Lake City," said Instructor Bill Cooper. "They were told by the tower that weather was okay, but upon approach they experienced something markedly different. Heavy rain. Light to moderate turbulence. A 20-knot tailwind. The crew discussed possible wind-shear conditions, mentally prepared for it. Then the wind-shear warning went on, and the crew immediately began avoidance."

He meant, they got the plane out of there fast.

"Which performance criteria were involved in this incident?" Cooper said. "And what lessons can we learn from this?"

The class decided the crew had acted well.

"Just because the preceding aircraft has a good landing doesn't mean you will," said a trainee at my table.

"Total crew awareness," Cooper said. "Each member of the crew knowing each other members' jobs in every event. Okay. You're riding jump seat, and the captain croaks. The copilot croaks. He's dead. *You've never been in this kind of airplane in your life*. And suddenly you have an engine fire. What are the things you do to put out an engine fire in an airplane, any kind of airplane? A 737. An L-1011. Power off. Pull T handle. Fire a bottle into the engine to get the fire out. Total crew awareness!"

Scenario number 2, read Cooper, behind a podium, peering out at the pilots over reading glasses older pilots wear. He was a vibrant, athletic-looking man with his sleeves rolled up. "You're a 727 pilot. Taking off but you have trouble with the left main landing gear doors. You have to land the plane without one of the landing gears. Take five minutes and write all the things to take into consideration before you put this bird down without one of the gears."

The three young pilots at my table conferred and wrote quickly. You should burn as much gas as you can so there's as little of the flammable liquid as possible in the wing tanks. You should fly as long as you can and let the plane settle down, don't just fall on the runway. Let the flight attendants know everything happening. Plan which side of the plane the evacuation should take place on. If there's no fire, the airplane will be lower on the left side, where the gear didn't come down, so evacuate on that side.

"And tell the passengers about the sparks. When you land there may be sparks but that doesn't mean there's fire. You don't want panic," Cooper said.

I figured it was a hypothetical exercise, but then Cooper showed an American Airlines training film movie of an American Airlines 727 which *had* experienced this problem on their way into Dallas one day. In the video the pilot, first officer, and chief flight attendant recalled how they'd talked to each other, told each other what they were doing, all the way down. I saw the crippled plane on the runway, mashed down where the gear should be, but intact.

"By the book. I did it by the book. If there's a better book, I don't know about it," the pilot said.

Afterward I flew the simulator, the $2.5 million re-creation TriStar cockpit allegedly so authentic that the FAA allowed pilots to train in it instead of using actual planes. New simulators can cost up to $15 million. From the outside the simulator looked pretty unimpressive, like an eight-sided windowless construction trailer on hydraulic stilts. It seemed impossible to imagine, watching the thing tilting backward and forward to a slight humming of hydraulic pumps, that anyone inside might actually imagine he was in a cockpit. The heaving simulator reminded me of the way dinosaurs jerked around in old black-and-white time-travel movies. I walked down a steel catwalk, across a ramp, and into the machine. Instantly the skeptical feeling vanished. Once the door closed, I felt as if I was in a real TriStar with the exception of a small computer screen and control board on the left rear side of the cockpit. This was the instructor control panel, pilot instructor Dean Berk told me.

An instructor could punch in airports: New York, Detroit, Honolulu, San Francisco, Dallas, Stuttgart, Frankfurt. He punched in Boston, and suddenly through the blank windshield, I was looking out at a real runway at night. Not a video of the runway, although the image was actually being projected down on the windscreen from hidden cathode cameras above. I gasped at the realness of it. I saw the Hancock building in the distance. I saw bright stars above. Ahead, on the runway, emerald lights stretched and converged in the distance, looking like candy dots.

Berk punched in fog. The dots on the far end grew hazy.

"If we fail an engine, the simulator will yaw, give you the same gut, seat-of-the-pants feeling you will get from an aircraft," Berk said. "You can do all the hazardous maneuvers that are required. We can fail an engine at critical point in takeoff. We can do turbulence, air pressure loss, thunderstorms, wind shear. We can do a two-engine-out approach. We can do a fog landing. If we were trying to do this with a real aircraft, it would be hazardous."

In fact, back in the 1960s, one Delta DC-8 crashed doing a practice two-engine-out-of-four approach.

"We can do a fog landing," Berk said.

When Berk turned on the simulator, there was a jerk and a throbbing noise sounding like engines. He "took off" and the machine seemed to roll down the runway so fast the runway "lights" rushed at us. In my gut I was taking off, never mind what my logical mind told me, that I was in the clumsy-looking box, inside a building at Delta headquarters. A box that from the outside hadn't even seemed to have the authenticity of a Coney Island ride.

"Pilots come out of here drenched in sweat," Berk said.

In the old days, barely twenty years ago, before the three-dimensional picture and six-axis motion system and computer keeping up with the pilot's movements, simulators simply showed a film on the windscreen. If a pilot missed an approach, the film kept running, and the instructor rewound it. If the pilot crashed, the film kept running its course.

In order to fly the simulator, were I a real pilot today, I would have to know the hundreds of switches and dials around me. Like the altimeter, which showed the height of 714 above sea level. Or the radio altimeter to read the vertical distance between the airplane and the ground, especially helpful in fog landings. The attitude directional indicator would tell me the angle of bank when I climbed, descended, or turned. Because in heavy fog a pilot can become disoriented without landmarks.

So many gauges. The horizontal situation indicator was designed to receive radio beams from the ground and tell me if I was on the right flight path, which Air Traffic Control had assigned the plane.

The flight management system, on the floor console between myself and the copilot, looked like a telephone keypad, so I could punch in coordinates to let the plane know predetermined points in a trip, locations of radio transmitters on the ground, so I would be alerted when to turn, or the autopilot could do it automatically if it were engaged. Beside the keypad was a small computer screen, which would display these coordinates, so all three cockpit crew could double-check them against a flight plan we would have before taking off.

Fortunately, the day I visited, all I had to do was steer the plane. And to do that I had to monitor one simple device. At least it looked simple. It was a blue ball behind a glass panel in front of me, and a little orange plastic airplane that floated above the ball.

All I had to do to keep the plane on course was make sure the plastic plane lined up in crosshairs in the middle of the ball. The principle, same as in a real plane, was that Berk had programmed all the information necessary for a flight—speed, angle, direction, route—into the TriStar simulator's computer. The computer presented the composite information in the location of the little plastic plane on the ball. If the plane was in the cross hairs, I was doing everything right. If the plane started drifting, I'd better correct it fast. I could do that by turning the yoke or pushing or pulling the control column.

I was eager to start. Berk explained that if the little plane drifted left, I could bring it back by turning the steering wheel left. Exactly the opposite move from the one I'd make driving a car. Or if the orange plane rose above the center of the ball I should gently push the stick forward. Gently. Like helping a grandmother across the street. Gently. That would make us descend.

Easy, I figured. Like a video game.

We would land in Los Angeles. Berk pushed buttons, and the ground shot away so fast I got dizzy. Suddenly we were 2,000 feet up. It really *looked* like we were 2,000 feet up. I saw stars. The simulator was bumping lightly, like a plane in flight. I heard our engines throbbing. I saw the airport and the lights of Los Angeles below. I eyed the little cross hairs and adjusted the yoke so the plane stayed in place. Within seconds it began drifting left. I turned the wheel right. Wrong direction.

"We're—uh—going to turn over," Berk said.

I yanked the wheel back.

"You're climbing at 5,000 feet a minute," Berk said.

I eased forward on the yoke. Now we were descending into Los Angeles again. The runway, bordered by green lights with a big red arrow pointing the way for me to land, started drifting left again. I tried to get us back on the path. A mechanical voice cried, "GLIDE SLOPE!"

I crashed into the United Terminal.

Next time I missed the United Terminal but took out the mushroom restaurant at the airport.

I figured, If pilots want $180,000 a year to fly this thing, give it to them.

Two months later I tried again. I told myself I would do better. On a hot, late spring night I went back into the simulator with Instructor Tom Kanaley, a twenty-four-year veteran pilot. Tom called up Atlanta airport, clear conditions, no particular wind problem. He put us up at 2,000 feet. He said, "You're flying."

This time I seemed to have everything under control. The plane moved smoothly. I looked up. The night was bright and beautiful. I said, "Tom, it really is peaceful up here. The stars look fantastic."

"Those aren't stars. That's Atlanta. You've turned the plane upside down," Tom said.

But despite the careful preparation, the unexpected can happen. In Jack McMahan's case, it was his pilot's raw skill that helped him save an otherwise doomed L-1011 one night in 1977, when he encountered a problem that had never been taught in any simulator. Because it had never happened before.

McMahan, a burly, affable, now retired pilot, a Texas-born ex-rodeo bull rider, was piloting Delta flight 1080 that night from San Diego to Los Angeles. He had forty-one passengers and eight stewardesses aboard. He was one of the company's most experienced pilots at the time. In fact McMahan was the pilot who had personally picked up ship 714 from the Lockheed factory in California and brought it back to Atlanta.

"The thing that amazes me is that a piece you can hold in the palm of your hand can cause you to lose a $40 million airplane and how many lives?" he told me one rainy day in his Atlanta basement, pointing to a softball-sized steel ring mounted on a plaque on his wall.

"That's what broke."

That night he was flying ship 707, one of Delta's first Lockheed 1011s. In thick fog the jet started down the runway. The first indication of trouble came at liftoff speed, when the plane rose into the air by itself without McMahan pulling back on the yoke.

McMahan checked the setting on the stabilizer, the two horizontal flaps on the tail, which control the plane's pitch. According to his instruments they were set at the right angle. Still ascending, McMahan retracted the landing gear.

But at 400 feet the plane pitched up sharply again, and McMahan went into emergency procedures. Although he was climbing at too steep an angle, he still wasn't worried because L-1011s have backup systems to do the same job. He tried the electric trim and manual trim, two more ways of setting the stabilizer. The pitch remained severe.

What McMahan didn't know, what he couldn't know because at that time there wasn't even an instrument on the control panel to tell him, was that the small bearing he had shown me in the basement had broken from water corrosion, jamming the left elevator in the up position. Elevators are small flaps on the trailing edge of the stabilizer. *The plane could only go up.*

McMahan reset all the switches responsible for determining the plane's angle of flight. It didn't help.

Copilot Wilbur Radford checked the cockpit warning lights to see if any part of the plane was malfunctioning. No clue. The engineer checked the four independant hydraulic systems. They were working too. But by 3,000 feet, with pitch getting higher, speed began dropping. Imagine a paper airplane looping toward the ceiling. As the angle of climb increases, it needs more power to fly. Finally it just stops and plunges to earth. The big jet was headed for a stall and crash into the Pacific.

"We were still going up and up," McMahan told me. "Normally San Diego to Los Angeles is a pretty short hop. The coordinating flight attendant sticks her head in the cockpit and asks if we want a cup of coffee. She came in and said, 'You guys want some'—and stopped dead. She could see the copilot and me bent over, trying to get the plane under control. Flight engineer Steve Heidt told her, 'You better sit down and strap yourself in.' "

By 5,000 feet the plane's angle was almost double what it should have been. McMahan knew that his minimum safe speed at this point was about 138. He was down at 130, and slowing. He was starting to feel the slight buffet that precedes a stall.

McMahan told me, "I had an out-of-body experience then.

"Suddenly it was like I was outside the plane, looking at it. There was a bright glow on my right. I could see us in the cockpit. It was a physical sensation, in fractions of seconds. I thought, Who's going to tell my wife. We'd just lost our sixteen-year-old son. What a tragedy this will be. I thought, accidents come in threes. The week before a Southern Airways DC-9 had crashed, killing sixty-eight passengers. And the week before that, Pan Am and KLM planes had collided in the Canary Islands. My God, I thought, we're Number 3.

"It was like there was a newspaper floating there. I could see the headlines. JUMBO JET PLUMMETS INTO OCEAN. JET CRASHES ON TAKEOFF. NO SURVIVORS."

McMahan also envisioned the National Safety Board report on the accident. "Under 'Probable Cause,' it would say, 'Pilot became disoriented on a night takeoff over water.' I'd seen that before in accidents. It teed me off. After all the night takeoffs I'd made off Iwo Jima and Guam and on coral strips with no runway lights and jeep headlights to show me the way.

"Pilot error? I thought, Not me. I thought, How does an airplane fly? There's thrust and pitch—and then suddenly I didn't think anymore. That was it."

What McMahan did amazed the copilot and engineer. With speed dropping, he *cut power* to the two wing engines. Then he shoved the throttle forward all the way on the third engine, the one perched higher than the others, on the tail.

The extra power coming from that angle forced the nose down. The speed started rising.

But his problems were far from over. He was at 9,300 feet, with no way to maneuver the plane, except by changing the thrust on the engines. "Where and how could I land it?

"I didn't want to go back to San Diego. The weather was bad. Palmdale and Edwards Air Force bases were nearby but they'd closed at 10 P.M. I considered Phoenix and Las Vegas. Phoenix would normally be forty-five minutes away, at 400 knots, but we were doing 190. At 190 it would take an hour and a half, and 25,000 pounds of fuel. That wouldn't leave much if something went wrong. Both Phoenix and Vegas have mountains around them. We would have to fly to 14,000 feet to clear the mountains, and if we ran into any turbulence . . ." In the basement, McMahan trailed off.

McMahan sighed. He decided the best chance of survival lay in the original route to Los Angeles. But even there, normal touchdown was out of the question. Even if he got the plane near the runway, if he couldn't get the nose down far enough, the TriStar might float on a cushion of air over the runway and crash on the other side.

"I also had to decide how to approach the airport. We could come in over the water or the city. Over the water we call the black hole. It's dark, and then you see the beach and the runway. It jumps out at you.

"The city had more light. But if we came in over the city . . . well, the mental images started again. I saw the plane rolling over and going upside down, like on TV, and there would be all these burned-out buildings and hulks and my God, what a tragedy."

He even considered ditching the plane in the ocean. "But visibility was bad. They had ships down there. And oil derricks. It was cold." He laughed. "I didn't want to do it."

McMahan advised LA airport of the emergency. He chose to come in over the water to save lives if he couldn't hold the plane steady.

He decided not to risk a normal more comfortable glide-style landing. He would try a hard landing. He needed to get the TriStar down fast. He needed to keep the nose as far down as possible. He would come in on a straight line, so less maneuvering would be required. Then he would try to jam the plane down onto the runway, and hope that although the nose was still pitched up, the tail wouldn't smash into the ground.

"We told the passengers we had a problem, didn't tell them what. We told them to pay attention to the flight attendants, who moved them up front to help get the nose down. Emergency equipment was standing by on the ground. I put the landing gear down, and the plane suddenly pitched up again. I was wrestling to get it under control."

"When we landed, we didn't drag the tail or blow any tires. Everything worked okay."

In McMahan's basement, which he jokingly called his museum, surrounded by mementos—books including *Women Aloft, The Giant Airships, Designers and Test Pilots*, and *The Road to Kitty Hawk*, a plaque commemorating thirty-five years with Delta, a souvenir-mounted turbine blade from a Delta jet after 6,500 hours of operation, equivalent to 156 trips around the world, a plaque from Lockheed commemorating McMahan's delivery of Delta's first L-1011, which he brought back to Delta from Palmdale, California, in 1973—McMahan laid the broken gear on the table and played the flight recording of the landing of flight 1080 on a Bass Booster boom box. Arms folded, brow furrowed, the bullet-headed pilot listened to the tape he must have played a thousand times by then. I heard the copilot say he saw the runway. I heard an automatic warning on the plane, "Pull up!" as they descended at a rate an automatic pilot would never have tried. The copilot said "Wooooo," when they touched down. I heard the chief flight attendant come into the cabin, and say, voice shaking, "You old sweetie pie!"

"She grabbed me and gave me a kiss," McMahan said. On the recorder, her voice said, "I'll have a cigarette with you. And I quit smoking."

The passengers had so little an idea of how close they'd come to dying that one sent McMahan a crabby note after they landed. It said, "You made me lose my connection. What are you going to do about it?"

"The whole thing happened in the middle of the night," McMahan said. "We got another airplane and continued on to Dallas before the FAA found out."

Later the FAA did find out. The distinguished service award they presented McMahan read, "As pilot in command of Delta Air Lines flight 1080, he maneuvered his malfunctioning aircraft more than 100 miles through 8,000 feet of solid overcast to a safe landing. His professional judgment and skill merit the gratitude of America's flying public."

In his basement, McMahan showed me a copy of the poem "High Flight," by John Gillespie Magee, Jr. It said:

Oh! I have slipped the surly bonds of earth
And danced the skies on laughter-silvered wings:

Sunward I've climbed, and joined the tumbling mirth
Of sun-split clouds,—and done a hundred things,
You have not dreamed of—wheeled and soared and swung

High in the sunlit silence. Hov'ring there,
I've chased the shouting wind along, and flung
My eager craft through footless halls of air . . .

Up, up the long, delirious, burning blue
I've topped the wind-swept heights with easy grace—
where never lark, nor ever eagle flew

And, while with silent, lifting mind I've trod
The high untrespassed sanctity of space

Put out my hand and touched the face of God.

McMahan said. "I remember when I felt like I was hanging outside the plane. There was this bright light, like an aura. It seemed like I could see a shape, but these are microseconds. Then something touched me gently, right here," he said, brushing his cheek with his index finger.

"I didn't say anything to the FAA or anybody about this. But when I got back to LA, my cheek burned. I thought nothing of it at the time. But it kept burning for three days. Then a long time after that, when the spaceship *Challenger* was taking off and blew up, my cheek started burning in the same place. And later still, a Delta pilot talked to me about a problem he had one night before he came to Delta, losing an engine—being upside down—my cheek started burning again."

McMahan looked me full in the face.

"Maybe God put out his hand and touched my face," he said.

And at the company, McMahan's experience became one more problem to be programmed into the simulator. The first two men to try it crashed. The problem might never occur again but what if?

And what if happened again almost twenty years later, when a United Airlines DC-10 heading for Chicago from Denver lost all its hydraulic systems. The pilot could only maneuver the plane by alternating thrust on the engines. That plane almost made a safe landing at Sioux City, Iowa, but crashed.

They never stop talking about the possibilities. What if? What if?

• • •

Back in the cockpit, we were reaching the end of the Great Plains. I spotted the snowcapped Rockies 200 miles ahead, over Malcolm's shoulder, and Denver, 40 miles away. From 39,000 feet up, the city looked like a dollhouse collection of aphid-sized homes and skyscrapers dwarfed by the mountains erupting in a solid wall behind them.

I walked into Coach and First Class. Tammy Mattiello was watching *Star Trek VI*, with William Shatner imprisoned by aliens on another planet. Sharon Lane had fallen asleep. B. L. Winfield read the Delta flight magazine beneath his overhead light. For them, as for 77 million passengers who flew with Delta in 1991, there were no flight 1080s, no operations in volcanic dust, no hijackings, no volatile liquids in the plane. *Because* of all the double checking. *Because* of the simulator rides. *Because* the rare mishaps are so endlessly analyzed.

Back at the cockpit, I gave the proper coded knocking sequence and the engineer, Smith, swung it open. It was almost time to land. Since Salt Lake City is surrounded by mountains, OJ Greene had already said we couldn't fly straight in. The flight plan called for an approach from fifty miles south, a right turn, and descent.

Greene told Malcolm, "Coming into Salt Lake City, you should turn on the seat-belt sign a little sooner than usual. Since Salt Lake City is at the base of mountains, winds can get turbulent once you get below 14,000 feet. When you get over the edge of those mountains and start making a turn, it can get real bumpy. Also, you come over those mountains fairly high, maybe 17,000 feet, and you're only forty miles from the airport. If Air Traffic turns you north, you gotta get down in a hurry. So instead of the normal twenty-minute warning, you might want to turn on the light thirty minutes out. Plan ahead. It's not like going to Los Angeles, where it's flat."

Like OJ Greene, 10 percent of Delta's pilots are line check airmen. They go to special ground school to get the job, then fly planes with the chief line check airman observing, and then give a line check as an FAA inspector looks on. "I like it because when you teach, you learn," Greene said.

At 30,000 feet we were descending over parched western cliffs. The earth rose toward us. At 20,500 feet we slid over pinnacles of white snow. A valley opened up, a little Shangri-la in the desert. I saw Salt Lake City and Emigration Canyon, through which

Brigham Young had led his followers, to establish the capital of the Mormon religion. There was the gray spire of the Mormon Tabernacle, and the biggest office building in town, headquarters of the Mormon Church. The ski resorts of Park City, Alta, Deer Valley, and Sundance were laid out ahead as long white strips, ski runs, on otherwise tree-covered mountains.

The pilots might have pointed these sights out to the passengers if this hadn't been a training flight. Many pilots I flew with kept maps of the country they flew over, read books on local history, and passed the information on to passengers. But pilots who weren't familiar with the landscape below could get help from those handy manuals that seemed to cover almost every eventuality and included information and even actual suggested announcements with jokes and pauses prescribed.

Here are three from Delta's *Flight Operations Guide to Passenger Communications*:

> Ladies and gentlemen, we've just been advised that we have some folks running to the gate from a connecting flight that just parked. (If applicable: Since ours is the last non-stop today, we're going to hold for, oh, 10 minutes or so to get them aboard.)
>
> Or:
>
> Ladies and gentlemen, I imagine most of you felt that big chuckhole in the road back there. Let me explain briefly what it was. Airplanes leave an invisible air wake behind them, similar to a visible wake of water behind a boat.
>
> Or:
>
> Idaho is the gem state. That's Twin Falls. Near here is where in 1974 Evel Knievel attempted to power his "skycycle" across the Snake River.

I remembered how, when I was flying into Salt Lake City several weeks before in the cockpit of TriStar 712, from Portland, Oregon, copilot Pete Hayden had looked eastward at the gouged-out snow-sprinkled Wasatch Mountains and said, "Those passes are where the Donner Party, the pioneer settlers, got slowed up on their way to California. They lost weeks, and later got stuck in California in the Sierras. You know the story. They ate each other."

"How long would it take ship 714 to go the same distance?" I'd asked. I'd been trying to figure out how to say just how fast 600 miles an hour is.

"Twenty minutes," Hayden said.

Now, in the cockpit, the crew went over the before-landing checklist. "Seat-belt lights!" "On!" "Air Speed Bugs!" "Set!" Dots became barns. Fields separated themselves from solid green into rows of irrigated crops. Vehicles on roads became large enough to look like cars or trucks. The shadow of 714 passed over streets, a suburban cul-de-sac, a tennis court. We were buffeted lightly in wind. A mechanical voice warned, "Traffic!" But it referred to a plane moving on the ground ahead, not to anything near us.

Engineer C. W. Massey leaned forward, watching from between the backs of the two pilots, monitoring our descent on the altimeter. Malcolm flew the plane. "Two hundred," the engineer said, meaning 200 feet high.

"Seventy, 60, 50 . . ."

We were down.

OJ and Malcolm would leave 714 and return to Atlanta on another plane. I would stay in the cockpit. The captain who would fly the next legs, to Los Angeles and Honolulu, was probably in the Delta flight operations room at Salt Lake City airport, looking over any weather advisories tacked to a bulletin board, studying information about weather in general around the United States and over the Pacific, reading company news, maybe looking over the flight plan to Los Angeles, maybe punching up his work schedule or bidding for next month's routes on a computer. Or maybe he was buying a hamburger, because on domestic flights Delta doesn't give the pilots meals unless there are extra meals left over from passengers.

The flight attendants on this flight would also be replaced by a new crew. Cockpit crews and flight attendant crews work independently of each other, and fly together as a group for a month at a time.

OJ Greene told me he'd been ready, throughout the flight, to take over for Malcolm if a problem arose.

"How'd Malcolm do?" I asked when we left the plane.

"Piece of cake," OJ said.

THE WINGED PRUSSIAN

Otto Lilienthal would have been amazed. At the height, the speed, the clarity of radio reception. I heard Air Traffic Control sign off on my earphones—"Good day, 795"—and the glass bubble rose higher into the sky for the second leg of flight today, to Los Angeles. Capt. Charles Violette was at the mike. Copilot Ron Scarpa, an ex-Rockwell engineer, at the controls. Engineer T .J. Carpender, three years out of the military where he flew F-16s, scanned the fuel gauges and lights on his control panel. It was a Salt Lake City-based crew. At 10,000 feet, we passed brackish salt flats, a vast marshy collection of spits, islands, and estuaries surrounded by arid brown American West. Bright sun broke through haze outside.

Lilienthal never imagined views like this. Never conceived that a flying machine could accomplish this much. Provo, Utah, grew smaller below. At 29,000 feet and Mach .793, over three quarters the speed of sound, we shot over desert valleys and bleak spiny mountains. A spade-shaped splash of red, Zion National Park, came up to the south. And Brigham Young's old winter headquarters, St. George, was on the left.

Lilienthal had not anticipated automatic pilots. Or retractable landing gear. Or pressurized cabins, where passengers watched movies as they dined and sipped wine.

But he helped bring them all about.

I thought about Lilienthal and a day in August of 1896, when a crowd of picnickers gathered near a grassy hill at Rhinow, near Berlin, to watch the forty-eight-year-old German experimenter fly through the air in a hang glider he'd built. The women wore leg-of-mutton sleeves and chokers, the men ties and starched collars. None of them dreamed that the tragedy they were about to witness would help lead to the construction of Delta ship 714 almost a hundred years later.

Among those who paid serious attention to the possibility of human flight, admittedly not too numerous in 1896, Lilienthal had a worldwide reputation as "the winged Prussian" or "the flying man." He'd built and flown over 1,000 gliders by that summer. He was a handsome man with full dark hair, brushed back, a neat mustache, and trimmed Van Dyke beard. In portrait photos he holds his head high, Roman style, and looks into the distance in a Victorian pose. In flight he wore flannel shirts and twill trousers. Three years earlier, he'd written, "The first obstacle to be overcome by the practical constructor is that of stability."

To the spectators that day, the contraption Lilienthal struggled up the hill with resembled a gigantic white bat. It was a wooden frame covered with white cotton cloth, and its upper and lower wings were canted upward. It had a cloth rudder that could not be moved. In old photos, Lilienthal in flight looks like a man being kidnapped by an H. G. Wells creature while he kicks to get away. But he flew by hanging on a wooden bar, trying to steer by heaving his body around in the air, changing its center of gravity.

Lilienthal ran down the hill, rose into the air, crashed when a gust of wind drove him into the ground, and began to die. To the men trying to save him he said, "Sacrifices must be made."

News of his death reached two brothers in the United States, who had followed his experiments with fascination. They too dreamed of building a flying machine. Wilbur Wright was serious, thoughtful, the shyer of the two. His younger brother Orville, co-owner of their bicycle shop in Dayton, was energetic, the snappy dresser, the driving force behind the team. Both brothers were bachelors and trophy-winning bicycle racers, athletes who understood that owning a good machine was not as important as having the skill to control it.

The Wrights knew that until Lilienthal's death most aspiring airplane inventors assumed that the main problem of manned flight was getting a craft into the air. Once that happened, they believed it would be stable.

But Lilienthal was dead because, no matter how much he twisted on his wooden bar, he had no way of overcoming the wind that drove him into the ground. "Get on intimate terms with the wind," he had written. The brothers decided to try.

Big deal. There was no reason to assume the Wrights would be any more successful in creating a flying machine than any other dreamers had been in the previous 500 years. As far back as the 1400s, Leonardo Da Vinci had sketched primitive hang gliders and helicopters. By 1804 a British baronet had built a glider shaped like a manta ray, called a "governable parachute." Then Frenchman Alphonse Penaud built a small rubber-band-powered "planophore," which flew 130 feet and resembled the wooden model planes children buy in candy stores today. It was a long way from manned flight, but it proved it was possible to build a stable aircraft.

By the time the Wright Brothers got around to trying their hand at it, steam and gasoline engines had been invented, and it was assumed that if a craft ever took to the air, steam or gasoline would power it. Hiram Maxim, inventor of the Maxim machine gun, built an 8,000-pound, three-crew, steam-powered plane in England. It took off down a wooden track and wouldn't fly. The "aerial steam carriage," patented by American William Henson in 1842, was presented to investors in the United States and Europe as a craft to carry passengers around the world. Henson distributed lithographs showing his single-wing plane trailing steam as it flew over the Pyramids. Nice picture, but in real life it never reached the sky.

In the United States, where typically the government was squandering money on big projects instead of supporting small ones, the hope for flight rested with Samuel Pierpont Langley, secretary of the Smithsonian Institution, who was trying to build steam-powered model planes and fly them across the Potomac River. Langley managed to launch two little powered models that stayed up.

Wilbur Wright wrote Langley a letter. "I am an enthusiast but not a crank in the sense that I have some pet theories as to the proper construction of a flying machine," Wright wrote. "I wish to avail myself of all that is already known and then if possible add my mite to help on the future worker who will attain final success."

Wright offered to pay for booklets Langley might send along.

It was the age of tinkerers, when an aircraft could be built in a backyard. Neither brother had gone to college. Even if they had, there were no aviation courses. Wilbur had finished high school, and Orville hadn't even done that. But they attacked the problems of flight in a scientific way. First they flew kites in Dayton to "get on intimate terms with the wind." Then they designed unmanned gliders, bigger kites with two wings, resembling World War I planes. Watching the way buzzards in Dayton used their wings to maneuver, Wilbur pulled a cardboard box apart one day and twisted the sides to show Orville his idea for improving control of their gliders. They should "warp" the wings in flight, he said. Raise or dip the edges to steer a craft. They tried it on kites, tugging wires attached to the wings from the ground. It worked.

Next they were ready to try manned glider flights. By 1900 they'd set up camp during the summer at Kitty Hawk, on North Carolina's Outer Banks, north of Cape Hatteras. They liked the strong winds that made gliding excellent, the soft sand that would cushion crashes, and the isolation, which was good for work. They built a shack and slept in hammocks. At night Orville cooked, and Wilbur washed dishes. During the day they took turns piloting the gliders, which by now resembled the "Flyer" that would make them famous. The pilot would lie in the center of the lower wing and warp the wings by moving his hip—which was in a harness attached to wires.

The warping improved control, but the Wrights were unhappy with the lift they were getting. They went back to Lilienthal's writing for help. The winged Prussian had made detailed recommendations about wing design. But instead of improving things the new shapes caused the gliders to pitch uncontrollably, climb and stall.

This was so discouraging the Wrights considered quitting, but Orville had a better idea. Back in the bike shop, he built the first wind tunnel, a small wooden box about one and a half foot square, shaped like a baby's coffin. A fan on one end blew air inside. The Wrights spent the winter designing and testing model wings or "airfoils" in the box. They learned they should design a wing slightly concave in the center to cushion air streaming by below. And that a wing slightly thicker at the front edge gave better lift.

By summer 1902 they were back at Kitty Hawk with a glider with 32-foot wings, essentially the Wright Flyer without an engine. But now they decided that the wing warping didn't provide enough control. When the pilot tried to raise the wing while coming out of a turn, the gliders would often crash.

They needed to supplement the warping. At night, in the shack, with the wind blowing outside and sand seeping in through cracks, the brothers sat around arguing, talking, reading about flight.

It was the way they'd tackled problems since they were children. "From the time we were little my brother Orville and myself lived together, played together, worked together and, in fact, thought together," Wilbur would later write. "We usually owned all our toys in common, talked over our thoughts and aspirations so that nearly everything that was done in our lives has been the result of conversations, suggestions, and discussions between us."

Now they were wrestling with the fundamental elements of flight that govern every plane, even today, whether it is Delta ship 714, a Phantom jet fighter, a Piper Cub, or a supersonic jet. Before they could successfully fly, the brothers needed to control "pitch," the way a flying machine ascends or descends. "Roll," the way an aircraft rotates its wings in a turn. And "yaw," the plane's right and left movement in the wind, a crabbing motion like a rubber raft's in rapids, when it shifts diagonally in the current.

The Wrights added movable rudders, vertical fins resembling a box kite, to help control yaw. They designed "elevators," canoe-shaped flaps in front of the Flyer, to help with pitch. The wing warping would have to do at the moment against roll, although within a few years planes would have "ailerons" for that.

Finally, if there were ever going to be manned flight for any appreciable distance, the Wrights needed to understand "thrust," or power. They needed an engine that would turn a propeller, and pull or push the plane forward.

That may sound easy in 1994, but in 1903 there weren't any airplane engines. Cars had engines, but there were only 200 automobiles in the whole United States. And the only propellers in existence were for boats.

Would boat and automobile parts work in the air? No, but the

Wright Brothers didn't know that yet. They wrote auto manufacturers asking if they would try building a small, lightweight, eight-horsepower engine.

"Most companies answered that they were too busy with their regular business to undertake the building of such a motor," Orville wrote.

So the guys in the shop built an engine. An employee named Taylor got the job, and the Wrights were pleased with the result.

As for the propeller, they walked over to the Dayton library and took out books on boats. "There was no way of adapting [marine propellers] to aerial propellers . . ." Orville wrote. "Our minds became so obsessed with [propellers] that we could do little other work. We engaged in innumerable discussions, and often after an hour or so of heated argument, we would discover that we were as far from agreement as when we started, but that both had changed to the other's original position."

In the end, they decided to use two propellers, mounted in the back to push the machine. And in the end the first manned flying machine was built with bicycle tools. The frail-looking beams separating the two wings would be made of spruce. Baling or piano wires would run from the pilot's hip cradle to the two boxy rudders and canoe-shaped elevators, and to the wings, for warping. The gas tank, no bigger than a small loaf of French bread, would be fastened to a strut. The engine would be carved out of a big chunk of aluminum with a drill press. The wings would be bed linen, unbleached muslin sheets sewed by the brothers on their dead mother's sewing machine, so translucent that anyone gaping up from beneath the Flyer when it passed overhead would make out the outline of the pilot in his soft peaked cap and tie and jacket, whizzing by at 30 miles an hour, lying between two bicycle sprockets that were turning the propellers.

On December 8, 1903, nine days before the Wright Brothers' most historic flight, Smithsonian Institution Secretary Samuel Langley's much publicized full-sized steam-driven flying machine took off and plunged into the Potomac River. Langley would never recover from the disappointment. Despite the $50,000 the government had poured into his effort, he'd ended up as just one more failure in the thousand-year-old effort of men to fly.

But on December 17, while newsmen hid in bushes near Kill Devil Hills, and as a stiff wind blew at 27 mph, Orville Wright climbed onto the Flyer, fastened himself in the cradle, and tested his controls. A simple wooden stick moved the horizontal elevator. Another lever in front controlled gasoline flow. The brothers waited for the wind to die down, but resolved to fly anyway when it didn't.

"We thought that by facing the flyer into a strong wind, there ought to be no trouble in launching it from the level ground about camp," Orville wrote. "We realized the difficulties of flying in so high a wind, but estimated that the added dangers in flight would be partly compensated for by the slower speed in landing."

It was so cold that puddles outside the Wright's shack had frozen. With four men from a nearby Coast Guard station as witnesses, Wilbur ran along with the Flyer as it started to take off on a wooden track, balancing the wings so they didn't hit the ground. The machine climbed into the air. When it returned to earth twelve seconds later, it had traveled 120 feet.

Wilbur tried next.

The brothers sent their father an understated telegram, considering their accomplishment:

> SUCCESS FOUR FLIGHTS THURSDAY MORNING ALL AGAINST
> TWENTY ONE MILE WIND STARTED FROM LEVEL WITH ENGINE
> POWER ALONE AVERAGE SPEED THROUGH AIR THIRTY ONE MILES
> LONGEST 57 SECONDS.

Eighty-nine years later, at 31,000 feet, ship 714 was over the desert, guided by Air Traffic Control hundreds of miles away, in Los Angeles. We were on an invisible highway, but one which to aviators was as tangible as an interstate is to a truck driver. If we deviated from the assigned path, Captain Violette would be fined. At all times in the air ship 714 was on a radar controller's screen, as men and women in dark windowless rooms around the country tracked us passing through "their" pieces of airspace, blocks of territory in the sky, one on top of the other, shaped like pieces of a jigsaw puzzle.

Yet the whole complicated system worked so smoothly that most of the time, other than regular position checks and monitoring gauges, crews had time to tell stories, gripe about taxes, make jokes.

QUESTION. "Hey, Bob, what's the definition of a successful flight as far as a cockpit crew is concerned?"

ANSWER. "The captain has a bowel movement. The copilot gets laid. The flight engineer gets a free meal."

QUESTION. "Hey, Bob, did you hear about the new automated cockpit? The crew will be a captain and a dog. Know why?"

ANSWER. "The captain to watch the controls. The dog to bite him if he touches them."

Below, drab and brown in the daylight, Las Vegas came up on the right. I saw a long cool splash of blue, Lake Mead, far away on the left, near Grand Canyon National Park. Sixty miles off, the canyon was just a jagged line. And Hoover Dam looked like an insect-sized parenthesis when we passed over it.

So much higher than the Wright Flyer. I was thinking that, back in 1903 when the Wright Brothers sent their telegram to Dayton, the air age had begun, but exactly what that meant was still unclear.

In 1903 there were no air highways or even roads on the ground to Las Vegas. Las Vegas was a small Mormon settlement. West Point graduates still learned to ride horses in the cavalry. George Armstrong Custer had been dead less than thirty years.

Man was flying but what was the point beyond show? You couldn't carry passengers on a Flyer. Couldn't carry freight. Before airplanes could become part of the everyday world they would have to become useful, and attract financiers or government support.

The 1903 Flyer was open to the elements. There weren't any runways. Or airports. Or even seats for that matter. There was no way to fly at night or in fog. If a pilot couldn't see landmarks, he would have no idea where he was.

In 1905 the Wrights offered their newer Flyer, capable of staying aloft for thirty-eight minutes, to the Army. It was rejected. There didn't seem to be any military need for a flying machine, although lots of civilians were starting to build them.

The big names of the future were still teenagers. Malcolm and Allan Lougheed, California brothers who would change their names to Lockheed and found the company that would one day build ship 714, were sixteen and seventeen years old on a fruit farm in the Santa Clara Valley.

Glenn Martin, whose company would build planes including the famous world-traveling Pan Am Clippers, a stuffy, shy, mama's boy who would never marry, was also seventeen, from Macksburg, Iowa, population 300. In 1910 his mother would receive a letter from the family doctor calling her son a "hallucinated visionary" and begging her to "call him off" aviation "before he is killed," wrote Wayne Biddle in *Barons of the Sky*.

Donald Douglas, who would one day found Douglas Aircraft, and supply most of Delta Air Lines' planes well into the latter part of the century, was eleven years old when the Wrights took the Flyer up, living in Brooklyn, born to an upper-middle-class family, father a Wall Street bank cashier. In 1909 he would go to Washington with his mother to petition his congressman for an appointment to the Naval Academy, and while there would watch the U.S. Army Signal Corps test-fly the Wright Flyer at Fort Myer, Virginia. It would change his life.

But at the beginning the only money to be made in aviation came from winning air meets.

The first big one was held in Reims, France, in 1909. A pilot named Legagneux stayed up forty-three minutes, a world's record. In the United States, posters advertising early meets proclaimed, "Flying Machines! Airships!" For 50 cents, crowds watched New York motorcycle racer Glenn Curtiss race his homemade airplane around a track at 38.4 miles an hour, against a car. There were shows in New York, Nice, Milan, Chicago. A program for the fourth Los Angeles International Aviation Meet in 1912, on display in Washington in the Air and Space Museum, advertised, "Sure Shot" Horace Kearny, "the aviator who is to fly in the Grand Canyon of Arizona." "Captain Tom Duck Gunn, only Chinese aviator in the world." "Sky High Irving. Irving will make a parachute jump while 4,000 feet high and travelling at a rate of 60 miles an hour."

The program featured famous daredevil Lincoln Beachey. "Beachey will do the turkey-trot, the ocean wave, the dip of death . . . He will perform with his hands off the steering wheel most of the tricks other flyers perform with both their hands and feet on the controls." In his "daring death dive," Beachey will "ascend to a height of 3,000 or 4,000 feet and after making a few reverse spirals will make an absolute vertical drop towards the earth. He will attain a speed of 130 mph. When within 50 feet from earth Beachey will throw his hand off the control and straighten out and land."

With each show, public awareness of flying grew, but the draw wasn't the passenger-carrying potential of the new machines but "the crowds' desire to look upon mangled bodies and hear the sob of expiring life," wrote *Scientific American*. At one 1910 meet in Denver, a crowd went berserk, rushed a crashed plane and tore souvenirs from the wreckage, and gloves from the dead pilot's hands before police cleared them away.

But the shows also attracted students of a more wholesale kind of death. The military. The Army Signal Corps had understood a little of the potential of airplanes as far back as 1908, when they bought and tested one Wright Flyer. But it was to be used for observation, not battle.

Aerial warfare became part of aerial shows. In 1912 in Los Angeles, Lincoln Beachey and Glenn Martin, flying two planes, destroyed a miniature city by dropping "bombs" on it while a crowd of 3,000 erupted in cheers. Since no real bombs had ever been dropped by planes, the performers had to be creative. The "bombs" were oranges, but nobody knew what an aerial bomb would look like anyway. The explosions were caused by powder dug into the ground beneath the "city" before the crowd arrived. "Such a spectacle has never before been seen on the Pacific Coast, or anywhere else," praised the *Los Angeles Express*. And Martin predicted in newspaper essays that planes would one day be used by armies and police.

The age of innocence was over. One year later, a French mercenary aviator named Didier Masson, in the pay of Mexican revolutionaries, flew a "bomber," made of wood and cotton-fabric wings and powered by a 75 horsepower engine, over Mexican government ships in Guaymas Bay on the Gulf of (Baja) California and tried to drop bombs on them.

Within two years the skies of Europe were filled with battling airplanes. In 1914 Congress authorized the establishment of the Aviation Section of the Signal Corps. It was the same year the first regularly scheduled air passenger service began in the United States: the St. Petersburg–Tampa Air Boat Line carried one passenger at a time, twice daily, across Tampa Bay for $5 for the twenty-mile trip. The airline used flying boats, planes that landed in water.

By 1916 the U.S. Army was asking for "squadrons" of observation, troop transport, and bomb-carrying planes. And the Post Office began experimenting in airmail delivery in 1918.

For the pilots, it was rough. There were no radio beacons for navigation or even weather reports. There was no way to talk to the ground by radio. If clouds were low, pilots flew close to the ground, dodging trees and buildings. Along the countryside they followed rivers or railroad tracks. In their open cockpits, they were at the mercy of the elements.

Just between 1920 and 1921 nineteen airmail pilots died in eighty-nine crashes. They carried guns because it was expected they would crash and have to guard the mail. They were empowered to deputize farmers whose fields they landed in. They flew 250-mile-long stretches, which would end when, out of gas, they would land in a field where two planes waited for them, warming up. The pilot would throw the mailbags into one waiting plane and take off. If the plane didn't seem to be working properly, which happened often, he'd return and try the second plane.

At night, farmers lighted bonfires along the way to guide pilots. The government began installing flashing lights at landing fields in Chicago and Cheyenne, and later, beacons flashing every twenty miles in between.

To give an idea of what airmail piloting was like, one famed pilot, Ham Lee, told a story later about one of his more memorable flights in 1919, from Philadelphia to New York. Lee ran into thick fog near Staten Island.

Author Carl Solberg quoted the story in his book *Conquest of the Skies*:

> It was the biggest fight of my life. I flew in that soup for maybe an hour while I tried to shake off the sensation that I was losing flight level when I wasn't. My experience in aerobatics saved me. I had to sit in that soup, letting down slowly, making turns, looking not for sky but for water. When I finally saw the water, I kept enlarging my turns till I saw the shoreline. I saw a field and was measuring it for landing when I had to pull up over trees.

Back in the soup, I had to do it all over again: careful turns, round and round, until I came out over the water, then wider circles till I saw the ground. This time I went for it. A treetop tore the fabric of my plane—a bough ripped through the fuselage and ripped my pants. I landed—on Staten Island after all.

I called up Belmont Park. They weren't surprised. They came with a barge from Long Island and found me near shore, and I went back to Belmont Park with them, the plane and the mailbags. They said, "You better not fly tomorrow." But I'd heard too many stories about that. When your nerves are on edge, you may lose it if you don't go right back up. I did, next day, but I shook all the way to Philadelphia.

By the 1920s the Post Office was awarding mail contracts to private air services, and with these government subsidies assuring incomes, the first airlines were formed. Aeromarine West Indies Airways published timetables and flew thousands of passengers and mail between Miami, the Bahamas, Key West, and Cuba. It used flying boats and went out of business after two of its planes went down in the open seas—the passengers were swept to their death off the drifting wreckage.

Aviation was growing, but slowly. Despite the government money, and Congress voting a five-year program of military aircraft procurement, and the passage of the Air Commerce Act of 1926, which authorized the government to set up licensing for planes and pilots, by 1927 only thirty airliners were flying in the United States, with combined seats for 200 passengers. What was needed was some dramatic demonstration of how air power was the future of transportation. Of how reliable a plane could be, and how far it could go. And that demonstration would be provided by Charles Lindbergh.

Lindbergh, twenty-five, was chief pilot and mail deliverer for Varney Airlines. A tall, slender, boyish ex-motorcycle racer and son of a Midwest Republican congressman, he'd grown up suffering nightmares about flying. He'd dream he was plunging, terrified, through space. The dreams didn't go away until Lindbergh made a parachute jump in 1922.

His fear conquered, he became a barnstormer, wingwalking and giving airplane rides at fairs. Delivering his mail to Chicago over Illinois one day, he decided to join a race to be the first to fly non-

stop from the United States to Paris. A $25,000 prize was being of-
fered by a New York hotel owner for the feat. Lindbergh persuaded
wealthy businessmen backers in St. Louis to fund the trip. The San
Diego-based Ryan company built his plane, *The Spirit of St. Louis*,
of steel tubing, piano wire, wood, and cotton fabric for the wings.
The Spirit of St. Louis had one engine. If it quit, Lindbergh would
die.

Unlike others competing for the prize, Lindbergh decided to fly
alone, to have more room for fuel, but that meant he would not be
able to sleep. He couldn't see out of the front of the plane because
a fuel tank blocked his view. His dream captivated the nation. At
7:50 A.M. on May 21, 1927, he climbed into a brown wicker seat in
the *Spirit of St. Louis* with a canteen of water and two ham sandwiches, two beef, and one egg in waxed paper. Reporters scoffed
at him for not carrying a radio, but he'd decided radios were too
heavy and unreliable. He had a hand-held periscope to see out of
the side of the plane to track where he was going. He also had a
magnetic compass on board, but because its needle was thrown off
by the iron in the gas tank, it had to be mounted behind his head.
Lindbergh borrowed a compact from a woman in the crowd so he
could read it. The *Spirit of St. Louis* wasn't exactly like ship 714.

In fact, Lindbergh's twenty-eight-foot-long plane inching into
the air from Roosevelt Field, Long Island, over Long Island Sound,
was more like a flying gasoline tank, it was so heavy with fuel. Six
men had died already trying to win the prize. The wind was blowing the wrong way and the engine barely gave enough power. He
cleared a tractor beyond the runway by ten feet. By Halifax, Massachusetts, he was up at 100 feet, wobbling. With his compass and
sextant, he headed over the black Atlantic. As the little monoplane
droned back toward the old world, 40,000 fight fans at Yankee Stadium, there for the match between heavyweights Tom Maloney
and Jack Sharkey, went dead silent as the announcer said, "I want
you to rise to your feet and think about a boy up there tonight who
is carrying the hopes of all true-blooded Americans. Say a prayer
for Charles Lindbergh."

New York radio stations broadcast the Bonnie Laddies singing,
"Captain Lindbergh, We're with You." And humorist Will Rogers
wrote in his column, "No attempt at jokes today. A slim, tall, bash-

ful, smiling American boy is somewhere over the middle of the Atlantic Ocean, where no lone human being has ever ventured before."

He had no radio. It was cold. He avoided thunderheads, but had no way to climb out of bad weather, because he would lose consciousness if he went too high, and even at 10,500 feet he suffered oxygen deprivation. He had no copilot to take over if he needed a nap. Fourteen hours into the flight he hit snow. Ice clouds. He used a flashlight to check ice on the wings. Then he started seeing things. "Trees outlined against the horizon," he would write. And islands. And ghostly forms. He fought off an urge to fly home. At seventeen hours, according to his grandfather's nickel-plated watch, he passed the point of no return. Ireland was now closer than Newfoundland. He was fighting off sleep, prying his eyelids open with his fingers. He tried smelling salts. He flew as low as 10 feet to fight monotony. At twenty-eight hours he saw seagulls and a fishing boat. He flew low enough to shout to the lone man aboard, "Which way is Ireland?" He got no reply.

By 9:30 A.M. Paris time huge crowds had gathered at Le Bourget Airfield, because word had come over the wireless from England: Lindbergh had been sighted over Cornwall. When the little plane came into view, pandemonium broke out. Adoring crowds stormed through lines of police and soldiers to surround him. In the United States, people danced in the streets.

He'd made it. "People who had been afraid to cross the street talked about flying the Atlantic," said *U.S. Air Service* magazine. Over the next three months roughly half the country would see the hero, funded by the Daniel Guggenheim Fund for Promotion of Aeronautics, at parades in all forty-eight states, in eighty-two cities. Airmail deliveries shot up. Investors pumped millions into aeronautics companies on Wall Street.

Lindbergh turned down offers to be in movies. He flew to Dayton and spent a night as a guest of Orville Wright. He had dinner at the White House. He met the big financiers in New York. They asked him what he wanted to do next, and his answer delighted them. I want to keep flying, and I want to help establish passenger carrying on a large scale in the United States, he said.

• • •

planes with jets. Eight years later, BOAC was flying passengers across the Atlantic on civilian jets.

And millions of passengers wanted to go. One big by-product of World War II was that people who otherwise never would have flown had gone airborne. The postwar passenger boom was on.

Just a glance at Delta's early 1960s travel posters back in Paulette O'Donnell's office had given me an idea of who the new passengers were. One showed a husband and wife, together on a plane, the wife looking delighted while a flight attendant served a meal on linen tablecloth with fine china. "SHE'LL like it," the words proclaimed. In another poster, a long, elegant banquet table was set for dinner on a runway, near a Delta DC-6. Beautiful stewardesses stood along the table, beckoning like maître d's to customers—er, passengers—on a night out on the town: "Dinner for 48!" Another poster showed a man, who is clearly a tourist to Hawaii—in a garish hip-high cotton shirt with flowers on it, and a hat set at a rakish angle, like Kookie on the old TV show, "77 Sunset Strip"—leaning in toward a beautiful girl, maybe his wife, more likely a girlfriend or a provocative stranger. Or then again, maybe the ad is for the girl—sitting in a wicker chair hung from a branch; she's in a two-piece bathing suit, with a coconut in her lap, and two long straws coming out of it. One for him. One for her. "Instant Paradise. Just add You," the poster said.

By 1960, 58 million people flew as passengers in planes.

Unfortunately, in the earlier days of flight some passengers and crew gave their lives so aviation could get safer. Crashes often brought new laws and technologies. After a United Airlines plane went down in a Wyoming storm in the early 1920s—a storm everyone at United on the ground knew about, but there was no way to tell the pilot—United installed the first ship-to-ground radios. They were filled with static, and the copilot had to dangle a wire out the window to improve reception, but they saved lives.

Wood, the principle material out of which airplanes were made in the early years, was replaced by metal after a 1931 Kansas crash when a three-engine Fokker carrying the famed Notre Dame football coach Knute Rockne plunged out of the sky into a field on a sunny, calm day. Wooden elements in the wing had rotted.

Passenger flight, once a crazy dream, was becoming ¡
day life. Five years after Lindbergh landed in France, ⟨
Roosevelt of New York became the first politician to
plane in a campaign. Roosevelt wanted to make a big
Democratic National Convention in Chicago if he wa
for president, so he flew to the Windy City on Ameri
from Albany. The future president ate peanut butter an
wiches and worked on his speech on the way. After his
wife Eleanor traveled the country on planes so much
Carl Solberg said in *Conquest of the Skies* that her natio,
cated column "My Day" read like a flight log.

Actors flew. Businessmen flew. But air travel wasn't ne
as it is today. In the early 1930s one in every 2,200 air
sengers was involved in an accident. Eight years later, U.
registered its first year without a fatality. Over 2 million ¡
reached their destinations in the United States without a
in 1940. Air travel insurance dropped until premiums cos
for travel on train or plane.

The planes flew faster, higher. Both World Wars brou
in technology. During World War I, both sides had expe
with using radio as a navigational aid. The U.S. Navy tried
ing boats. The Germans used it to help guide their ¿
bombers toward British targets.

With World War II came radar. Pressurized planes able
high altitudes, over bad weather. And most of all, jets.

The idea for jet power had been around for some tim
wasn't until 1938 that an actual German experimental pla
by using it. The principle was the same one explaining wh
loon shooting out air flies around a room: Thrust comes f
caping gas. In a turbojet, a pump called a compressor pun
into a main compartment. A burner in the compartment ign
fuel. The explosion shoots toward the back, providing thr
also turning a small windmill called a turbine. The turbine ¡
the compressor. And the whole process starts again.

The German Heinkel He 178 Vl could fly at 373 miles pe
By 1943 Westinghouse had an American-designed turbojet. B
the U.S. Air Force announced plans to replace all piston pro

During the mid-1930s a whole series of crashes were caused by faults in the radio navigation system. At the time pilots followed radio beams across the United States to get from one place to another. But in places like the Rocky Mountains, the beams could bounce around, and in bad weather planes sometimes followed them into mountains. Also, the beams would go off the air during periodic weather reports. During one such eight-minute blackout in 1936, the crew of a TWA DC-2 carrying Sen. Bronson Cutting of New Mexico missed air traffic instructions that might have saved the plane, and later it ran out of gas and crashed, killing all aboard.

After that, air laws, which had been issued piecemeal, were codified into the Federal Air Regulations. The government increased spending on radio and navigation equipment. Under the Civil Aeronautics Act of 1938, the government began studying how to build airports.

A year later another air tragedy brought more change. A British seaplane bound for Bermuda went down in the Atlantic, split open, and sank. There were no lifeboats aboard. Within months Pan Am was phasing out their Clippers and buying land planes, and from then on all transoceanic flights had to carry rafts.

In 1956, in one of the worst air disasters ever to occur in the United States, a TWA Super Constellation with seventy passengers on board, and a United DC-7 with fifty-eight, hit each other over the Grand Canyon. The passengers were slaughtered. The government ordered long-range radar for air traffic controllers, and for the first time, required all flights to be under Air Traffic Control surveillance at all times. Pilots were required to retire at sixty.

The accident rate went down. The equipment got better. The numbers of passengers kept growing, so much that by 1960 the airlines were contemplating widebody jets, enormous craft able to carry over 300 passengers at a time. Boeing Aircraft unveiled the 747, and Lockheed and Douglas Aircraft companies were about to embark on one of the bitterest fights in airline history, a battle between the makers of the DC-10 and the L-1011 for supremacy of the smaller end of the widebody market—if a 300-passenger plane could be considered "small" at all. At stake were billions of dollars and thousands of jobs. The loser would be so crippled it would have to be saved by Congress from collapsing. It would drop out of the civilian end of aircraft manufacturing altogether. It would produce a dream plane loved by pilots for its maneuverability and by passengers for its comfort, but the superb quality would raise the price so much, and bad luck would wreck the delivery timetable so badly, that the company would lose the race in the end.

I planned to talk about the battle in a chapter about Lockheed and the building of ship 714. In fact the fight would erupt near Los Angeles, just coming into view below. The second leg of 714 was over. We were descending. Capt. Charlie Violette, a tall, gregarious native of Salt Lake City, talked to Air Traffic Control while Ron Scarpa flew the plane. They would switch jobs on the next leg, to Hawaii. Ship 714 had been in the air so far today for less time than it takes to drive from New York to Burlington, Vermont, and we had already crossed the continent. Below, Los Angeles seemed suffused by the sort of gray pollution haze that once seemed reserved for Third World cities that Americans pitied when they saw aerial photos of them. I saw palm trees. Blue swimming pools. Freeways filled with traffic. As we touched down and taxied to the gate, I saw passengers waiting for the next leg pressed to the glass, watching us approach, eagerly awaiting the flight to Honolulu.

Otto Lilienthal would have been astounded. The ease of it all would have amazed him the most. Even back at Delta, Paulette O'Donnell, in arranging this trip, had worried about whether I'd sleep on the plane, or that I might start to smell after two days in the cockpit, or that the plane might get diverted to Portland or Cincinnati or Miami, and not get to Hawaii. But she'd never fretted about storms. Or radio transmissions. Or beams bouncing in the Rocky Mountains misleading 714 into a cliff. All the thousands of problems that had been overcome in a scant ninety years.

Now Captain Violette stood at the door to the cockpit saying good-bye to the deplaning passengers. Outside, in a drizzle, and with less than an hour to go until the next takeoff, a line mechanic was walking beneath the belly of 714, peering at the condition of the wheels, the landing gear, the wind pressure measuring equipment, the flaps and slats. Engineer T. J. Carpender would also make his "walkaround," or visual inspection, before we went back up.

A Dobbs Food Service truck pulled up outside the plane, and

catering attendants began loading steaks, chicken, little bottles of mai tais for the next leg of the trip.

Baggage attendants crouched inside the luggage compartment and also at the bottom of a moving ramp, checking bags leaving the plane by tag, loading them onto appropriate carts labeled by destination.

Cleaning personnel moved quickly through the plane, straightening up after the passengers who had left.

Like a racing car at a pit stop, 714 was getting a touch-up before continuing over the Pacific, toward the most isolated islands on earth.

Captain Violette and I walked out to the terminal area, where he punched a secret code into a lock on a door. We walked downstairs to the Delta Operations Center. In a small functional-looking room, he stood near a locked safe where flight attendants put liquor money, nearby a computer terminal where he could bid for routes for the next month's schedule, and he scanned eight separate weather maps tacked to a bulletin board. One just showed winds across the Pacific at high altitudes. One showed showed Metro Alerts, areas in the country experiencing more severe weather. Forecasts are updated on the boards every six hours, he said.

So far it didn't look like there was any weather to worry about all the way to Hawaii, but weather could change, so crews never took it for granted.

It occurred to me, watching him check the maps, that almost a century after Otto Lilienthal crashed and died outside Berlin, Delta Capt. Charles Violette as well as every commercial pilot flying today, even every airline flying today, was still following his advice before and during every flight. In a thousand operations centers and in a thousand airports, pilots were looking at tens of thousands of weather maps. Checking low pressure centers. Memorizing highs. Noting the speed of winds at levels they would fly. A century after the Winged Prussian failed to build the stable aircraft he had dreamed of, Capt. Charles Violette was getting on intimate terms with the wind.

ELOISE TANI AND THE INVISIBLE MAN

She nestled into her First Class seat, a small, pretty nurse on her way home to Honolulu. She'd been hiking and skiing in Utah, but the real reason she'd gone off was to have time to think. "I told myself, if you're not going to marry him, you better cut it," she said. In her condo back on Hali-aka Drive, living with her boyfriend and his son by a previous marriage, she'd felt confined. "I didn't tell him what I was thinking. Just that I needed to be by myself."

The seat-belt sign went off. The flight attendants got up and began preparing service. We broke from the clouds, and the Santa Barbara Channel was calm and deep blue below. The Channel Islands green, volcanic-looking.

"For two years we hadn't been alone for one evening," Eloise Tani said. "And his son is nice, but he's a whole other person."

She looked lovely in tight jeans, a waist-length white jacket, a purple T-shirt from Moab, Utah. Her finger- and toenails were painted red. Her black hair fell to the small of her back. She wore two small earrings in each lobe. She carried a paperback romance novel she'd been reading in the terminal.

"The girl in it is in love with her best friend's brother, but he treats her like a friend," she said.

In four and a half hours, Shawn Sweeney, her disc jockey boyfriend, would meet her at the terminal in Honolulu, having no idea how close they'd come to breaking up.

"I was only gone a few days," Eloise Tani said. "But I missed him so much."

I'd met her in the terminal area. She'd walked up to me when a Delta gate agent announced over the intercom that I would be on the plane. This was part of a compromise I'd reached with Delta Public Relations Vice President Bill Berry, over how to talk to passengers.

"If Ron Allen [the chairman] gets one letter from a passenger complaining about you, this book will be over," said Berry, who worried passengers might feel put out if they felt trapped by an interviewer. This was frustrating for me, but typical of Delta management, who fretted about the sensibilities of anyone I interviewed, from their own baggage handlers to the public who paid for seats. It was more than commerce. A paternalistic attitude was at play. "We're Southern," is the way Paulette O'Donnell mysteriously explained it. I'd known that, among airline analysts, Delta's reputation was that their strength lay in extra-quality service. That allegedly they were much more loyal to their own employees than most American corporations. So much so that Delta had managed to operate pretty much without unions. But I also knew that even the meanest, stingiest, most selfish companies bragged in the 1990s they were "people companies." I was skeptical of the claims at first. But not after a while. I planned to talk about them in a chapter on management and labor relations.

In the meanwhile, the deal between Bill Berry and me was, I could approach passengers in the terminal area, where they were free to escape. I could talk to them on the plane if we'd agreed beforehand on the arrangement, and I kept out of the way of the flight attendants. Flight attendant happiness was important to Berry too. Later, after a single complaint from a flight attendant who said I'd "scared her" with a question about a crash, Delta would bar me from cockpits. But at the moment, Delta was telexing their gate agents at different cities, asking them to make the announcements.

"Ladies and gentlemen! We have a special passenger on board! He's writing a book about this very plane! He doesn't want to bother you, but he'd love to talk to you," the agents would say while I stood around like a gawky teenager about to give a piano recital.

Usually, in the dead silence that followed, between one and three hundred passengers stared back at me. This being Los Angeles, they'd broken into applause.

But then Eloise Tani had walked up and introduced herself. She seemed like a person who takes pleasure in everything in life. The way she'd been the only passenger to come up. The way she smiled when she tasted the champagne in First Class. The joy in her voice when she told me how the passenger agent had given her a First Class seat even though she'd not paid for one. The way she loved her book.

I joked, "Is your heart hammering with anticipation now, about seeing your boyfriend again?"

She blushed. "Every time I saw something beautiful, I wished he was there."

I got up and walked to the cabin and gave the coded knock. When the door swung open, the vista jumped out at me. The whole sky seemed to be in the cockpit. Engineer T. J. Carpender pored over a stack of long computer printouts, key information enabling 714 to make the flight safely. The printouts were "flight plans," usually delivered to cockpits by gate agents half an hour before takeoff, although Charlie Violette had picked this one up at the gate.

For Eloise Tani to reach Honolulu tonight, for every plane to reach its destination safely, the printout had better be right, with the hundreds of facts on it. The weight of the plane at the gate, 430,360 pounds for us today. The expected amount of fuel we'd burn just on this leg, 92,130 pounds. The amount of time we'd need to reach an alternate airport if Honolulu was closed, nine minutes. The number of passengers on board, 282. Even the amount of fuel we'd burn taxiing to takeoff.

Crucial information. The weight determined how high and fast we could go, how quickly we used up fuel. The latitude and longitude checkpoints were where the engineer would calculate if we were burning fuel at the proper rate, and radio Oakland Air Traffic Center to let them know we were on course, on time. The "equal time point" told Captain Violette when 714 would be equidistant from Hawaii and the West Coast, if we lost engines and had to decide whether to turn around or keep going. The reserve fuel on board, an FAA-mandated 10 percent extra, was there in case 714 had to circle on the other end or had a course change.

Looking over T.J.'s shoulder, I made out a name on the upper left-hand corner of the printout. Rick Knell.

Eloise Tani had been introduced to Captain Violette over the intercom. Had heard the names of the cockpit and flight attendant crew. But unless a disaster occurred today and she survived and read about the investigation, she would never know Rick Knell existed. He was the invisible man. The fourth crew member on the plane. The "dispatcher" back in Atlanta at Delta's Operations Center, who might never in his life set foot in 714, but who to the FAA was as legally responsible for our safety as Captain Violette. Rick had checked and sent out this flight plan.

"When a pilot gets on a plane, he's betting the dispatcher did his homework," Delta Vice President of Operations Buddy Doll had told me in Atlanta.

For all Captain Violette's power here, he could not change route, or even take a sick passenger to a different airport unless the invisible man agreed.

I sat in the jump seat and watched T. J. Carpender checking gauges against the flight plan, to see if our fuel burn was the proper rate so far, and I remembered Rick Knell. He was a tall, slightly rumpled looking forty-two-year-old I'd met at 1 A.M. in the Operations Center on the fifth floor of Delta's complex near Hartsfield Airport. A native of Los Angeles, an ex-cargo loadmaster at Korean Airlines, now licensed by the FAA to dispatch planes. A man who drove his Ford pickup to work from Atlanta's suburbs every day.

Knell had a deep voice, a glance full of instant appraisal, a quick, efficient manner when he worked flights. At 1 A.M. he fortified himself with black coffee and an enormous plastic cup of cold water he kept filled on his desk.

"A captain has one flight to think about. I have twelve in the air right now," he said.

The nerve center of the airline's minute-by-minute operations was a big split-level room in soft grays. Dispatchers worked at desks separated by waist-high partitions, below television weather monitors and in front of computers. Supervisers were on the upper tier.

The muted intensity reminded me of a newspaper city room,

when reporters worked on stories. Even the soothing colors seemed to compress the energy and make it more palpable. To the hum of computers and the bursts of printers in the meteorology section, Rick Knell and twenty-five other dispatchers talked low and seriously into telephones, with pilots in the air all over the world.

They worked by region. Eastern Europe. The North Atlantic. The Pacific. The Northern United States.

"We deal with problems instantly here," Vice President of Operations Buddy Doll said. "Elsewhere in the company there's time to send a committee out to study problems. Dispatchers decide right now."

These were the action junkies. The guys who liked to work under pressure. Who liked balancing twenty flights at a time. Who thrived on the adrenaline rushes of airport closings, passenger reroutings, ice storms, heart attacks.

"We like punishment," grinned Rick Knell. A dispatcher's job is so important he can't even go to the bathroom unless he alerts another one to watch his station in case there's an emergency.

For ship 714 today, Rick's job had boiled down to its two usual aspects. He'd planned the safest, most economical, most comfortable flight. And he would react instantly if something went wrong. Back in Atlanta, even as we flew, his tools were all around him. There was the computer where he could access data systems on weather, equipment, routes. There was a meteorology staff whom he periodically consulted for updates on weather. Even though the computer could access weather, the meteorology people might have important new information affecting his planes.

At Rick's desk were special speed-dialing phones so he could talk directly to pilots. Or wake up the sleeping station chiefs in any city Delta serves, if a plane needed the station opened in the middle of the night for an emergency. He could rouse Chairman Ron Allen at 3 A.M. Which is what one dispatcher did shortly before I visited, when movie star Zsa Zsa Gabor dealt "with considerable vulgarity" with Delta personnel in First Class on a flight from Los Angeles to Atlanta, after flight attendants asked her to keep her two dogs, Genghis Khan and Macho Man, in their cases, said company spokesman Bill Berry.

Delta had the Atlanta police escort Zsa Zsa from the plane.

Zsa Zsa's version was, "If I live to be a hundred I'll never understand why five policemen would take me off the plane. As long as I live I don't want to hear the word Delta."

"Dispatchers also handle medical emergencies somewhere in the system about twice a week," Russ Crawford, director of flight control, told me. "Heart attack. Coma. Baby. Or maybe there's a mechanical failure. The captain will probably call. He'll say, 'We need to put down.' He'll give the name of the sick passenger. But suppose it's 2 A.M.? And the captain wants to land in Charlotte, and our Charlotte operation is closed. Or suppose the plane is an L-1011, and Charlotte doesn't have the jetways long enough, or passenger steps so people can get off the plane. You don't want to land the airplane where you can't get the passengers off. The dispatcher has to know this stuff."

At the operations center, the "what ifs?" had started again.

"What if there's a thunderstorm ahead," Russ said. "A dispatcher has to know how high different planes can fly. A plane needs to clear a thunderstorm by at least 2,000 feet. An L-1011 can fly to 41,000 if it's light. A Boeing 727 stays at 37,000 feet or less. Even with radar, a captain may not have as good information as a dispatcher as to what lies ahead. If a thunderstorm is sitting on a route, the dispatcher needs to know if his plane can climb over it or should go around it. He has to be familiar with mechanics, principles of aviation, electrical systems.

"He has to know his planes."

That's why in written and oral tests Rick took from the FAA, he had to answer questions like, "What's the maximum gross weight for an L-1011," or "What are the limitations on the 737 if the rotating beacon [which indicates that an engine is running] is out." Before he could get his certificate, he had to complete test flight plans and calculate fuel loads. He took a psychological test at Delta.

"The shrink was wearing a baseball cap during the interview," one dispatcher told me. "He asked, 'What do you think of it?' 'I don't mean to be offensive,' I said, 'but I don't think about your cap at all.' "

"What if there's a hijacking?" I asked Russ. "Does the dispatcher come into it?"

"Fortunately, it hasn't happened in a while, knock wood. But there are procedures. We get a call from the plane, they have some-one from Cuba on board. He's homesick. There the concern is, Do we have enough fuel? You have to negotiate with the hijacker, you may have to land to *get* fuel. You have to talk to the FBI, the FAA. Make arrangements through the State Department for the ground handling of the plane on the other end. I think we go through the Swiss Embassy."

Rick Knell said, "Every day, it's something different."

One time, in 1965, a Delta plane was hijacked in Kentucky, and the hijacker wanted to go to Algeria. But the plane didn't have fuel to get from the American Southeast across the Atlantic. It didn't have equipment for navigating over water. And the hijacker said the captain was lying when he tried to explain it to him.

Just like planning a regular flight, a dispatcher had to handle this one.

"First we had to figure out how to get it across the Atlantic," said Mickey Tierney, who'd been a dispatcher on the case. "With a full tank we could make it from Boston. But we had no facilities at the time in Boston. So we contacted Northeast Airlines, which agreed to handle the plane on the ground. Then we contacted TWA, which flew to Europe from Boston, and we arranged for our plane to follow one of theirs, which had the right navigational equipment. Our plane spun off at Portugal. There Air Traffic Control took over and got it to Algeria. The passengers got home safely. The Alger-ian government took the crew out and gave them a big party. Two months later they sent Delta a bill for it."

During 714's flight to Honolulu today, Rick Knell would be called if *any* emergency arose. Mechanical problem? The calls to the me-chanics would be routed through Rick, because he'd need to agree with Violette on any solution. Turbulence? Violette would call Rick Knell, Knell would discuss possibilities with Violette, and when they agreed, Violette would relay the request for an altitude change to Air Traffic Control.

A dispatcher has to "reason like a pilot, interpret like a meteo-rologist and think like a passenger," writer Jerome Chandler wrote.

At the Center, Rick had shown me how he plans Hawaii flights. He'd gotten out of his swivel chair, walked to a long table behind him, and picked a map off a pile. It was an "upper atmosphere map," a chart of the air, not the land. When he unfolded it, it gave me the impression of being inside a glass globe, looking out. Land masses on the map seemed elongated as they would stretched over a sphere. The land was blue, the sea white, accentuating the notion of looking at something backward, as in a photographic negative. On the map, dark blue tracks ran from a dozen points off the west coast to converge on Hawaii.

"These are invisible roads in the sky," Rick said. Each track had arrows on it to denote which way traffic flowed on that particular road. When you threw in altitude changes, there could be dozens of ways 714 could get to Honolulu. Sixty-seven routes existed just between Los Angeles and Dallas!

"Three hours before a flight, the computer calls it up automatically and calculates the best, most economical route," Rick said. "It figures in wind. Fuel consumption. It lists airport conditions. Weather alerts. Winds at different altitudes. By the time I get in, if I'm on a morning shift, I'll have six or seven flights to Honolulu to look at. My job is to make sure the information is correct, change it if it's not, pass it along if it is.

"If things are going smoothly, working a flight can take ten minutes. If not . . . " He smiled and trailed off.

I knew this smile. By the time I visited the Operations Center I'd been around Delta for two months, and it was a very particular kind of smile. It was usually accompanied by the person looking off into the distance. And it always appeared when I was trying to figure out exactly how complicated one problem could get.

"Okay, your flight 714 will burn less fuel at a high altitude," Rick said, nodding as if this fact was a given. "But what if there's a stiff frontal wind at that altitude? What if Air Traffic Control won't give us that altitude? Here's another one. Your plane 714 will burn less fuel carrying less weight, and less if it travels a shorter distance . . . " He started smiling. "But what if Air Traffic Control only lets us fly the shorter distance at the lower less-fuel-efficient altitude?"

I was getting a headache, but he wasn't finished. What if a thunderstorm was sitting in the middle of the best route? Better yet, what if the storm *wasn't* sitting in the route yet, but two hours from now, when the plane reached that location, it *might* be? Or what if there was a strong tailwind on the *longer* route, which would speed the plane up and save fuel?

Then there was the comfort factor. Suppose, dispatchers told me, chuckling at their beloved complexity, there was a *tiny bit* of turbulence on the cheaper route? Just for a couple of minutes. Nothing terrible. Was that itty-bitty minute of passenger discomfort, just an instant of coffee sloshing around, worth 4,000 pounds of savings in fuel? How *much* passenger discomfort was worth the savings? And how much savings exactly to the dollar? Profits were on everybody's mind. Everyone I met at Delta, from baggage handlers to mechanics to schedule makers to flight attendants to dispatchers to pilots, worried about profits. "This is my job we're talking about," one flight attendant told me. "Airlines are going down the drain right and left."

"My license, my job is on the line just like the pilot's," Rick said.

People took their jobs seriously at the Operations Center. And just when I thought I'd gotten a handle on how complicated the job was, Rick pointed to another man in the upper tier, hunched over another computer. Rick Goodman, it turned out, was a "systems coordinator" whose job consisted of monitoring all the L-1011s and international aircraft in the fleet.

"I juggle planes," he said.

While dispatchers worried about individual flight systems, people like Rick Goodman made sure the right type of plane was always available for the right trip. The horrible what-ifs were about to start again. Okay, Rick said, the weird recognizable smile appearing, let's say an L-1011 is scheduled to fly from Los Angeles to Honolulu at 1:40 P.M. Los Angeles time. It *has* to be an L-1011 because only that kind of plane can accommodate the 300 passengers on the flight today. Except what if the particular plane that is supposed to make the trip just broke down in Chicago? Where do we get another L-1011 from? There's another L-1011 scheduled to fly from Portland to Salt Lake City around the same time, and it's only carrying 100 passengers. I could switch that L-1011 for a 737, except *after* Salt Lake City, the second L-1011 is supposed to carry 280 passengers to Orlando, so I can't send that plane to Los Angeles. Or what if there's an ice storm in Atlanta, which meant the first plane was late in leaving this morning, and won't get to Los Angeles for another two hours? Or what if it *did* get out of Atlanta on time, but at its interim stop, Salt Lake City, it was held at the airport because 200 Los Angeles-bound conventioneers, due to take it, were delayed by a tornado watch that closed *their* departure point, Cincinnati Airport?

So how to fix the problem. Huh? *Huh?*

No matter how well managed the airline was, there was nothing any airline could do about weather.

I hated that smile.

"Right now," Rick Goodman told me on another visit, during the day, "Atlanta's fogged in. It's supposed to stay fogged in for six more hours. That means we can't land as many planes here as we usually can. So we have to cut back on arrivals. But *how* do we cut back and still get all the passengers that are coming to Atlanta *to* Atlanta?"

Rick scanned information on incoming flights on his computer. "Here's two Miami to Atlanta flights," he said. "Leaving a couple hours apart. Both L-1011s. One's scheduled in with 133 people. The other with 253. An L-1011 holds 302 people. That means I can get *some* of the passengers from one L-1011 onto the other one. But there are still some left. Hmmm."

Rick punched buttons and called up all the planes flying from Miami to Atlanta.

"Ah, here's a 757 coming in, but it's full. I can't use that one. Hmmm."

Rick changed tactics.

"Okay, not all the people coming into Atlanta from Miami are staying here. Some are going on to other places. Maybe I can get them to those places without sending them through Atlanta."

From Reservations, Rick found out that ninety passengers from the two L-1011s were only using Atlanta as a jumping-off point for the next leg of their trips.

In the end, Rick was able to get all the Atlanta-bound passengers into one L-1011, freeing the other to be used elsewhere, cutting back on the number of flights Delta was sending into the fogged-in, slowed-down airport. He contacted a "coordinator" at Miami airport and told him to "protect" the ninety passengers originally scheduled to use Atlanta as a hub departure point for their next destination. Ticket agents in Miami handled each individual passenger.

Rick smiled. End of problem.

Almost three thousand flights a day.

I hadn't even talked to the weather people yet. I walked back to the meteorology department and met John Pappas, who headed it. He was an older, balding man in a side office, wearing a translucent maroon shirt, and he clearly loved his job and grew excited talking about it. If the sky was filled with highways to a dispatcher, to a weatherman it was an ocean, with all the fluid properties of liquid affecting the airships like 714 that navigated it.

"Waves," John Pappas said, rolling around in his swivel chair and undulating his hands. "You sit on the beach and watch waves build up, build up, build up. And all of a sudden they break. The water tumbles chaotically across the sand. That's what happens in the atmosphere. That's what you call an air pocket. There's no such thing as a real pocket, a vacuum a plane falls into.

"It's waves. Especially along fronts, which are transition zones between air masses. That's what we do here, define where the changes in the atmosphere are. You get an air mass that's 80 degrees replacing one that's 30 degrees? *That's where things are gonna happen!*" He grinned. He waved his hands. "Snow! Rain! Turbulence!" he cried. "We identify these transition zones! We have radar! Satellites! We know it's moving fast! These troughs and ridges can be a hundred miles long. Fifty miles can separate waves in the sky. And fifty miles is nothing to a plane. Flying between waves. And meanwhile the waves are building, building, building."

Pappas shoved his palm down, as if suppressing the plane. "Breaking and tumbling across the sky. It pushes you down momentarily." He laughed. "But inside the plane, it feels like nothing is there.

"To me, wind, he's like this *wind guy*," John Pappas said. "He's what the wind looks like to me. Fat. You know the way Dizzie Gillespie's mouth works when he blows the trumpet? He's blowing like that. And we're looking for him. We're the wind seekers. We wanna find that max wind. We wanna put the plane in the max wind if it's going in the same direction. We want to avoid it if he's going the other way."

Pappas took me outside the office and introduced me to Jeff Hubright, the meteorologist who would later study the weather across the Pacific before 714 took off with Eloise Tani inside.

Hubright was much younger looking than his thirty-five years, in his khaki pants and plaid shirt and tie and wire-rimmed glasses. He was an ex–Air Force weather forecaster and high school mathematics teacher, who had decided he wanted to make a career in aviation when he was fifteen, taking flying lessons in Alma, Georgia, where he'd grown up.

"I was at the airport one day, and there was thunder and lightning all over the place. And my best friend's dad was a flight service station weather forecaster. He was talking on the radio to a guy in a little Cessna trying to get around this thunderstorm. I thought, This is something! This guy, sitting here in this weather station, it's like he's rescuing that plane. I wanted to help guys flying around in airplanes."

At Delta, Jeff concentrated on upper atmosphere forecasts, although the meteorology department also had staff who just studied weather near the ground at airports serviced by Delta. Not only wind and precipitation but pollution too. "The air temperature impacts takeoff," John Pappas broke in. "How much runway you'll need to get off the ground. And pollution, the man-made things in the atmosphere may effect our predictions. Let's say Spokane, Washington. We have a flight that gets in at 7 A.M. If you have a big factory on the north side of town emitting smoke, well, smoke is made up of lots of little particles. Hydroscopic nuclei. For fog to form, it needs something to condense around. A factory emitting smoke changes the climatology of the airport."

For Jeff and other meteorologists at Delta, "the problem is persistence versus climatology," Jeff said. "Persistence is what the weather is doing now. It's clear over the Pacific. Will it stay clear? Or will it go to climatology, if it's typically raining this time of the year in that area?"

The weather people were the linchpins in the scheduling process that seemed to be getting more complicated by the minute. Hundreds of thousands of dollars could ride on a weather prediction, especially if that prediction meant canceling flights. In the Operations Center, wind meant money. Snow meant money. With the hub system of travel in effect in the United States, a blizzard in Atlanta would change the travel plans of a lawyer in Chicago who was heading *west*, a tourist in San Francisco, a convict scheduled to be moved on a plane from Cincinnati to LA. Would the weather turn bad? When exactly would it turn bad? If Jeff told the dispatchers the weather would get ugly, really ugly, planes could be rerouted, passengers rescheduled, flights canceled. The company would put hundreds of travelers in hotels. The reservations offices would have to find flights for them tomorrow. The equipment that would be needed for other flights might not arrive, and then the systems managers would come into it, trying to find replacement equipment from somewhere else.

If Jeff decided bad weather was indeed on the way, but it wouldn't show up for just one more hour, that would mean one more hour of smooth scheduling for dozens of flights, and thousands of passengers, all through the United States.

To Jeff it was a contest. "Who wins? The weather? Or me?"

"See, I'm guessing the computer," Jeff said. "A couple of weeks ago I had a 180-knot wind off Japan. Would it increase? Or turn south? Or dissipate? Would it be pushed north? Or sit there? That's the jet stream. If I could get a plane into that, it would move pretty fast. It's a game between the wind and me. I looked at the history. I decided that in a few hours the jet stream would be pushed north, so I recommended we change our flight plans to take advantage of it. And the dispatchers did change the flight plan. Only when I came back the next day, I found out that the warm air never got pushed north. It pushed east. The airplane, instead of getting a 180 knot tailwind, only got 70.

"So the wind beat me," Jeff said.

"Did you get chewed out for what happened?" I asked.

Jeff looked surprised. "No, they understand it's an art."

Jeff explained basic meteorology. "The sun heats the earth up at different rates," he said. "It hits the equator and the lower regions more. The hot air rises. This develops different pressures. One section of the earth is high pressure and one is low, and the wind flows between them. There's entropy; the earth likes to balance everything out. That gets the wind flowing. Gets your moisture field involved. That's the basics."

To break these basics into forecasts for pilots like Captain Violette, Jeff had started work at 6:30 A.M. the day I met him. "When I get in, the early planes in the Pacific Fleet—to Japan, Tokyo, Seoul—are departing, lifting into the sky, their flights planned last night. They'll send me reports to verify or discredit the most recent computer forecast, so I can change it."

Jeff laid out another map of the Pacific on the drafting table, but if Rick Knell's map divided the sky into roadways, Jeff Hubright's treated it like a fluid. Jeff's map showed an area stretching from the eastern Rocky Mountains of the United States in the east to China in the west, and from the Bering Sea between the United States and the old Soviet Union on the north, to Hawaii at the south. Every few degrees of latitude and longitude along the way, the computer had printed blocks of information: temperatures, wind velocity, and air pressure at five different flight levels.

"We operate between 24,000 and 43,000 feet," he said.

Jeff said the maps were constantly being updated as new information came in. The computer got it from satellite radar, ground radar, the United Kingdom Meteorological office, weather balloons. "Twice a day," Jeff said, stretching his hands wide to show the diameter of the balloons, "at 7 A.M. and 7 P.M. eastern standard time, weather forecast services all over the world send up their balloons. They each carry probes for temperature, humidity, and pressure. They float right up to 60,000 feet, and a couple of hours later we get the information from the National Weather Service in Kansas City, which processes it, formats it, and sends it out to the Delta main computer."

The numbers on the map transferred in Jeff's mind's eye to wind, rain, turbulence.

"A couple of weeks ago I saw wind shear off Hawaii," he said, referring to the sudden and violent winds that could smash a plane into the ground during takeoff or landing, and which in fact destroyed a Delta L-1011 in Dallas in 1986. "I saw winds at 120 knots at 39,000 feet, and 60 knots at 34,000 feet. I went over and told the dispatcher, 'I got an idea this area off Honolulu is rough. We better watch out for it.'"

Jeff said he's also always looking for the "tropopause," a 4,000-to 6,000-foot-thick boundary in the atmosphere separating the troposphere, or lower atmosphere, from the stratosphere, where flight tends to be smoother. But the tropopause itself tends to be "bumpy."

"Pilots should fly above or below it," he said.

"What else do you look for?"

"You always want to get the difference between speed and turbulence. Like with the jet stream. Think of the wind as a rapid river at a sharp bend. A lot of times you see the river bubbling up on the rocks and splashing on the bank. But in the middle of the stream the current can be fast but smooth. I'm always looking along the edges of my jet core and seeing how rapidly speed decreases on either side of it. If it's gradual," he said, nodding, "no problem. But if it's a marked difference, 130 knots near Maui, say, and 30 knots a hundred miles away, I know we have a strong 'speed shear' or 'horizontal shear.' That would mean turbulence, which the pilots should avoid. And I'm looking at temperatures. Very strong temperature contrast can indicate turbulence."

Like Rick Knell, or the systems coordinators constantly monitoring the Delta fleet, Jeff kept checking and rechecking, and getting new information throughout his shift. Pilots throughout the world send in reports as they fly. And get reports over the radio if weather changes suddenly along their route.

By the end of the day Jeff was ready to make up a new map for the next meteorologist, to add statistical enhancements to what the computer had sent. The result would be sent out over the telex machines and tacked up in flight operations offices at airports around the world, so Delta captains like Charlie Violette could look at the maps before taking off.

First he typed into the computer the new sets of weather data he'd come up with. The information would be attached to the flight plans for upcoming planes. A large translucent printout emerged from a printer, with the blocks of information on it. Working at a drafting table, Jeff began drawing what looked like musical notes on the map, long thin shafts with small black barbs at the bottom. Except the shapes were really wind information. The barbs pointed in the direction the wind was coming from. By the number of barbs and how filled-in they were, a reader could tell speed. A symphony of air flow through the upper atmosphere. Dizzie Gillespie, John Pappas's *wind guy*, was playing the trumpet at 37,000 feet.

Jeff said, as he worked, "Sometimes pilots come in here for a tour. And often ask, 'Do you really use the information I send you? It's the middle of the night, and I'm over the Atlantic, and I send this information over the radio. Does it mean anything?'"

Jeff looked up from the drafting table. "Does it *mean* anything?" he repeated, shaking his head. "I tell them it's absolutely crucial for the flights behind theirs."

Now, in the cockpit, I watched T. J. Carpender filling in weather information on the flight plan, to be sent back to Atlanta. We had passed the equal-time point. On the basis of our weight and the wind that Jeff Hubright had worked on, the flight plan told us it should take three hours and thirty-four minutes to reach an airport from midpoint in the trip, and that 714 would need 52,919 pounds of fuel to do it.

"One time I had a plane lose an engine exactly at the equal-time point," Rick Knell had said. "But an L-1011 should be able to descend to 6,000 feet and get safely to land. Which it did."

I'd told Rick Knell about my experience losing an engine on the Swissair flight two years earlier. "That captain should have turned around instantly," Rick said. "You lose an engine, you turn around."

I read the flight plan. Under "Computed En Route Winds," it told us that the rougher air of the tropopause sat at different elevations between 36,000 and 50,000 feet along our route today, which was fine since Air Traffic Control in Oakland had us flying at 33,000 feet all the way. But just in case we hit a problem, or Air Traffic Control changed our altitude, the flight plan listed the wind speed, direction, and tropopause location at 29,000 feet, 31,000 feet, and 37,000 feet.

The flight plan told us that runway 4L in Honolulu was reduced in length today. It was being worked on. It was good to know in case we were heavy and it was raining in Hawaii when we arrived. "A heavier L-1011 needs more runway to stop," Rick had said.

The weather was beautiful, the blue sea calm below, and peaceful-looking cumulus clouds hung, tremendous but easily avoidable, like white islands in the sky. In the glass bubble, I could swear I could see the curve of the earth in the distance. Working from the flight plan, Ron Scarpa was on the radio with Oakland Center, re-

porting our position and speed so Air Traffic Control could make
sure we were separated properly from flights ahead and behind us
on the highway in the sky. Unlike flights over land, where planes
are on radar at all times, flights over water are only observed as they
leave or approach land. The rest of the time Air Traffic Control
works by calculating speed, direction, and position.

It was an uneventful flight. Plenty of time for talking. Amiable
Charlie Violette told me about his side businesses. Most pilots had
side businesses, he said. He owned real estate. A trailer camp. He'd
built houses.

"I'm a workaholic," he said.

He said he'd grown up in Southern California, wanting to be a
test pilot. "I got out of the Navy, finished school at Ohio State. I
started at Delta as an engineer in the old piston-driven DC-6s.
Pretty primitive," he said. "You felt everything was held together
with baling wire and upholstery. It leaked a lot of oil. It was a long
way from this."

I left the cockpit, and T. J. Carpender locked it behind me. I
walked back to where Eloise Tani was reading *Marriage of Incon-
venience*.

"The girl wants a child so badly she was going to adopt one but
she couldn't," Eloise said, as the other passengers watched *Fried
Green Tomatoes*. It was like a silent movie in color to us, the lights
playing on the faces of the passengers in First Class. On screen, Jes-
sica Tandy told Kathy Bates a story. Kathy Bates started crying. One
of the passengers with earphones on was crying too.

"Then the woman met a guy, and he was going to do it in vitro
as a favor," Eloise said. "They'd been friends for a long time."

I asked how she'd met Shawn Sweeney.

"I was working in the intensive care unit at Kuakini Medical
Center. It was a weekday night," she said. "He's a disc jockey,
pretty well known in Honolulu, and he was having a contest on his
show to win tickets to *Green Card*. The thirteenth caller would get
the tickets. I was the thirteenth caller."

She blushed. "Then we were flirting on the phone. He kept saying, 'Don't hang up.' He has this humor about him."

Once they met they were inseparable. They did everything together. "I always wanted someone with patience," she said. Other

boyfriends had always wanted to be alone, or not include her in things. But not Shawn. He moved into her condo with her, she said. But then his son Tony moved in too.

"Until living with them, I had my space. I could come home, dance around, do what I wanted. Now there was this seventeen-year-old there."

"I needed time to myself," she said. "So I flew to Salt Lake. My sister Leila lives there. As soon as I arrived, we got out the coffee and started talking. I'd missed him on the flight, but I still felt good. But when I saw things with Leila and her husband, I thought there's nothing better than being with someone. I was only away a short time, but that's all I needed." She smiled blissfully thinking about it.

"So now you must be excited coming back," I said.

Eloise blushed. "Yes."

"You'll marry him now?"

The blush got deeper. "If he asks."

The movie ended, and after a snack of cheese and chocolate and more champagne, the seat-belt sign came on. We were approaching Honolulu, the head flight attendant announced. I went back to the cockpit, and the guys were all staring at the radar screen, at a white blip pulling up on us from behind. Apparently a race had developed since I'd left, although neither of the planes involved was speaking to the other.

But monitoring Air Traffic Control frequency, it was clear that a Honolulu-bound Hawaiian Airlines L-1011 at a lower altitude was trying to overtake us and land first. They increased speed. We increased speed. They got on the radio with Honolulu, asking to land.

Honolulu radioed that we were to land first. Charlie, Ron, and T. J. shouted and pounded on the windscreen. The little white blip fell back.

At 10,000 feet, going into sterile cockpit silence, Rick Knell's flight plan had us crossing a latitude/longitude fix arbitrarily named BAMBO at 250 knots. On the left, from the glass bubble, I saw the island of Maui. Peeking from a cloud bank, the long, spiny black ridges thrust out of the blue Pacific. And now I could see Honolulu harbor ahead. The white high-rises by the sea. The peak of Diamondhead crater. We passed over a white breakwater and pleasure boats and marinas in the harbor. I saw little platforms in the water below, for divers. "Aloha" was written in red letters on the main terminal at the airport.

The flight plans had worked perfectly today so far. Although we still had one more leg to go.

Charlie Violette, Ron, and T.J. would spend tonight in Honolulu and fly a plane back tomorrow. A new cockpit crew would fly 714 to Maui thirty minutes from now. The new captain was probably down in operations now, getting the new flight plan.

I found Eloise Tani in the terminal, holding hands with a heavyset, Polynesian-looking man in a pink cotton shirt, shorts, and sandals. As soon as we saw each other, we both started grinning. "So you really *are* a writer," Shawn Sweeney said. "When she told me she was talking to a writer, I said, 'Eloise, you are so gullible.' "

They were so happy to see each other. They never stopped holding hands. I had the feeling her worries about leaving him had never been serious. Sweeney wanted to show me around Honolulu. "Call us if you're coming back. I mean it," he said.

He retold the story of how he and Eloise had met while she smiled and blushed. By the time he was finished, the plane was boarding. The new captain, a short, heavyset man who reminded me of the actor Wilford Brimley, walked past with his copilot and engineer. Time on the ground was lost revenue from ship 714.

"You know," Shawn Sweeney said, grinning and holding Eloise's hand, "I wrote a poem about her."

"Oh, stop," Eloise said.

"No, I did."

"You don't have it, do you?" I said.

"Cut it out," she said.

"I remember it," he said.

Ukulele music played in the terminal, which was filled with tan people in thonged slippers and floral shirts. Shawn Sweeney drew himself up.

He recited his poem as 714 boarded.

"If life were but a moment," he said, while she blushed and looked down, "blowing in the breeze . . . I'd gladly spend that moment, in the arms of Eloise."

FROM THE BOLL WEEVIL
TO BULGARIA

Monroe, Louisiana, lies ninety miles west of Vicksburg, Mississippi, forty-five miles south of Arkansas, in the northern third of its boot-shaped state. It is the seat of Ouachita Parish, which gave ex–Ku Klux Klansman David Duke a majority vote in Louisiana's 1991 gubernatorial election. Delta Air Lines executives flying into Monroe for their annual meetings pass over cotton fields and piney woods. There's a GE parts plant and a factory for plastic trash bags. Spanish moss drapes willows in residential sections. Downtown, at the Central Bank, the second-story conference room features a watercolor of a Delta four-engine Convair jet over Monroe, the town lighted up at dusk. And a 30-foot conference table near a penny bank collection in a glass cabinet. Little hands come out of boxes and yank money into dark depths. There's the clown who throws pennies in his mouth. The Jonah who drops nickels in a whale. The rifleman who shoots money into a plastic tree stump.

A month before boarding ship 714, I'd cruised through Monroe in a Ford pickup belonging to Delta's local manager, Jim Mann, an amiable, chubby, twenty-eight-year veteran with the company. It was a muggy day, and we were sweating. Mann parked near abandoned railroad tracks and low-income housing on the poor side of town. He'd warned me to wear hiking clothes. We moved into thickets of sticker and huckleberry bushes, which Mann poked with a stick. "Watch out for snakes."

Late afternoon sunlight dappled the mulchy ground. There was no sound; no traffic, jets, even birds. We reached a ruin in the woods, a half-wrecked one-room brick building the size of a country school, roof gone, trees and bushes sprouting where the floor had been, poking through arches that had once contained windows, rising so high they were twice the height of the walls. I saw trash on the ground. A coke can. A blackened paper where someone had started a fire.

"This is it," Mann said. "Delta's headquarters until 1941. Mr. Woolman's office. Ticket office. Name it."

The tininess of the place astounded me even though I'd been told what to expect. I couldn't help but contrast it with the complex in Atlanta, acre after acre of five- and twelve-story buildings, footbridges over streets, parking lots, guard booths, meeting rooms, projection rooms, a credit union, cafeterias, miles of corridors and little partitioned-off cubicles, dormitories for new student attendants, instructional rooms for pilots, mock-up planes, gigantic hangers, and shops for maintenance.

Mann kept poking the bushes in the ruin. Just the reservations department in Atlanta alone was bigger than this building. I didn't even think Pres. Whit Hawkins's office would fit in here.

"Delta did everything we could to make money in those days," Mann said, steeped in company lore since he worked at the birthplace. "We flew mosquito control. Stored airplanes for people. Crop-dusted. Sold fuel."

Now, on ship 714, his words came back to me as the glass bubble rose into the Pacific sky at dusk and the red "Aloha" sign on the Honolulu terminal grew smaller. Only a handful of passengers had boarded for the last twenty-minute leg of the day, and 714 was so light even I could tell the difference in the way it had leaped off the runway into the sky.

I was tired and eager to get to the hotel. But what had started me drifting back had been something Capt. R. E. "Roscoe" Diehl had said when he introduced himself.

"I'm Western."

Western meant Western Airlines, merged into Delta in 1986. Western, which back in 1930 had been the operator of the biggest commercial air network in the United States and by 1992 had become a mere footnote in Delta's history. Western, which had provided ship 714 with the routes we'd flown today, from Salt Lake City to Los Angeles and on to Honolulu after that.

How had Delta, the little backwoods airline, clawed its way out of obscurity, survived deregulation, absorbed Western instead of the other way around? How had it avoided the financial problems still wreaking havoc in the industry? In the competitive world of aviation, just in 1991 and 1992, Trans World Airlines had gone bankrupt, and so had Braniff International. And America West. And Midway.

At least TWA was still hanging on. Others hadn't been so lucky. Eastern, once Delta's principal competitor, was defunct, its buildings and hangers empty, its thousands of employees out of work. Pan Am, once the flagship airline of the United States, its blue logo as familiar to people overseas as the Stars and Stripes, was finished. Pan Am's Clipper Goodwill, from Barbados to Miami, its last flight, had completed its journey on December 4, 1991, as Capt. Mark S. Pyle wept at the controls and an honor guard of airport firetrucks shot water over the taxiing Boeing 727 during its approach to its final gate.

Other companies had disappeared in mergers. Frontier had been bought by People Express and merged into Texas Air Corporation, which had gone bankrupt. North Central Airways and Southern Airways had merged into Republic, which was bought by Northwest. Ozark had been absorbed by TWA.

But Delta, the old laughingstock of the big guys, had prospered, at least into early 1992.

Tracing the history, I thought back to an oil painting in the Monroe airport, of a severe-looking man in a brown suit, cut to show the blocky body underneath, a white hanky in the breast pocket, eyeglasses in the man's right hand draped over the arm of his sitting chair, silvery hair parted a third of the way across his head, eyes boring into the viewer as if sizing him up. The picture hung in the public terminal near a display of Monroe's wood and paper products, as if the town considered both the man and the forest natural resources.

During the months I'd spent at Delta, whenever founder C. E. Woolman's name came up, it was pronounced with reverence even though the man had been dead for years. He was always "Mr. Wool-man." Never just "Woolman." Or "C. E." Like he still might walk into the office any second.

In old photos he looks so tall that the top of his head is often the same height as top hats worn by men beside him. Mister Woolman. The acutely private patriarch who grew orchids in his greenhouse and gave them to secretaries and stewardesses. The workaholic who was said to know everyone by name at Delta for years. The tight-fisted manager who would walk around scavenging rubber bands and paper clips at the company, who was said to have a hand-shake like a lumberjack, who liked to play country boy with strangers. The man whom one early Delta investor described as having a knack for "making himself firmly but gently understood."

In the stories he was always quieter and less visible than his com-petitors in the business. And in reality it's the same management style that fools Delta rivals today.

"Sometimes people think we're not very aggressive," Delta Pres. Whit Hawkins had told me in his Atlanta office. "But our aggres-siveness is masked by the way we do business. I remember one time Frank Bormann of Eastern was testifying before the Civil Aeronatics Board, and one of the lawyers said, disparaging him, 'Well, you're just competing with Delta, and Delta is not very ag-gressive.'"

Hawkins grinned. "Mr. Bormann said, 'Anyone who thinks Delta is not aggressive has been smoking pot.' We keep the pressure on and do aggressive things without fanfare. People confuse flam-boyant and aggressive."

It had sounded a little boastful, so I'd said, "What's a quiet ag-gressive move you've made lately?"

"Acquiring Western Airlines. Acquiring Pan Am. Growing from 38,000 employees at the time of the Western merger to 80,000 to-day. Growing from a fleet of 265 planes to 560 today."

Hawkins smiled. "I'd say that's aggressive."

Woolman had started it, shaped the company, defined its style. In one old story, the patriarch had attended a banquet in the 1950s, where a mechanic was being awarded a pin commemorating years with the company. Woolman jokingly reminded the man, before several hundred people, of a time years before when the mechanic had thrown away a small piece of wire on a hanger floor, and Woolman had retrieved it for reuse.

Just a little incident, but it showed how Delta still functioned. Awarding their people on one hand. Scrupulously monitoring at least small resources on the other. For instance, just before I arrived in Atlanta, Delta management issued an across-the-board 5.7 percent raise to employees, making them among the highest paid in the industry, despite the fact that the company had posted multi-million dollar losses the two preceding quarters. Then at the same time, management had announced companywide expenditures cutbacks and asked employees to help identify ways to slice costs. A flight attendant had suggested eliminating a decorative piece of lettuce in meal service. Management was amazed to learn the savings exceeded $1.4 million a year. A food service employee modified a machine to cut cakes into fourteen instead of thirteen pieces. A flight attendant designed a new way to package napkins. By perforating the packs they came in, they could be removed one at a time, and the unused napkins saved instead of thrown out after each flight because in the old days there was no way to keep them. By the end of my time with Delta, the cutbacks would be deepening.

But nothing epitomized to me the way management watched resources more than a trip I took with Senior Vice-Pres. Harry Alger. Alger, former chief pilot, was one of the most powerful men in the company. His Operations division employed over 27,000 people, including pilots, flight attendants, and dispatchers. He called me at home one day to ask if I wanted to come to New Orleans with him and attend a banquet for a retiring pilot, and sit in while Alger addressed a meeting of Delta Air Lines Pilot Association representatives.

Alger flew our 727 himself to New Orleans, to keep himself current as a pilot. When we landed, a Delta flight engineer driving his family Chevrolet took us to our hotel. No taxicab or car service for the VP. The hotel turned out to be a Holiday Inn where Delta got rooms for $30 a night. We ate dinner in a seafood restaurant, where the average entree cost about $10. The next morning we were picked up by another pilot in his family van, and driven to the ALPA meeting. Alger sat in the back seat, near an empty baby seat, as the van crawled through New Orleans rush-hour traffic toward the French Quarter. He read the lead article in *USA Today* about management styles at automobile corporations.

"What do you think of the salaries those guys get?" I asked.

Alger shook his head. "Terrible."

To C. E. Woolman, scrounging pieces of wire and paper clips back in the 1920s, the billion-dollar issues facing Delta today probably would have seemed like science fiction. *Mister* Woolman. Like many giants of aviation, he was born before the Wright Brothers' first manned flight, before the turn of the century. His father taught physics at the University of Illinois, at Champaign–Urbana, where Woolman spent most of his youth and attended college, majoring in agriculture. He got his first experience with an airplane on campus when one made a forced landing there, and Woolman helped fix it. He got a summer job taking tourists to France so he could see the World's First Air Meet in 1909 at Reims.

Despite his interest in aviation, he went to work in agriculture when he graduated, first farming in Mississippi, then becoming a county agricultural agent for Ouachita Parish and the extension department of Louisiana State University. Woolman advised farmers and agricultural businesses.

In the end he entered aviation because of an insect and an accident. The insect was the boll weevil, which was destroying millions of dollars of cotton a year in the Mississippi Delta. The accident was another forced landing that would provide a profitable way to destroy the pest.

At the time, Woolman was working with an entomologist named Dr. B. R. Coad, who had come up with a lead arsenate powder to kill the weevil and whose problem was how to spread the powder on fields.

Coad got a congressional grant to experiment with crop-dusting, using airplanes to drop the powder. At first the operation used old U.S. Army World War I Curtiss Jennys for the job. Then a New York businessman's plane was forced down in Tallulah, Louisiana, with mechanical problems. The businessman, George Post, worked for an airplane manufacturer, Huff Daland Company in Ogdensburg, New York, which had lost its government customers after World War I, and needed to find new uses for planes. Post persuaded the home office to set up a new division, Huff Daland Dusters.

By 1925 Woolman was a vice president of Huff Daland, with its fleet of twenty-five dusters. But the business was seasonal and the equipment lay idle during winter months. Woolman started up a winter crop-dusting operation in Peru, where the seasons were reversed. He also landed an airmail contract to carry mail from Peru to Ecuador, establishing a foothold for U.S. aviation interests in South America. The business flourished, but the heady era of small airplane company expansion in the United States was coming to an end with a wave of consolidations as big holding companies grabbed control of the industry. Huff Daland was acquired by Wall Street interests, and their representative, financier Richard Hoyt, decided to liquidate the dusting division and switch the South American mail contracts to another aviation company the new owners were backing, an outfit called Pan Am. To the new owners, Huff Daland had achieved its purpose, securing the crucial foothold in South America.

Woolman went to local businessmen in Monroe and raised money to buy the dusters.

The new company, headquartered in the little brick building I'd visited in the woods, was called Delta Air Service. They still dusted crops, but by 1929 Delta was also carrying passengers between Dallas, Texas, and Jackson, Mississippi, with stops at Shreveport and Monroe, on five-passenger, 90-mile-an-hour single-engine planes.

"SAFE. SWIFT. CLEAN. COMFORTABLE," read the ads, which showed the fabric-covered Stinson plane, lone prop whizzing, wheels locked in landing position, flying over an enlarged map of parts of Alabama, Mississippi, Louisiana, and Texas.

Again the future looked bright but *again*, in the back rooms of the Northeast, secret deals would nearly crush Delta. This time it was a Republican Postmaster General and the big airlines at work. They would destroy scores of smaller operations before the scandal was made public and rocked the country. It had to do with mail.

Mail was the only way an airline could make a profit in the early years, because there simply wasn't a steady supply of passengers who would risk flying. In 1929 Woolman was holding on, bidding for the government contract to deliver mail on the routes Delta already flew. But in 1930 the Post Office awarded the contract to a big airline holding company named AVCO, allegedly after competitive bidding, but it would turn out AVCO (later American Airlines) got the job in a secret deal. AVCO had never flown the routes.

Without mail, Woolman was forced to sell out, at a loss, to the combine. It was the end of his passenger service. And with the depression on, and farmers cutting back on boll-weevil spraying, it looked like the dusters would go out of business too.

The next few years were probably the source of Woolman's habit of scrutinizing small expenditures. The weather turned bad for crops. To stay afloat Delta Air Service rented hanger space to airplanes belonging to AVCO and private pilots, sold quarts of oil to them, had its mechanics service them, had its pilots give flying lessons. Woolman managed to get a crop-dusting contract in Mexico. Delta's entire Louisiana state tax bill, for one depression year, was under $26.

But the bleak years ended in 1934 after Democrat Franklin D. Roosevelt took over the White House. Pressure had been building in Washington to investigate the mail contracts ever since Hoover's Postmaster General Walter Folger Brown gave them out. Under Brown, twenty-four of the twenty-seven mail contracts had gone to TWA, United, and American Airlines, all owned by Wall Street holding companies at the time. With the Democrats back in power, small airlines rushed to Washington to push for hearings. Sen. Hugo Black of Alabama, who would later become the famous Supreme Court justice, ordered Interstate Commerce Commission agents to spread out across the United States, raid the big airlines, and seize records without warning.

As the scandal broke in the press, Brown, accused of burning records, said he'd lost them but turned up with a suitcase of papers, claiming to have "found them." Black ordered Pres. Calvin Coolidge's old Assistant Secretary of Commerce for Air arrested for contempt of the Senate when he refused to produce records of meetings with airline representatives. Federal agents went through the trash at Northwest Airways and pieced together letters that company Vice-Pres. L. H. Brittin had tried to destroy.

The letters described regular meetings at which the big airlines carved up mail routes among themselves, with Brown as a kind of referee. One letter, quoted by Carl Solberg in *Conquest of the Skies*, said, "The Postmaster General was not able to get the necessary legislation in the Watres Bill enabling him to grant airmail contracts to the passenger-carrying airlines without competitive bids. He has made up his mind to do this anyway. . . .

"To work things out he called the operators together, handed them this map and instructed them to settle among themselves the distribution of these routes. The operators have been meeting every day for two weeks. . . . The Postmaster General meets with them about once a week, stirs them up and keeps them going."

Supporters of the old Postmaster General claimed he'd only wanted to create a strong airline industry that would cover the United States. That he didn't want to waste government subsidies on small airlines that might not survive. Detractors claimed the deals were nothing more than a fraud to enrich big money interests.

C. E. Woolman appeared before Black's committee to testify how Delta had been shut out of the contracts on its own routes. Black asked him, "Did the company who got the [mail route] have any experience of any kind on it?"

"No one had flown that route but ourselves," Woolman replied.

"Did you sell out because you *wanted* to sell out?" Black asked.

"We sold out because it seemed the expedient thing to do. . . . It would be impossible to compete with a line carrying airmail, and it is impossible, and has been proven repeatedly, to make money carrying passengers alone."

Enraged, President Roosevelt canceled all mail contracts and ordered the Army to fly the mail. But the Army pilots were inexperienced in night flying, and the country was being wracked by winter storms. By the end of the first week, five pilots were dead, six were injured, and eight Army planes destroyed.

Roosevelt relented. The mail would be delivered by private contractors, but this time there would be bidding.

And this time Delta got "route 24," the contract to carry mail between Charleston, South Carolina, and Fort Worth, Texas, with stops at Columbia, Augusta, Atlanta, Birmingham, Meridian, Jackson, Monroe, Shreveport, and Dallas.

Woolman had an airline again. He started flying passengers again, although conditions were primitive by today's standards. On the Atlanta–Charleston route, for instance, "passengers were scarce . . . and there were no beacon lights and no emergency landing fields east of Atlanta," one pilot told authors W. David Lewis and Wesley Phillips Newton, who wrote *Delta: The History of an Airline*. Eight passengers could travel in Delta's three-engine Stinsons, capable of flying 160 miles an hour.

In old photos the Stinsons lack the symmetry of a modern air ship, and look like engineers took a narrow boat hull and stuck a wing, motors, and wheels on it. Struts ran from the body of the plane to the long single wing along the top. Landing wheels were permanently locked in place.

Inside the plane copilots served box lunches: two sandwiches, an apple or banana, a piece of cake, and a thermos filled with coffee. Pilots rarely saw other planes in the skies, Lewis and Newton wrote. And when sudden, vicious southeastern thunderstorms came up in summer, the Stinsons couldn't climb over them.

But the small regional airline was growing. This time the government helped. The Civil Aeronautics Act of 1938 created the Civil Aeronautics Authority, and its offshoot, the Civil Aeronautics Board (CAB), which would regulate the industry—grant new routes to airlines and make sure the fledgling companies weren't hobbled by too much competition.

"Regulation came about because of the depression," Jim Callison, Delta's senior vice president of corporate and external affairs and former chief counsel, told me in Atlanta. Callison had spent the bulk of his career dealing with regulatory matters. "The government wanted to give young industries a chance to grow. There were always more airlines wanting a route than traffic to support them. When we wanted a new route, we'd get in this long legal fight with other airlines who wanted it too, a fight that could last five years sometimes. We'd go before 'examiners' from the Civil Aeronautics Board. Five members up there, like judges. We'd go through all these economic and legal arguments about why we should get the route, if there was more than one applicant.

"Then after a while the government started creating *new* routes where none existed. They would look at telephone calls between the two cities, mail, try to figure out if there was a community of interest sufficient to justify an airline service.

"They treated airlines like public utilities in those days. Called us quasi-utilities," he said. "They limited competition and only put on as much competition as traffic would support."

Meanwhile, the planes got bigger, faster, safer. In 1935 Delta started replacing the fabric-covered Stinsons with metal Lockheed Electras, able to cruise at 160 miles an hour and which had two-way radios. The first Douglas DC-2 went into service for the airline in 1940, with an enlarged capacity for fourteen passengers and a top speed of 165. DC-3s would carry up to twenty-one passengers at 180 mph. In 1945 Delta Air Corp., renamed Delta Air Lines, was flying four-engine DC-4s nonstop from Chicago to Miami.

Delta's ads in the *Chicago Tribune* said, "Fly Delta to the Magnetic South." Flights had names: The Day Rocket. The Night Rocket. Posters showed the Chicago skyline in the distance, beneath blustery tornadolike winds, with the sleek DC-4 shooting away from the inhospitable weather, toward a smiling, waving woman in a swimsuit, beneath a palm tree, sitting between the arms of a magnet, which wrapped the Florida peninsula and pointed north, as if pulling the oncoming plane toward the girl.

"As blizzards blow and your compass swings to the magnetic south, fly Delta," the ad said.

In the early days, in the government-regulated world of airline travel, each company had its territory. Companies made "interchange agreements" to ferry each other's planes and passengers into each other's air turf.

For instance, under one agreement Delta had with TWA, Delta passengers traveling from Atlanta to Detroit would board a Delta or TWA plane in Atlanta, and stay on the same plane through the whole trip, but Delta crews would pilot the plane south of Cincinnati, and TWA crews would have it after that. The same system worked for TWA passengers going south.

In 1953 Delta got some new routes in a different way, by merging with Chicago-based Chicago & Southern Airlines. St. Louis came into the Delta system, as well as cities including Little Rock, Houston, Indianapolis, Detroit, Havana, Caracas, and San Juan.

And in order to control passengers going from small cities to larger ones, Delta marketing people invented the hub-and-spoke system, which characterizes major airline travel in the United States today. "We did it because so many of the cities we served in the Southeast were small," Jim Callison said. "Columbia, South Carolina. Savannah, Georgia. Even Atlanta wasn't very big then, although it was bigger than they were. They couldn't support direct air service to places. To provide them with links to the national system we started bringing flights into Atlanta, using Atlanta as a hub, with the flights out to other destinations the spokes. This way we could control our traffic, keep passengers in our system for the whole trip."

Despite the steady growth, Delta was still shut out of the most profitable part of the country, the Northeast Corridor, between Washington and New York, where 45 percent of all air traffic in the United States originated. "The New York barrier" was what Delta personnel called it. At CAB hearings Delta lawyers complained that American, Capital, Colonial, Eastern, National, Northeast, Northwest, TWA, and United Airlines had all been given access to New York. And that only one airline, Eastern, flew from Atlanta to New York. They trotted witness after witness before the board, Southern businessmen who thought a Southern-based carrier should get the business, passengers who had had bad experiences on Eastern, the mayor of Atlanta, who complained that Eastern just flew three planes a day to New York from Atlanta, the president of a department store who told the CAB his business had a rule that no more than ten executives could fly on the same plane at the same time. Without another carrier going to the Big Apple, sometimes forty of their executives would be on the same plane. "Relief from monopoly is needed," said one brief filed by Delta.

A 1950 *Time* magazine piece on airlines jokingly told a story how, after a meeting of airline executives in Washington, the participants crammed into taxicabs to get to the airport. When C. E. Woolman squeezed into the last seat, Eastern's Pres. Eddie Rickenbacker asked if he could ride on Woolman's lap.

"I've been helping support you for years, so I might as well do it some more," Woolman said.

By 1956 the CAB was ready to grant a new route from the Southeast to New York and lots of companies applied for it. Braniff. Capital.

Eastern's lawyers argued that more service wasn't needed.

Delta got the route. "I never felt better," C. E. Woolman said, abandoning the country-boy pose when he got the news, "and I never had more."

By now Delta had moved its headquarters to Atlanta. An aerial photo of their facilities taken in 1958 implies growth so explosive that construction can't keep up with it. There's the long Quonset hut of the terminal and prop airplanes everywhere, at the gates, in the background, waiting for space to pull in.

Within two years jets would be arriving at those gates. Delta's Convair 880 could cruise at 606 miles an hour, 880 feet a second. The delivery flight, from San Diego to Miami, took three hours, thirty-one minutes, and fifty-four seconds, a record.

Delta got a southern transcontinental route. It started serving Las Vegas, San Diego, and San Francisco. Cabin service improved. In the 1960s, passengers on the direct morning flight from Atlanta to Los Angeles breakfasted on cantaloupe and fresh strawberries, southern-fried quail with butter sauce, scrambled eggs and cheddar cheese, hominy grits with quail gravy, hot biscuits and pecan muffins, wrote Lewis and Phillips. A far cry from management squeezing fourteen pieces out of a cake in 1992, instead of thirteen.

Delta got the Chicago to Nashville route, Dallas to Phoenix, Miami to San Francisco, Miami to Houston. In 1972 another merger, this time with Boston-based Northeast Airlines, brought Boston, Montreal, Bermuda, Nassau, and twenty other new cities into the system. The era of widebody jets had arrived. In 1974, ship 714 went into service, carrying passengers from Atlanta to Chicago, Atlanta to Philadelphia, LaGuardia to Atlanta. A big plane carrying heavy loads up and down the Mississippi Valley, over the big summer thunderstorms the old DC-6s had flown around.

For the airlines, these were the last golden days of government regulation. Routes were protected. Fares were protected. Profits were practically guaranteed. "Oh, in those good old days of regulation," Capt. Malcolm Simpson had said to me wistfully during 714's first flight today, "when it came time for contract renewal, the company would say to the pilots, 'Well, what do you want?' And then they'd give it to us."

Then came deregulation.

The end of having to get permission to fly routes. The end of being protected from competition. The end of having to wait years for decisions in Washington before an airline could make a move.

It would destroy companies, create millionaires, bring thousands of new jobs to aviation, and then drive thousands out of work. It would fundamentally change the industry.

"We were against it. We fought it," Jim Callison told me in his office in Atlanta.

"The Republicans were pushing for deregulation," he recalled. "The industry had gotten big and strong, and government regulations were stifling competition, they said. The Democrats were for it too. Congress was saying, 'We thought you were a quasi-utility all these years, but we were wrong. You should be treated as an industry, no different from steel.' They were saying the airlines had gotten too plush. Salaries were too high. Costs in general were too high from lack of competition.

"We made speeches against it. We wrote articles against it."

Callison said he regularly went to Washington in those days to testify before Congress against the proposed deregulation.

"I used to stay in these small hotels in Washington. The night before testifying we'd cram ourselves full of information just like taking an exam in college. And like college, you know you'll be sharper on the next day if you sleep." Callison laughed. "But you don't sleep. It's scary. It's like testifying before a court, but there are some pretty august people up there. Senators. Congressmen.

"The committees would listen to us, but once things get on the floor of Congress, it's too late, they've already decided," he said.

We pretended I was a congressman in a committee. "Why do you fear deregulation so much?" I asked.

He leaned back. He was a fast-talking native of Buffalo, New York, in a dark pin-striped suit with a white hanky in the pocket and a monogrammed shirt. There were hunt scenes on a lampshade on his big wooden desk. He had lightly freckled, delicate-looking hands, and he waved them to make points. "We fear it because we think you won't really deregulate. We think Congress'll change the system in a way that'll hurt us," he said, heating up the way he'd probably done in front of the Senate Commerce Committee in 1976.

"It's the best airline system with the most competition and lowest fares. Why mess with it? If you change it," he warned in a slightly hoarse voice like actor Richard Dysart's in "L.A. Law," you don't know what the effects will be. You're probably going to wind up with all the big carriers going to the major markets, but the markets won't support all of them. And at the same time smaller cities will wind up with no service, or service from smaller carriers with smaller airplanes.

"The industry will concentrate into a small number of large carriers, fewer carriers than you have today," Callison said. "You'll wind up with *so* few carriers that the government could get concerned and say, maybe we ought to nationalize this industry."

Still playing congressman I said, "Aren't you just afraid of competition?"

Callison shrugged and returned to the present. "They used to tell us that with deregulation anyone could buy a used airplane and start a company. That'll keep you honest, they'd say. That was the theory. New companies would undercut our prices. We'd say, that's true, but go too far, and you'll undercut the whole industry, undermine service, affect safety, even weaken competition in the end."

Callison sighed. "Which is what happened. But we'd go back and forth with these economic theories."

But the tide in Washington was running in favor of deregulation. "When it passed," Callison said, "nothing really happened at first. We weren't surprised. But then it started sinking in. We had to do a 180-degree flip-flop in management. We'd grown up for forty years in a little tiny industry under regulation. Everything airlines did, we thought in terms of regulation. How could we get a route *from the government?* What would the government's reaction be to a fare? Will *they* put competition on this route we've had a monopoly on for all these years? *What will the government do?*

"Now we had to train ourselves to think the other way around. We were free to use our resources any way we wanted. Free to charge what we wanted. I remember going to a sales managers' meeting after deregulation started. I was the main speaker, because I'd been the guy in charge of getting the new rates in the past and defending the fares. I said to them, 'We're passing the ball to you. You gotta go out there and decide where we'll go, what we'll charge. The lawyers aren't going to do it anymore.' "

"You had to keep pounding it on them."

Callison smiled. "We had an awful time, not just Delta, the whole industry. American. United. We all lost money. We'd never *been* in a real free market before. You'd get carriers on the East Coast charging real low fares, doing exactly what the economists said they'd do. Going out and buying old planes and hiring young folks, like People Express. Or Air Florida. And we thought the only way to compete with them was to lower all our fares, but our costs were higher. We lost tons of money."

Callison talked a mile a minute. "We later learned that there was a differentiated market out there. We didn't have to lower all our fares. Some people preferred a reservation. A meal. Full services. Versus some who had never flown before, hadn't been able to afford more than a bus ticket. We learned we could attract businessmen at regular fares. That's what airlines do today. Appeal to a differentiated market."

Callison said some of the politicians who had voted for deregulation weren't so happy when it came about.

"Up until then, we'd been proud that we had applied to serve all these cities, big and small, and never left any of them. But one of the first things we did after deregulation was stop serving Meridian, Mississippi, which had been in our system for years. I got a call from Senator Stennis from Mississippi, pleading with us. He said, 'Don't do it. We depend on you. You're important to our economy.' And I said, 'Senator, that's what I tried to explain to you when you voted for deregulation.' "

Callison leaned back. "He said, 'I didn't know that's what I was voting for.' "

"How'd you feel?" I said.

"Bad. But we'd lost money in Meridian, and once we were free to shift resources, we did."

With deregulation also came new pitfalls for Delta, like the danger of antitrust suits, said Callison.

"The airlines had never been subject to the antitrust law. Regulated, like we used to be, we were exempt. But now we had to train our people to think in those terms. I set up conferences in the marketing division, which is the most sensitive because they set prices and sell the product. Our lawyers showed them movies about guys going to jail for antitrust violations," he said, chuckling and remembering the new concept at the time: "This could happen to *you*. You have to learn that a normal thing you might do as a salesman, like . . ." he said, changing his voice to play salesman, " 'I won't raise my price past this level if you won't' . . . A very casual remark—somebody overhears it. It snowballs. Pretty soon you're a witness in an antitrust suit."

"It sounds like those old scare-sex education movies they used to show in high school," I said. "The dangers of VD. Don't get pregnant."

Callison laughed. "Yeah, it was like that," he said.

But the real pitfalls weren't from government prosecution, just from bad management now that airlines were more responsible for themselves. Pan Am, for instance, was basically an overseas carrier with no feeder routes inside the United States to get passengers to their international flights when deregulation started, Callison said. They could have created the domestic routes they needed, but they didn't. It was one reason they went downhill.

In the end, contrary to Delta's fears, deregulation turned out to be one of the best things that ever happened to the company. "We got dragged into it kicking and screaming, but then we played it to the hilt. If the government ever wanted to start up regulation again," Callison said, "I'd probably finish up my career here arguing *against* it."

Under deregulation Delta added more routes. Atlanta to Cleveland. Atlanta to San Antonio. New York to Orlando. But success wasn't just a question of *where* an airline went but how often it flew there. Airlines with a heavy presence on a route usually carry a bigger percentage of passengers than their percentage of flights. Under deregulation, Delta was free to put as many flights as they wanted on a route. No more begging the CAB.

In 1987, a merger with struggling Western Airlines brought another wave of new destinations into Delta's system and eliminated the biggest rival on those routes. The airline now flew to Anchorage, Calgary, Mexico City, and Vancouver. Cities like San Francisco, San Diego, and Denver, already in the system, became links to more destinations and offered more Delta flights.

So far the mergers had added complementary chunks of the United States to the system. The Chicago & Southern deal had given Delta access to the Midwest. The Northeast merger had brought in New England, and 714's destinations of Boston and Montreal, and their links to Florida. The Western merger had given Delta a strong presence through the Far West, in Salt Lake City, Honolulu, Portland, Seattle. By 1991, Delta was poised to buy part of an international carrier. The stormy, much-publicized acquisition of Pan Am routes meant ship 714 would be ferrying passengers to sister planes linking the U.S. with twenty-one overseas destinations Delta had never before served. Moscow. Warsaw. Bangkok. Bombay.

Announcing the acquisition, Associated Press said Delta had become a "full-fledged aviation superpower."

That year the little ex-crop dusting operation carried 15.3 percent of all U.S. air travelers, just behind American, with 18.5 percent, and United, with 18.3 percent. Way up from 1935, when Delta had flown 4,104 passengers for the whole year, fewer than half the company's boardings from Salt Lake City alone on an average day in 1992.

"I remember," Jim Callison told me, "when Eastern wouldn't give us the time of day."

But nothing underscored the explosive growth to me more than the daily briefing at company headquarters in Atlanta, which I'd attended on my first day there.

At 9 A.M. that morning, men and women, steaming coffee cups in their hands, had trickled down the nondescript halls of Widget City, as Delta headquarters is called, into a bland-looking meeting room with bare walls and a long wooden table in front. Chairman Ron Allen and two other men sat down at the table. From the drowsy mood it seemed that whatever happened would be pretty boring. The only bright color in the place was the blue stripes on Allen's shirt and more blue on the glass-covered Delta route map behind the table.

But suddenly the men were rapping out reports concerning *every single Delta* flight, over 2,800 of them, that had flown within the last twenty-four hours. Boston had had gusty wind yesterday. Salt Lake City had suffered thirty-minute early morning delays because of fog. The overall on-time percentage for the system had been 85.5 percent and 94.3 percent for the Washington–New York shuttle. Ship 763 had had an air turnback out of Taipei. Ship 005 had had a two hour and twenty-four minute delay out of Kennedy, because of a window problem. A computer snafu in Salt Lake City had caused fourteen delays. An airplane out of London, Gatwick, had shut down with an electrical problem.

I was astounded. I'd sat around in plenty of airports in my life, during delays, blaming it on the airline instead of weather, or grumping with other passengers that whichever company we were flying didn't give a damn about us. But the people in this room were clearly concerned about every single delay. Not only that, it was crucial to the jobs of all present that it was raining today off Japan, that Hawaii enjoyed sunny skies, that there was a little turbulence in the upper Mississippi Valley, that the Caribbean and Asian operations looked "routine."

I looked at the route map again, the red lines arcing around the world, as a voice reported, "Passengers on the books today are 177,000. Atlanta, 38,293. Dallas/Fort Worth, 12,969. Orlando, 6,581. Kennedy, 2,190. . . . On Monday we flew 4,530 hours. . . . Our total delay time yesterday in the system was forty-nine hours and twenty-nine minutes. . . ." Suddenly those red lines became real planes trailing condensation, over Asia, over Europe, over the Pacific, up at 39,000 feet.

After the meeting and in other visits to headquarters, I'd ask senior management what they were working on whenever I talked to them, to get more of an idea of the reach of a modern airline.

"We bought three gates from Eastern at Los Angeles for $21 million," said Rex McLelland, senior vice president of administrative services, which manages airport facilities. We sat in his modestly furnished office at a small round conference table beneath another route map, this one with colored pins stuck in it. Dark blue ones denoted cities Delta had served pre-November 1991. Red marked Rio, Singapore, Jakarta, Kuala Lumpur, where Delta was applying for permission to land. Light blue pins meant new Pan Am cities, including Athens. Istanbul. Geneva. Helsinki. "I had to grasp where Pan Am flew, and where we're gonna fly," McLelland said.

Harry Alger, senior vice president of operations, said, "I talked with the director of in-flight scheduling about a bill in Washington, which we are fighting against, to change flight attendant rules. Shorter work days. Longer sleep periods. And I've been looking at how to adjust the presentation of snacks in flight to reduce costs without loss of service. Do you really need to put a piece of cake, intended to be light fare, on a dish? Or how about more yogurt for breakfast or fruit, as opposed to scrambled eggs and sausage?"

I said. "Why don't you just order it?"

"I need to know what the consumer wants first."

Alger had also met with Jenny Poole, his vice president of in-flight service, who wanted him to ask senior management for authorization to hire outside consultants to track the way Delta employees use sick leave.

"Delta departments don't have budgets," he said. "Most companies give you a certain amount to spend each year. With us senior management gets up on Monday morning and reviews all expenditures over $1,000. It's not unusual for another VP to say, 'Harry, why the hell are you putting up all that money!' " Alger laughed. "I've had lawyers assail me on the stand when I testified in an accident several years ago. One ranted and took off her shoe and pounded it on the podium." Alger imitated the lawyer. "*What do you mean you don't have a budget! That's scurrilous! How can you not budget for safety!*

"She was trying to intimidate me, but she didn't. Believe me, when I want something for safety, I get it. We probably end up spending more that way.

"Anyway, I told the vice president of in-flight service, let's see if we can track sick leave without hiring outside help."

After Alger I put the "what did you do today" question to Tom Roeck, chief financial officer, a lean, shy-looking, soft-spoken ex–vice president of Western Airlines, who'd come over in the merger, and whose windowsills and shelves were lined with momento paperweights commemorating deals. It was a particularly busy time for Delta, because two days earlier American Airlines had announced a change in the way they priced tickets. They'd eliminated all special fares and said they would charge only three rates. No more special prices for the elderly, the military, special business customers, the government, or anybody.

Nobody at Delta thought the new fares would last, but until they broke down again, everyone was scrambling to react.

"We've been trying to come up with long-term financial forecasts and adjust fares," Roeck said. "We're looking at the numbers of full-fare passengers versus discount traffic. Talking about the like-lihood of other carriers going out of business, trying to predict when that might be. In this industry nothing is static, even by the hour. When I started at Western, I'd fly somewhere for a press confer-ence, and when I'd get there, the first question would be 'What do you think of the fare action earlier this morning?' I'd say, '*What* fare action?'"

Roeck seemed to relish the volatility. "In the oil and gas busi-ness where I came from, things were slower. We'd deal with them on a monthly basis. At Western I was stunned. We'd have our Mon-day morning meetings, and the guy from Marketing would say, 'We don't have the numbers for the weekend yet, but I can talk about last week.'" He laughed. "Like working for a television network. You come in overnight and look at what's happening. Aviation is one of the most difficult businesses, because everything is interrelated in one big system. You can't change anything without having a whole series of ripple effects."

"Like what?"

Roeck sipped a Coke. His expertise at Delta was in financing new aircraft. In the past week he'd announced the company was instituting a $5 billion capital savings program, cutting back on air-craft acquisition, letting staff dwindle by attrition because the in-dustry was in one of its periodic slumps, and because Delta had extended itself financially to buy Pan Am assets, a one-time chance they thought they had better not pass up.

"In the contract drilling business, you'd have the North Sea op-eration and the Gulf of Mexico operation. The North Sea was deep water, the Gulf shallow. They had nothing to do with each other. In aviation," he said, flashing the weird complexity smile I'd seen at the Operations Center, "everything relates to everything else. If we change an aircraft rotation in Atlanta, it will effect the workload in LA, but we're still not exactly sure how.

"I remember when I got to Western, Western was flying Boeing 767 airplanes they'd bought in the 1970s. Looking at those planes,

I thought that seemed like the dumbest thing I could imagine. Western didn't need bigger planes. They needed smaller equipment, like 737s. But it turned out they'd bought the right plane, but had the wrong system. They'd *ordered* the 767s before deregulation, at a time when Western flew point to point and needed bigger planes. But the lag time between ordering and getting a plane is so long they *got* the 767s *after* deregulation, when they'd gone to a hub-and-spoke system, and carried smaller loads."

Roeck lifted up an index finger, as if testing the wind.

"A lot of decisions we still make like this," he said.

I asked Roeck about the paperweights lining his windowsill. One was an attractive obelisk shape encasing a paper with "$60 million" written on it. Roeck said the figure represented money Delta had borrowed to lease aircraft, MD-88s.

"Wait a minute," I said. "The paperweights commemorate money you *owe?*"

"Well, the banks and investment houses who raise the money for us like to give out momentos as a marketing tool. They're saying, when you look at these things, remember that we do a lot of business with you."

I looked at another paperweight, three little windows with gold certificates, the first for $228 million in notes due in 1998. The second for $200 million due in 2011. The third for $350 million worth of 9.4 percent notes due in 2021.

"Isn't this like commemorating money you owe the IRS?" I asked. There were dozens of the momentos all over the place.

Roeck smiled. Without the money they couldn't get the planes.

Vice President of Sales Al Kolakowski was next, an open, genial man whose office was decorated with posters by French impressionists. One, by a potted tree near his drawn blinds, showed a winter scene. Snow on a field.

Kolakowski said most of his department's work involves getting travel agents to book passengers on Delta instead of other airlines. "Eighty percent of our business comes through agents," he said. Some of the agents serve the general public, others the government or big corporations. Up until two days ago, he said, with the American Airlines fares announcement, the marketing department negotiated ticket prices with bigger customers and cargo shippers.

"Let's say a travel agent handles Procter & Gamble. We go to the agency. We've identified that they're a big producer. We say, where's your business coming from?" He lowered his voice. "But we already know. We say, are you willing to share with us Procter & Gamble?" He shrugged. "Sometimes yes. Sometimes no. Now we're working with that travel agent, trying to book as much business with us."

He held up his index finger. "But then we also go to Procter & Gamble. We say, hey, is your travel agent making a decision whom you fly on? Or are *you*? Or maybe Procter & Gamble will have a cadre of people in the company who watch the travel agent. Or maybe inside the company there might be different people handling relocations, training. We identify and cultivate them."

Kolakowski said airlines often give perks to travel agents, special deals or trips or discounts to encourage business. I said, "Is that legal? I mean, if a customer goes to a travel agent and doesn't know the agent has a sweetener deal with an airline, is that against the law?"

"It's legal," he said. "It may not be ethical, but it's legal. That's a debate around the country. Should a travel agent tell a customer whom he deals with?"

On the day I met Kolakowski, he was scheduled to meet with one of Delta's biggest travel agent customers. "A Chicago agency, they do about $100 million of business with us a year. They've been big in coordinating regions for companies. The president of that travel agency is probably concerned about the new fare structures American introduced. He's afraid Delta and the other airlines will cancel their special negotiated deals—corporate discounts, meeting fares, relocation fares. The playing field will be leveled. He'll lose his edge. Before, when he went in to gain an account, he could tout the fact, 'I can sit down with the airlines and because of my volume, my clout, I can negotiate deals for you.' "

"You'll assure him things will stay in place?" I said.

Kolakowski laughed. "No. Things are changing. Until we see which way the industry is going to go, we're going to start leveling the playing field too. He may have to adjust."

I said, "But what if he says, 'I just met with United and *they* said I can keep my special deals?' "

Kolakowski softened. "We'll see. What we're doing now is keeping people in check. You don't want to burn your bridges."

Kolakowski said another part of the marketing department's job was dealing with organizations Delta had an official relationship with. Pro football teams. Disney World.

"I see on commercials that Delta is the official airline of Disney World," I said. "But what does that mean? You get an advertising benefit but what does Disney get?"

Kolakowski laughed again. "Cash. We pay," he said. "The relationship is different from many other cooperative arrangements, because Disney feels they have leverage. The Mouse is known worldwide. It's recognition. For a cash payment over $10 million, a fifteen-year agreement, we get the right to call ourselves the official airline of Disney, no one else can do it. We get the right to use their logos, to portray their characters, to give kids on board those cardboard Mickeys.

"Disney gets to be affiliated with a major carrier serving Los Angeles and Orlando. A carrier with a reputation for service. They get a whole sales force throughout the world. Us. Delta people go out and put together programs, visiting hospitals, children, working with different groups—travel related or not—we do all the legwork. Set up promotion. And they join us on the visits to the hospital or shopping center. We have a full-time staff of six working on Disney. On meetings. On conventions at Disney. There are Disney-owned hotels. Ship 714 regularly carries Disney customers in and out of Orlando and Los Angeles.

"We also have a relationship with the PGA, PGA officials and staff. Pro golfers at country clubs around the U.S. have special discounts and an 800 number for reservations and discounts."

Eight-hundred numbers hadn't existed when C. E. Woolman signed the lease for Delta's little office in Monroe. It was impossible in the United States to make a transcontinental phone call without operator assistance until 1951. After Kolakowski, I went down the hall to talk to Bob Harkey, Delta's senior vice president and general counsel, whom I spoke to about legal suits against the company and who, in proper lawyerly fashion, talked a lot but revealed so little in an hour that I had less than half a page of notes.

But Delta's legal staff, the full-time attorneys in Atlanta and the private firms for hire, were dealing with several big legal actions at the moment that C. E. Woolman never would have envisioned when he was sending out his duster planes to kill boll weevils in 1916.

- Delta was being hit with a $2.5 billion breach of contract suit by creditors of defunct Pan Am Airlines, who claimed Delta had backed out of an agreement to save the airline, had cut off promised financial support for Pan Am, and that move had killed it. Delta officials were furious over the suit. They said they'd agreed to lend Pan Am $80 million to keep it operating and had actually forked over $115 million before they finally refused to pay more in the face of "substantially lower revenues and higher costs" than projected.

- Another suit involved computerized reservation systems, which travel agents use but are owned by airlines. Delta and other big airlines were being challenged to stop steering travelers in their systems toward their own flights. At the moment, Delta owned the Worldspan system with Northwest Airlines and Trans World. Sabre system was owned by American Airlines. Apollo by United Airlines. And System One by Continental. Soon after I met the evasive Bob Harkey, the Worldspan companies agreed to be the first to design an unbiased system. New York State Attorney Gen. Robert Abrams, who had brought the suit, said, "Worldspan is establishing a solid example that others in the travel business would be wise to follow."

- Then there was the price fixing suit. The Justice Department was accusing Delta and the other big airlines of collusion in the way they set prices. The government's reasoning worked like this, Al Kolakowski explained, since I couldn't get any information out of Bob Harkey. Because there are so many fares ("Some days there are literally a million fare changes"), airlines needing to track what the competition is doing need a central location where they can get minute-by-minute information. They all subscribe to an automated monitoring system called the Airline Tariff Publishing service. When an airline announces a fare change, it's immediately posted over the service, and everyone else can see what the competition has done.

Kolakowski told me that when companies lower fares, they announce them so they go into effect instantly. But when they *raise* fares, they announce the price will go up some time in the future.

"Because it's not done instantly, the government considers this a communication, a trial balloon," he said. "Historically, the way it works is, you put a fare increase in, scheduled to go into effect June 1. June 1 comes around, and some carriers matched it, and some didn't. Some modified prices a little. Or maybe you get a situation where all the airlines matched it. Or maybe you're at May 31, one day before the higher fare is supposed to go into effect, and one airline is still out there hanging on to the old fare, and everyone says, that guy will be cheaper. The other airlines cancel the raises. "The government is saying, No trial balloons. You wanna raise fares? Raise them and hold to it."

Personally, I liked the government's position. But Delta management had other ideas. Pres. Whit Hawkins, whom I met next, likened Delta in this suit to "a guy who owns a gas station at an intersection where each corner has a station. The guy on one corner will put up a sign saying, gasoline, 99 cents a gallon. Well, the guys on the other corners aren't going to keep the price at $1.20 a gallon. The government seems to think we decide what fares to put out together. No. We decide and put it out. That suit is a gross misunderstanding of the way the computer system serves the traveling public."

"I think the government is more interested in how prices get raised, not how they get lowered," I said. "They're saying the current system is implied communication."

"It's not a method of communication with each other," Hawkins said.

I asked Hawkins about the Pan Am suit too. After the smooth way Delta had combined with Western, Northeast, and Chicago & Southern, what had gone wrong with Pan Am?

Hawkins sighed. He'd been the one to start the negotiations with Pan Am, and Chairman Ron Allen had finished them. He was an ex-native of Sterling, Kentucky, who had joined Delta in 1955 as a ground agent. "In the Western and Northeast mergers, we had months to work out details," he said. "And those mergers went so seamlessly that people still say to us, Wasn't there some airline you were going to merge with? What happened with that? That's how smooth it went.

"But Pan Am went fast. The first trip I made to New York was April 19 last year. We had a deal August 12. During that time we had to talk about the shuttle, then the North Atlantic routes, then what people go with this operation, what office goes with that operation, what parts go with what airplanes. It was a very difficult thing to put our arms around. And we had to think about how everything would affect our employees. Some people think we aren't so serious about this people stuff, but it's a very big consideration with us."

In the end, Hawkins said, Pan Am hadn't turned out to be as profitable as Delta had been led to believe, not only in terms of the part of the deal they changed their mind about, but in terms of the assets they bought. "When we purchased the Pan Am assets, we didn't have a lot of time to look at everything. We had to take some on faith. I'm not saying we got it in bad faith, but we assumed some things. Like parts. You assume there will be so many parts for so many airplanes. We couldn't possibly inventory all the parts in the limited amount of time before acquisition. So we made some assumptions based on the way we do business."

Hawkins blew out air.

I said, "If this business is so hard, and the profit margin so small, and everything is so complex all the time, why is the airline business so intoxicating to the people in it?"

He burst out laughing. "I wish I knew," he said.

As for the what-did-you-do-today question, Hawkins said he'd been cost cutting like the rest of management. Working on combining accounting systems and reservations offices.

I asked Hawkins what a $160 million loss last quarter meant. "I know it's bad," I said, "but was it expected? Did you plan a temporary loss, considering the expansion?"

"It was expected, but it's worse than we expected," he said.

We talked about the old days, when Delta was still a southern regional carrier. "When we started flying to New York, if we had a flight on at nine o'clock, Eastern would put on one fifteen minutes earlier, and another fifteen minutes behind. They tried to cut us out."

Now Eastern was gone. And Hawkins was helping run a global carrier. Just today he'd given permission for flight operations to cancel an L-1011 into Bangkok because antigovernment riots there threatened to spill over to the airport.

"We're monitoring the situation on an hourly basis," Hawkins said. "Yesterday, with the flight forty-five minutes out of Bangkok, with the disturbances not near the airport, we decided we'd turn the airplane around on the ground, not leave it there overnight, get the crews out. We've canceled flights to Bangkok for the next few days."

Which meant, in the complex world of aviation, that ship 714 and dozens of other Delta jets thousands of miles away in the United States would be carrying fewer passengers on their runs to Salt Lake City and to Portland, passengers on their way to Asia who would have been alerted by Delta's reservations people not to bother coming to the airport.

I asked Hawkins if he was used to the global reach, or whether, in those daily morning briefings, listening to the weather over Hong Kong and the flight reports from Tel Aviv and looking at the route map in front of the room, he ever grows amazed over how the company has grown.

"Yesterday," he said, "we had a problem with somebody in Bulgaria who decided Bulgarian airspace wouldn't be open to us that day. "But our flights to Istanbul and Tel Aviv needed to go through there. I kept thinking, Bulgarian airspace? Of all the things I'd be worrying about one day, who would have thought it would be a problem with some bureaucrat in Bulgaria who decided we couldn't go there. But we straightened it out," Hawkins said.

He sat back. He grinned. He shook his head.

"Bulgaria."

BATTLE OVER BAJA

Crimson sunset. Pastel sky. Ocean the color of pink coral.

Ship 714 coasted through Pacific dusk, at 13,000 feet, during the eighty-seven-mile flight from Honolulu to Maui. Haleakala crater came up to the southeast, highest point on the island, thrusting blackly from white mist obscuring its base. I saw sugarcane fields. Towns with lights coming on. Maui's last windsurfers of the day skimming toward beaches.

In 1772, Capt. James Cook of the English Royal Navy, first western visitor to the South Pacific, had needed a year to reach it. And two more to get home.

But two hundred years later, ship 714 made the journey so unremarkably that Capt. R. E. "Roscoe" Diehl had spent the whole flight griping. Delta management had too rigid a style, he said, not like the good old days at Western. Delta pilots didn't appreciate how well off they were compared to pilots at other airlines.

"Goddamn broad sits there and forces the FAA to make a political solution to a technical problem," he snarled, referring to Transportation Secretary Elizabeth Dole's order that U.S. airliners carry radar warning devices. Ours had just gone off as we descended toward 10,000 feet, but we saw no other planes nearby.

"It doesn't work. And anyway, you want me to look at this thing? Or you want me to look where the hell I'm going? My job is to look where the hell I'm going, not at some goddamn gadget."

"Flaps!" We were coming in.

"Check."

"Altimeters!"

The griping didn't affect the way the crew did their job. Captains always set the mood in cockpits. Crews I flew with always performed in standardized ways. Maui grew closer, the island so far from Atlanta it was impossible to imagine they occupied the same country. By this time tomorrow the passengers would be lying on beaches below, driving past cattle ranches at the foot of Haleakala, hiking in wonder down footpaths inside the dormant volcano, through lava beds that went on for miles, making them imagine they'd been cast back to the Pleistocene era. They'd be admiring the African tulip trees and hibiscus along Maui's two-lane roads. Gazing at the setting sun from a Shinto temple overlooking the sea. Sipping mai tai's or eating mahimahi in the little hill towns occupied by aging hippies.

Or maybe 714 was taking them to the big resorts. The Sheraton. The Intercontinental. With their private beaches and coral reefs and guests speaking German, French, and Japanese. Bobbing in rented flippers above schools of needle fish. Putting on golf courses. Donning tropical whites for the nightly hula show.

Maui. The payoff for frequent fliers. Delta actually loses money flying to Hawaii, since such a high percentage of travelers are cashing in free trips. "People come here to get their attitudes adjusted," ticket agent Mel Ames had told me on a previous trip.

For Maui residents looking back at us, 714 was part of a battle over tourism raging on the island. A jet coming in meant jobs for some, destruction to others.

"When I see your plane coming, I see loss of life-style, loss of shoreline access, strained sewer systems, clogged highways, no place to get away, real estate going up so people who live here can't buy a house," Dana Hall had told me on a previous visit. She led a faction on the island that opposed lengthening Kahului Airport's sole 7,000 foot runway so it could accommodate bigger jets.

"Without the longer runway, the hotel industry is dead in the water," one hotel manager told me. With it, he said, 747s could fly into Maui. Which would mean direct flights from Japan. Thousands more tourists.

Kahului's runway was so short that on peak travel days Delta ground personnel counted children boarding outgoing TriStars to better calculate allowable weight limits for safe liftoff. They barred Delta personnel flying free from open seats. They even rarely had to turn away paying passengers.

But 714 was practically empty this evening. With a recession on, planes to Hawaii carried fewer vacationers. Even passengers flying free lacked money for hotels.

The control tower rose from sugarcane fields. We descended toward the runway. Captain Diehl touched down so smoothly the crew whistled and clapped, and I wasn't sure of the exact moment we made contact with earth.

I was tired. Back in Atlanta, one reason I'd chosen 714 was that it was scheduled to go to Hawaii. Now all I wanted to do was sleep.

But I woke up a little when we taxied to the gate, and I saw the plane beside us. It was 714's old archrival, a United Airlines DC-10, McDonnell Douglas's entry against the L-1011 when both planes were conceived of in 1966. After spending time alone in 714, flying in it, eating in it, sleeping in it, staying in the cockpit as crew after crew came and went, on some level the jet had stopped being a machine to me and had begun assuming a personality.

I liked 714. I liked the way it shot down the runway. I liked the way it felt weightless lifting off the earth. I liked the way the dials glowed orange in the cockpit at night. I liked how close the full moon looked from the glass bubble.

Even though logically I knew there was nothing strange about two airplanes parked side by side, mine was alive now, and the one close by had tried to harm it. Imagine Napoleon checking into a hotel and finding the Duke of Wellington in the next suite. Or Elliot Ness buying a house and discovering Al Capone mowing the lawn next door.

If inanimate objects had consciousness, even after twenty-six years, these two could never spend the night together.

In airline history, the battle between the TriStar and DC-10 for prominence in their market is still considered the most vicious ever to occur, and still shows how every commercial jet flying today, whether a Boeing 747, MD-11, Fokker Jet, or Airbus, is conceived, built, and sold to the public. The story of the Lockheed–McDonnell Douglas war still illustrates how airlines play manufacturers against each other and ultimately gamble millions of dollars and hundreds of lives that they've made the right choice.

Because the truth is, for all any airline knows about a new plane, for all the scrupulous supervised tests and retests and certifications of every system aboard, all the bragging companies do when their ships are unveiled, in aviation the unforeseen brings tragedy. That's what happened to the DC-10. And came close to destroying 714.

But those mishaps were still in the future when the airlines had to decide which plane to buy. Many of the people who had made the choice at Delta were still at the company in 1992. I'd met them, talked to the engineers who designed 714, the test pilots who flew it, even the man who had personally handed over the $20.5 million check for it, in those days when Delta paid cash and the company chief financial officer didn't have his windowsills lined with paperweights commemorating acquisition loans.

The legendary battle started innocently enough in 1966, during a rainstorm over New York City one night. Trapped in an air traffic backup, American Airline's chief engineer, Frank Kolk, was coming into LaGuardia from Cincinnati, heading home after inspecting a new General Electric jet engine. He realized the airlines needed a new kind of plane. One big enough to carry lots of passengers and still land on short runways like LaGuardia's. A jet that would cut down on the number of planes clogging the skies and still accommodate growing passenger traffic, increasing at 14 percent a year.

Kolk decided to try to convince a manufacturer to build a twin engine jet able to carry 250 passengers up to 1,500 miles at a stretch, burn less fuel, and land on short runways.

He flew to the West Coast to run his notion past the big three airplane builders. Boeing, whose business was booming with the 747, wasn't interested. McDonnell Douglas was lukewarm at first. Lockheed was building only military planes at the time, having fled from the civilian market nine years earlier after its last entry turned into the kind of nightmare that no amount of preflight testing seems able to anticipate. The Electra, Lockheed's turboprop plane, a propeller/jet driven combination, had won rave reviews when it took to the air in the late 1950s. But within two months two

Electras crashed, killing all aboard. It took a year to figure out why. It turned out that when the plane flew at its recommended speed of 405 miles an hour, between 22,000 and 26,000 feet—*only* at that altitude, and *only* at that speed—a deadly vibration started that fractured a supporting structure on one of the plane's propeller shafts, making the propeller wobble, making the engine jiggle, making the wing shake so badly it would tear itself off the plane.

Once Lockheed knew the problem, it was easy to fix with extra structural support. But turboprops were a thing of the past by then. Jets were supreme. And Lockheed's reputation was damaged.

Now Frank Kolk's idea came at a perfect time for Lockheed. The perennially struggling company needed business. They'd just lost a competition with Boeing to build the SST supersonic airliner. Listening to Frank Kolk, Lockheed engineers got excited. His idea dovetailed with a notion they'd been toying with on their own, a modification of one of their military planes into a commercial airliner. They pulled out their early sketches, and *Kolk* got excited. The design was "close to what he had in mind." He wondered if Lockheed would consider designing the plane. And mentioned that he was heading over to Douglas to ask the same question.

The opening guns of the battle had sounded.

In the end two companies would almost go broke. Two governments would be sucked into corporate bailouts. Tens of thousands of workers would get jobs and then lose them.

But on that first day, when Kolk left, "we had about 1,200 surplus engineers from the SST program," Lockheed's chief engineer Bill Hannon told Douglas J. Ingells, author of *L-1011 Tri Star and the Lockheed Story*. "We transferred most of the top people to the new project and jacked up [the designing] to full speed ahead."

But exactly what kind of plane would they design? It wasn't enough that just American Airlines might be interested. If other companies weren't going to buy the new plane, there would be no profit in building it. While Hannon's engineers began sketching out possibilities, Lockheed salesmen canvassed airlines, asking about their needs and suggestions.

TWA and Eastern both wanted a new plane, but preferred something heavier than Frank Kolk's, to accommodate their traffic between Chicago and the West Coast, and New York and San Juan, respectively. TWA vetoed a two-engine jet. What if a plane lost one engine over the Rockies with a full load? No jet engine existed at the time that would provide enough power to keep the plane flying within FAA safety limits. Besides, the public preferred three engines.

"Frank Kolk's idea to have a little short-range 'shuttle bus' started to stretch a bit," Bill Hannon told Douglas Ingells. "The obvious thing was to lean toward a trijet."

"It would be a great big gamble, building the plane," Elliott Green told me.

Green, whom I met in Tarzana, California, was Lockheed's chief engineer of production design on the TriStar, then director of commercial engineering, then vice president in charge of all Lockheed commercial aircraft programs. He'd been involved in all phases of the plane's life.

"It was exciting, but it was scary. If a project that size failed, it could doom the company."

He was a big, tall man, retired since 1987, with a mellifluous voice like a late-night radio host. And his home was a small, airy ranch amid orange trees, azaleas, and camellias, with oriental silk screens and statuettes on tables and shelves, and a combined living/dining/family room open for square dancing, which he and his wife, Dot, love.

Green said Lockheed decided to take the plunge and accept orders for the new plane, only to discover that McDonnell Douglas had come up with a model too. In fact the two jets looked much the same, except for a few differences hardly visible to the naked eye. The DC-10 would have three engines like the TriStar, two on the wings, one on the tail, but the Douglas's engine would sit a little higher up. Both planes would carry about 260 passengers at first, and later, 330. Both had two aisles and eight-across coach seating. Lockheed decided to put Rolls-Royce engines on the TriStar. Douglas opted for General Electric. The sticker price would run somewhere around $20 million.

The race was on. Lockheed and Douglas salesmen rented apartments in St. Louis, Chicago, Atlanta, New York, home cities of the big airlines. They bumped into each other daily coming in and out of meetings with management and engineers, as the airlines put together teams to analyze the contenders.

"The salesmen were tactful," said Joe Davis, a Delta engineer considering both planes. "They were always available if you had a question. If need be, they'd bring in an engineer from Burbank to talk to us. We'd go to lunch with them sometimes, but it wasn't Let the Good Times Roll. It wasn't, Go with the guy with the most booze and steaks."

For the airlines, a battle between Lockheed and McDonnell Douglas was the best thing that could happen. "It was great," *Fortune* magazine quoted an anonymous airline official saying. "The longer negotiations lasted, the more we would get." He meant bigger payloads. Better performance. Better galleys. Cheaper prices. Better financing.

It was an unequal battle at first. "Lockheed was the dark horse," said Joe Davis. "At the first meetings we were pretty skeptical, because they'd literally gone down in flames with the Electra. They had a black eye."

But Davis said the more Delta engineers looked, the more they examined thousands of technical components on the planes, the more they leaned toward the TriStar.

"One thing we liked was that the TriStar had plug doors, and the DC-10 didn't," Davis said, naming an innocent-sounding factor that would make the difference in the slaughter of hundreds of DC-10 passengers a few years later. Plug doors are like corks, Davis told me. They're wider on the inside, narrower on the outside. When the door is closed and the plane pressurized, pressurized air pushes against the door, and the cork shape becomes an added safeguard with the lock, preventing the door from blowing out.

Unlike the TriStars, the proposed DC-10s had cargo doors locked only with latching mechanisms. Some engineers thought the locking system was so complicated the doors could *seem* locked when actually they were only partially that way.

The difference in doors would be tragically demonstrated on March 3, 1974, when a Turkish Airlines DC-10 plunged into the forest of Ermenonville outside Paris right after takeoff, killing 346 aboard.

Visiting the scene afterward, Capt. Jacques Lannier of the French Gendarmerie Nationale said, "On my left, for 400 or 500 meters, the trees were hacked and mangled. In the valley, trees were even more severely hacked, and the wreckage greater. There were fragments of bodies and pieces of flesh which were hardly recognizable. Not far from where I stood, there were two hands clasping each other, a man's hand tightly holding a woman's, two hands which withstood disintegration. . . . "

Reeling from the carnage, investigators tried to piece together what had caused the crash. The weather had been good. There had been no turbulence. The plane had been climbing without problem when suddenly the mishap occurred.

But then investigators, listening to the flight recorder and the crew's voices just before the crash, heard the whoosh of violent decompression on the tape. Then the howl of the pressurization system working overtime to replace escaping air. On the tape a klaxon began blaring. Copilot Oral Ulusman's voice said, "The cabin blew out."

It turned out that the small rear cargo door, only 48 inches tall, had been improperly latched. With five tons of pressurized air pressing against it, the door blew. It was clear to investigators what had happened next, wrote Paul Eddy, Elaine Potter, and Bruce Page in *Destination Disaster*. As pressurized air escaped from the cargo bin, there was no pressure inside it to counterbalance the force pushing down against its ceiling from the passenger cabin above. The cargo compartment ceiling caved in, plunging two rows of passengers through the fuselage, 11,500 feet into a turnip field below. (The cargo compartment ceiling is the cabin floor.) The collapsing ceiling also severed the plane's control cables. For Turkish Airlines ship 29, that was the end.

I asked Joe Davis, at Delta, "Did you really anticipate that could happen in the 1960s?"

"One of our engineers said it specifically."

Davis also said Delta engineers favored the TriStar hydraulic control system—which operated the plane's rudders, elevators, and ailerons—over the DC-10's. The TriStar had four separate systems, he said. And the cables for each never came together anywhere inside the plane. That meant if one was severed somehow, the other three would keep operating. Davis said the DC-10 had three systems, which was good, but they ran together in one tiny spot in the plane.

"It was such a small area we didn't think anything could take out all three systems," one McDonnell Douglas engineer told me. "But we were wrong." Again the fluke wouldn't happen for years, until July 19, 1989, but on that date a United Airlines DC-10 was headed from Denver to Chicago, when a jet turbine fan broke loose, spun through the fuselage, and severed all three hydraulic systems at the spot where they came together. In a fraction of a second, the plane lost all controls. Capt. Al Haynes tried to land the plane at Sioux City, Iowa, using "differential power"—steering by alternating thrust on the two engines he had left. He almost made it. A hundred and eleven people were killed, but 185 were thrown clear and survived.

Who could anticipate these things? How could they tell? In the late 1960s, at the major airlines, hundreds of engineers pored over the plans for the TriStar and DC-10. And not only engineers. At Delta, Pre Ball, chief pilot and vice president of flight operations, was in charge of analyzing the entries from the pilot's point of view. He was a short, no-nonsense ex-barnstormer, whose boyhood goal had been to be a mail pilot, and who, when I met him long after his retirement, still conveyed the impression that it would be unwise to get on his wrong side. Ball inspired reverential loyalty among the men who had flown under him. Ball was the best man in the world to back you up in a tight spot, they said. We talked at his home near Hartsfield Airport, in a suburban section where signs on lawns advertised noiseproofing, and where Ball joked he was responsible, since he'd brought in the first jet. He had a slow, southern, courtly manner, a deep sense of humor, and a quick wit revealing steel underneath.

"When Lockheed decided to get into the big jet race, they took an unusual tack," he said. "They went to the airlines and said, We're contemplating building a large jet, and we want to be sure it is not just a creature of our thoughts but a product the airlines themselves can live with. Five companies interested in an airplane of that type—TWA, Eastern, National, Delta, and Air Canada— formed committees of pilots for cockpit performance and maintenance people to look at access to pumps and hydraulics. We had flight attendants give information on aisle spacing, ovens, buffet location. I went out to California. They'd pick us up in the morning, and we'd go off to Lockheed as if we were going to school. This was two years before the airplane was built.

"At the same time Douglas was trying to get us to buy the DC-10. My job was to recommend one or the other."

Ball was interested in getting automated pilot systems on any new plane. "We got in the room with this Lockheed gentleman, and he said, 'What do you want the automated system to do?' We told him. When we were finished, he said, 'You've given us an awesome task. You want this thing to take off, climb, acquire proper altitude, maintain speed and fuel flow, pick the point of descent, make the approach, and land. Would you like it to apply the brakes too?' "

Pre Ball grinned. He was eighty-seven years old now and couldn't drive a car because of bad eyes.

"We told him, Hell, yes, that's what we want. And the truth is, none of us really believed the airplane would do all those things. But it did."

In fact, in 1992, twenty-two years after the revolutionary automatic system was developed, pilots still loved it. "The plane lands itself," they told me. I assumed they meant the automated system was so excellent, it *seemed* like the plane landed itself. I didn't think the plane really landed itself.

Then on my first cockpit flight, coming into Portland, Oregon, from Salt Lake City, Capt. Magness Lindsey turned to me and asked, "Want to see it land itself?"

"Sure," I said, thinking, No, I don't want to see it land itself. I want *you* to land it.

Next thing I knew, Lindsey had his camera out and was taking pictures of Mount Hood, which was going by on the left. Copilot Pete Hayden was picking a piece of lint off his pants. The captain's and copilot's horseshoe-shaped yokes were turning by themselves as if moved by ghost hands in a movie. The Columbia River seemed to come up at us, and there were barges down there, I could see the frothing wakes behind them, and the dive got steeper and beeping started, and I looked back through the open cockpit door at a woman reading a *Glamour* magazine in First Class, and I thought, Boy, if you only knew what's going on up here.

I was relieved when Hayden finally put his hands back on the controls. We touched down smoothly, rolled down the center of the runway. "Beautiful," Lindsey said. Hayden said, "How did you like that?"

"It was good," I said, "but I was glad when you flew it in the end."

Hayden looked surprised. "I didn't touch it," he said. "My hands were guarding it in case I had to take over."

I stared at him. "You mean when the flaps moved—when we cut back on speed—when the landing gear came down—what about when we went down the middle of the runway? You weren't doing it?"

They nodded.

Retired pilots told me they'd been amazed too when the system was installed. "I remember the very first run I made into Atlanta, in fog, in a prop plane, when I was starting out," one said. "I was copilot. The pilot said, 'Put your head out the window, and when you see the trees, holler. Then they told me we have some kind of automated landing system. I had my doubts. The first time we tried it, it didn't feel right. The second time, better. The third, I was elated."

Another pilot shook his head. "I told them, wait a minute. This little gadget with two needles is going to take me down the runway? Who was gonna believe that?"

Pilots told me:

- The L-1011 was the first airplane I ever flew where I didn't care what the weather was.
- I never had to go to alternate airports anymore because of weather.
- I never missed a golf game in London after we got that landing system.
- The L-1011 was high tech before the term "hi tech" became popular. I used that landing system once in San Francisco. I had thirty acquaintances on board, and they told me, "We want a smooth landing." I put it on autopilot. I never told them. After we landed, I took my bows.

• We'd be over the Rockies, and we'd hear United and American asking for altitude changes. And we'd be sitting there on autopilot. Smooth.

In the end, Pre Ball recommended that Delta buy the TriStar over the DC-10, and even today the instrumentation on Lockheed Tri-Stars is in use in about 50 percent of airliners.

But back in the 1960s, the design stage, Elliott Green and the Lockheed engineers were under the gun to help invent the new systems. To make sure they worked. "I was in charge of the 'ilities' at first. Productibility. Reliability. Maintainability."

During the design work, in Burbank, "I'd get up early, thread the freeways and get home ten or eleven at night. Day after day we'd be modifying. Remodeling. Reps from the airlines would come in to ask questions, probe, test, oversee."

Green shook his head, sipping coffee on his couch. "I was a driven man. I remember one night when I was caught up on a problem, I forgot to call home. When I got there, I found cold supper on the table. Dot had gone to bed and left our son's sleeping bag for me on the floor, and a note, 'If you think that much of Lockheed, why don't you stay there instead of coming home.' "

At Lockheed, the engineers were confident their plane would blow Douglas out of the water. They figured Douglas was behind them in the race. These illusions were cruelly crushed in February 1968 when American Airlines became the first big airline to place orders for their choice. For twenty-five DC-10s, at a cost of $400 million.

"Lockheed's chairman Dan Haughton called a meeting and told us, 'I've got the price too high and we're going to cut it,' " Bill Hannon said.

Within a month Lockheed won the next round, pulling in $2.58 billion worth of orders from TWA, Eastern, Delta, Northeast, and Air Holdings, Ltd., a British company, which would market the planes around the world. The race had turned around. Lockheed almost had it won. If United Airlines, the last big holdout, went for the TriStar, the McDonnell Douglas program would fail, and the whole company might even go under. But United chose the DC-10. United's Pres. George Keck phoned Dan Haughton and told him, "If the DC-10 isn't built, Douglas will be out of the business. And I think that would be a bad thing for the airlines." What he meant was, We want to keep competition fierce.

With the first phase of competition over, the new focus of the fight became, Who would get their prototype plane into the skies first? The winner would probably capture the public imagination. And attract the interest of foreign buyers.

At Douglas, banners went up in the Long Beach plant: "Fly Before They Roll."

At Lockheed, the center of activity moved from Burbank to the Mohave desert at Palmdale, where a gigantic TriStar factory took shape. On the 667-acre facility just the final assembly buildings took up 868,522 square feet.

"It was exciting, and it was scary," Elliott Green said. "We were going to see hardware from the dream everyone had in the beginning. We would certify an aircraft the likes of which had never been certified before. For the first time in aviation, there would be no direct connections between the cockpit and the control surfaces. It would all be hydraulic. For the first time you had the autoland.

"But the scary part was you have this new equipment, but it doesn't always work right. So is it a design problem? Or a manufacturing problem? The tooling is brand new. Things don't fit quite right. You have to do redesign on the spot. You get engineers into it. You get the FAA in the loop and get it approved."

On Lockheed's monstrous assembly line, parts came together from subcontractors all over the United States. The evacuation slides came in from Air Cruisers Company of Belmar, New Jersey. The antiskid system came from Goodyear Tire & Rubber of Ohio. The navigation instruments from Sperry Flight Systems in Phoenix. The bulkheads and flooring from Northwest Industries in Edmonton, Alberta. Crew attendant seats came from Kent, Washington. Fuselage doors from Gifu, Japan. Automatic flight control systems from Cedar Rapids, Iowa.

Thirty thousand jobs were riding on the TriStar, and every employee knew they could be out of work if more orders didn't come in. Twenty-four banks funded the project, including the First National City Bank of New York, the Girard Trust Bank of Philadelphia, the Mellon National Bank & Trust Company of Pittsburgh, the Wells Fargo Bank of Los Angeles, the Crocker–Citizens National bank of San Francisco, the Trust Company of Georgia, from Atlanta.

Elliott Green could hike up to the top of the factory twenty-four hours a day and look down and watch the planes being assembled. The prototype leading the way. The other jets behind. But this was an assembly line in slow motion. It took months to build a plane. The fuselage arriving in sections at first, like big water pipes. The interior; the hydraulic systems and electrical wires added after the fuselage was intact. The wings "mated" to the plane, and the landing gears. The Rolls-Royce engines to be attached last.

"The most amazing part was watching them install the wiring," said Milt McKnight, Delta's man in California who would design the crucial manuals Delta would use for pilot training and TriStar operation. Manuals which had better be clear to the last tiny detail, because they would be what crews turned to in emergencies. "Twenty-five thousand miles of electrical wire." McKnight shook his head in wonder. "How they got all those wires, reading lights, audio, movie lights on amazed me. Peel back the outside of an airplane, and you have these huge bundles of colored wires, each going to a different place."

Listening to McKnight talk reminded me of my own visit to an airplane assembly line at the McDonnell Douglas plant in Long Beach, in 1992, to watch new MD-11s being completed. I remembered that the building was so huge, the planes so immense, the workers so tiny against them, that the sense was not of an assembly line, where machines were being constructed, but of a movie set or a museum, where the half-finished jets were frozen in different stages of completion. Workers welded, wired, inspected, tested, hung inside shells of planes, riveting, but their efforts seemed puny when looked at one by one. Outside the hanger, wings sat on a dolly, without any airplane attached to them. Inside, I saw a long bullet-colored fuselage without wings. I saw an engine hanging from steel scaffolding. The parts didn't seem to have anything to do with each other.

In the assembly plant I felt industry, energy, and it was hard to imagine that such a vibrant scene, which would have looked almost the same at Lockheed, could mask impending bankruptcy, but at

Lockheed that was the case. For all the hard work at Palmdale, Douglas rolled out its prototype first. The July 1970 ceremony was attended by California Gov. Ronald Reagan and a bagpipe band in kilts. And a few months after that, the bottom really fell out. In February 1971, Lockheed Chairman Dan Haughton went to a luncheon in London hosted by Lord Cole, chairman of Rolls-Royce Ltd., builders of the TriStar engines. Over sherry and cold salmon, Haughton gave Cole the good news that Lockheed production was on schedule and funding problems were solved. He asked how work was coming on the engines.

Rolls-Royce is going into receivership, Lord Cole said.

Haughton was bowled over. Receivership would mean no engines for his TriStars. Cole said costs on the engine had exploded. Development was falling behind schedule, and Rolls couldn't afford to pay the tough penalties stipulated if the engine was late. Worst of all, England's Prime Minister Edward Heath, a Labourite not sympathetic to business, was refusing to authorize government help. Pretty ironic in light of the government stand in 1968 when the man who had swung the British end of the Rolls-Royce–Lockheed deal was knighted by the Queen for his contribution to the country's balance of trade.

Things were so bad at Rolls that down in the lunchrooms embittered engineers were chanting a parody of the Lord's prayer during meals.

> Give us this day our receiver
> And forbid our redundancies
> As we forgive them
> That did nationalize us
> But deliver us from creditors
> For ours was the Merlin
> The Spey and the Conway
> Dart and the Avon
> Rolls-Royce Men

The Merlin, Conway, Dart, Spey, and Avon were old Rolls-Royce military engines.

Suddenly the TriStar program was in danger of collapse. And this time it was the Douglas people watching, hoping for a funeral. If Dan Haughton was to keep his company afloat, he would have to "perform one of the most delicate balancing acts in the annals of modern business," wrote *Fortune* magazine. He would have to keep the airlines from canceling orders. Would have to keep his funding banks from backing out. He would have to try to convince the British to bail out their company.

"The outcome depended on simultaneous commitments by six airlines, twenty-four banks, and two governments," *Fortune* wrote.

Haughton ordered gigantic layoffs at Lockheed, and work proceeded but at a very slow rate. The chairman became a kind of corporate diplomat, winging his way between London, Washington, California, and the home offices of the banks and airlines, struggling to help come up with a way of funding Rolls-Royce.

A reporter asked Haughton how he stood the pace.

"I sleep fast," he said.

The difficulty was compounded by British fears that even if Rolls-Royce became solvent, Lockheed would fail and drag down Rolls. After months of negotiating, Prime Minister Heath swallowed his opposition to Rolls on one condition. The British government wanted guarantees that if it lent money to Rolls-Royce, and the TriStar program failed, the money would be repaid. Those kind of guarantees couldn't be provided by Lockheed. They could only be provided by the United States government.

So now, while Lockheed employees held their breath, Haughton met with Pres. Richard Nixon's treasury secretary, John Connally, who met with Nixon and announced that the administration would send the loan-guarantee legislation to Congress.

For Elliott and Dot Green and thousands of other Lockheed employees, this was the worst time. Their jobs, their years with the company, their pensions, their houses—everything would come down to a roll-call vote in the Senate, and newspaper reports predicted the vote would be close.

"That vote was a dark day, a *dark* day," Dot said. She was a small, cordial, outspoken woman whose expression went black when she remembered.

"We lost friends during that period," she said. "It was awful. Elliott had worked at Lockheed since college, and some of our friends would *still* say to him," she said, still furious, " 'The government can't go around bailing out companies.' One friend kept getting on Elliott, wouldn't leave him alone. I could never speak to her again."

On the day of the roll call, Dot sat by the radio listening as each Senator voted. California Sen. Alan Cranston, who was pro-Lockheed, had estimated the vote would go against the company, 49–48, with the swing vote belonging to Montana's Lee Metcalf. Cranston had been working on Metcalf for weeks, trying to get him to change his mind.

With six votes to go, Metcalf told Cranston, "I'm not going to be the one to put those thousands out of work."

The guarantee passed by one vote. People danced in the streets in Burbank that night.

Lockheed would get the Rolls-Royce engines. But Douglas was clearly the front runner now.

"There was a lot of pressure to get the planes done," Elliott Green said. "I flew down to Palmdale in the first week of March 1972. Just for a couple of weeks, they said. Ha! I got home the end of August."

Elliott was overseeing hundreds of tests, changes, suggestions. With a new plane, modifications keep occurring throughout the process. Engineers did fatigue testing on the TriStars. Using hydraulic jacks they simulated stress on the plane, putting models through the equivalent of 52,000 flights. They used infrared equipment to find "hot spots." "Where temperatures are higher, we can expect components not to last as long," Green said.

To show one test, Green got up and disappeared into his study and returned with an infrared photo of his own head. In the thermograph, heat showed up as colors. Elliott's eyes glowed magenta, the hottest temperature, which also radiated from his long neck. Dark blue, next hottest hue, coated the outer fringe of his skull, below cooler yellow fuzz, his hair. His greenish nose was cooler than the light blue face around it.

"I had hair once," Elliott joked.

He said at Lockheed, engineers used a "boroscope" to look into the engine.

"Have you ever gone to the doctor to be checked for polyps?

That's a boroscope," he explained. "Imagine a light and a transmitter. We stick it inside an engine to examine for cracks in turbine blades or stress from heat."

He also said the metal was x-rayed.

"You put a plate in an area. You use a radiation device, just like in a doctor's office. Same technique. Different energy level. It shows discontinuities in the metal, which look like ripples. A crack shows up darker than the area around it because more radiation goes through."

In another test, in a lab, engineers assembled the entire electronic system of the plane for tests.

Finally the first TriStar was ready for its first test flight. "I stood on top of the hanger, holding my breath all the way," Green said. "It went beautifully." But testing would last for months.

Don Moor, who piloted the second L-1011 up, told me many tests were designed to establish the limits of the new plane. Airlines would have to know exactly how takeoff would go with different weights. Exactly what would happen when the weights were combined with different flap settings. Exactly how to set the throttle for takeoffs and landings. All the theories were being tested now. "We had to establish the procedures for single-engine landings," said Moor, a lanky, amiable man with light-colored eyes, gray hair, and a brushy mustache. "We had to establish procedures for what happens if three out of four hydraulic systems are out. It was our job to come up with procedures so the FAA," he said, making the sign of the cross across his chest, "could bless them."

How high would the TriStar go? How fast at different altitudes? How would the plane hold up when it went that fast? Don Moor tested the brakes under emergency conditions. He raced down the runway at full speed, jerked the engines into idle and stood on the brakes, seeing if they could stop. Some day, somewhere in the world, a pilot with a full passenger load might be faced with this situation, and he would have to be trained how to handle it.

"From 160 knots to the brakes," said Moor. "Can you imagine the energy going into those wheel brakes?

"Test flights could be as long as eight to ten hours. We'd generally go off the coast of Baja, run up and down over the ocean. We'd see the DC-10s going by, being tested too. We'd rag each other over the radio."

In still another test, Moor said, he kept increasing the angle of takeoff until he intentionally brushed the tail of the plane against the runway. Pilots in the future would have to know exactly how high they could aim the nose in an emergency.

Each night when Don Moor and other test pilots got back to Palmdale, Elliott Green and his team would be waiting. "I'd go have dinner, then at midnight drive back to the field and the big bird would come in," Green said. "With that gritty desert wind blowing. We'd go into a room and debrief. During the day decisions were manufacturing ones. At night, after the airplanes flew, the engineers and I would go through every item and write a plan to fix them."

"We were working three shifts. Twenty-four hours a day."

Test flights aren't limited to the early life of a plane. I was surprised to find out that in 1992, Moor and Delta pilots *still* regularly tested 714 and other L-1011s over Atlanta, to check their performance after heavy maintenance, look over modifications, or examine used planes the company has bought.

"Want to go on a test flight?" Paulette O'Donnell asked me at headquarters one day. She said Capt. Reuben Black, Delta's chief pilot, was planning on taking up an L-1011 Delta had purchased from Eastern Airlines. I'd been hearing for weeks that the Eastern planes were in deplorable condition. And now this one had received some preliminary repair and would be flown to Germany for more work. That is, if it passed the test flight.

"Come in early, 8 A.M.," Paulette said. "We'll go over to Captain Black's office. They have to do some things before the flight."

Things? *What* things, I thought. I had a vision of myself in a G-machine, strapped in, face distorted out of a "Saturday Night Live" skit, spinning like an orange peel in a Cuisinart. Do things.

I thought about the words, "test flight." Not "flight." "Test" flight.

"What's the worst that could happen?" Delta Capt. Fred Gordon joked on the phone when I told him. "Thirty seconds of terror? A plunge to earth?"

"Test" flight. "Don't let them talk you into going to the back of

the plane," Public Relations VP Bill Berry told me. "The pilots like
to have you stand in the tail, and they kill the power, and you fly
up in the air."

"Gonna write your will?" a friend asked.

On the morning of the test, I met Reuben Black in his typically
modest office, where the desk lamp was shaped like a trout fishing rod, and wall decorations included a family picture by a beach
house, a book on a shelf called *Taking Charge*, Reuben's name in
needlepoint, and a Japanese symbol that Captain Black said meant
crisis. "Danger on the top. And the bottom means opportunity. A
friend told me the Japanese expect crisis, and we're always surprised by it."

"Do you believe that?" I asked.

"Nope." Reuben was a soft-spoken white-haired man in a camel-
hair jacket. "Anyway, probably some Japanese guy'll come in here
some day and tell me the symbol means taking a crap."

We drove to the big maintenance hangers where mechanics were
final-checking ship 789 before Reuben took her up.

"These Eastern planes were pitiful when we got them," he said,
angry that anyone would allow an airplane to get run down.

"Were they dangerous when you got them?" I asked.

"Yes."

The twenty-year-old TriStar had been stripped for its Deltizing.
There would be two avionics mechanics on board, a Lockheed
representative, a Delta inspector checking off tests, and a copilot,
the company's chief instructor pilot, Bill Gibson. Reuben strapped
himself in, and I walked back in the plane. It felt like an office
building under construction, not an airplane. The seats were gone
except for two out-of-place leather lounge chairs, which the engineers would ride in during the test. Wires dangled from the ceiling. Aluminum padding coating the walls. The carpet was gone.
The floor was metal panels with tape X-ed on areas like actor's cue
marks.

An hour later we were up at 10,000 feet over Augusta, Georgia,
checking the controls. Reuben did three automatic landings, touching down and taking off without stopping. TriStars need to have
their automatic systems regularly tested for them to stay certified.
Reuben checked takeoff power. Temperatures on the engines. He

made sure the "rudder felt good." He checked pitch. Pedals. Brakes. Air pressure.

At 29,000 feet he leveled off in a white haze, and we bumpily did a "speed trim test." "You might have no problems at low speeds but get a completely different kind of performance at high," said Inspector Steve Greene, who stood in the cockpit writing all the statistics down on a clipboard as Reuben went through test after test.

In back of the plane, like drunks on a dance floor, the engineers and I stumbled around without anything to hold on to, peering out the windows at the control surfaces. Ship 789 was a little unstable at 3,000 feet, but it was fixable.

"Next time stay longer," Augusta Air Traffic Control joked as we headed back toward Atlanta.

"You happy?" Gibson said.

"I'm happy," Reuben said.

Inspector Greene gave a thumbs up. "Top-notch so far," he said.

But these were the final years of testing L-1011s, of flying L-1011s. As fit as these TriStars were, even their biggest fans at Delta said they'd be gone from the company in another decade. But in the early days there was a heady feeling in testing those brand-new planes. Don Moor tested the TriStars, and then Lockheed put him to work presenting the plane to buyers overseas.

It was the final days of the competition between Lockheed and Douglas. Moor flew from air show to air show, from capital to capital, to show off the plane. "I flew it to Athens to demonstrate it to Olympic Airlines. To Cairo for Egypt Air. We made a swing across North Africa. Down to South Africa. Up to the Middle East. We carried a marketing rep and about seventy people. We had to be self-sufficient because there weren't facilities for this kind of plane. We had mechanics on board. A fly-away maintenance kit. No parts. We were on our own. The CEO would meet us sometimes, fly demonstrations with us.

"At Accra, Ghanian officials met us at the airport wearing swords. In the Mideast we had to fly in big circles to avoid sensitive airspace. Instead of taking thirty minutes between Beirut and Damascus, we needed one and a half hours. We flew into high-altitude airports in Bolivia. In Africa we had an air-conditioning problem:

When we rotated the plane, water would spill out. It soaked one of our executives."

"At the air shows we'd have demonstrations. Take the airplane out. Do a takeoff, a six-minute show, come back quiet and fast. Make a wide turn. Nobody likes doing air shows, but you do them because if you don't, buyers are suspicious about the plane. *Why didn't you come?* We'd take up potential buyers, then we'd come back and have selected management guests on board, refreshments. Hors d'oeuvres. Beer. It was a party atmosphere for the management types."

"Girls there?" I said.

"Certainly."

"We'd demonstrate the plane to people who'd seen the DC-10 the prior week." Moor sighed. "We were like shadows chasing each other around the world."

At each stop the marketeers would meet with customers, talk prices, argue the TriStar's merits, cajole, coax. In 1976 Dan Haughton would resign from Lockheed amid charges that the company had been selling TriStars and other planes by bribing foreign officials. Not only Lockheed was doing it. It was a widespread practice in the industry. Some industry proponents argued it was a necessary way of doing business abroad.

In the end, the L-1011 sold to Air Portugal and All Nippon Airlines. A Portuguese Catholic priest blessed the first delivery into Lisbon, as Elliott and Dot Green, who had flown in with the plane, watched. A Japanese Shinto priest blessed the first plane sold to Japan.

Other national airlines were interested but what would kill the TriStar would be a lack of hard orders. "The day the program ended was sad, but foreseen," Elliott Green said. "Our management could see a slump in the market. We were looking at a recession, cyclical in the industry. Boeing had the 747 and enough orders to keep up production. Douglas had sold a version of the DC-10 to the military. That kept the line going. We formed a team that went out to customers—at the time we had a letter of intent to buy TriStars from Air India. Quantas was very interested. We said to the other people, we're facing a decision. We'd like you folks who are considering us, who need the planes, to provide us with orders so we can keep going.

"The airlines, being conservative, said, 'We can't do that now.' "

Then Elliott Green surprised me by getting up off the couch, disappearing into his study again and coming back with a computer printout. He still had the week-by-week performance record of every L-1011 he had supervised, up until his retirement in 1987. "Lockheed still tracks what every L-1011 does, every week. We still track every engine," he said, flipping pages in the printout. "Ship 714, let's see, it was the ninetieth TriStar to roll out. In 1987, its average flight lasted 2.7 hours. It was in use 9.8 hours a day that year. By summer of 1987, it had 40,437 total flight hours."

He pored over the printout. Looking at his planes.

"When you're out on your lawn," I said, "and you look up and see TriStars coming in," and he nodded to confirm that this happened regularly, "do you still feel any affinity with them? Or is it something from the past now?"

Elliott Green shook his head. A slow, warm smile spread across his face. "When I see them, I think, That's my baby," he said.

Don Moor also had good feelings for the plane, twenty years later. And he was still test-flying them, coming down to Delta regularly from Lockheed's Marietta, Georgia, facility, working with the planes when they were revamped.

"When the program folded, I couldn't believe it," he said. "I was coming back from a training assignment, with LTU German Airlines. We got word as we coasted into the States. Just a news announcement on the radio. I knew the program wasn't making money, but it looked like it was turning the corner. . . . We would have sold more planes."

Moor told me that in 1992, besides being a test pilot, he worked as a designated engineering representative for the FAA. "If the FAA doesn't have the people to handle a test flight, they'll designate me to do the job."

When he said it, I remembered OJ Greene, the pilot on my first leg out of Atlanta on 714, who also acted as a surrogate for the FAA in analyzing his own company. OJ Greene and Delta pilots and management had claimed there was never a conflict for the FAA designatees in overseeing their own planes and pilots. They always said, and it sounded logical, that they would be endangering their own friends and families who flew on the planes if they didn't oversee them properly.

But if that logic worked across the board, how come the Eastern L-1011s had arrived at Delta in such horrible shape? Hadn't the Eastern FAA designatees done *their* jobs too?

It occurred to me that perhaps the designatee system worked well when a company was healthy financially, but put a strain on the inspectors during times of fiscal crunch.

I asked Moor, "What position do you think the FAA designatees were in at Eastern in the final days of the airline, when the company was cutting back on maintenance?"

"Very tenuous," he said, shaking his head. "Believe me."

"As in, If they tell the FAA about problems, they're hurting their own company? And if they don't report it, they're not doing their job?"

"You have to be very careful," Moor said delicately. "You can cut your own throat. Ideally, you go to management if you see problems and try to change them."

"That doesn't seem to have worked at Eastern," I said. "Do you think the FAA designatees at Eastern felt caught in the middle?"

"I'm sure. With Eastern going down the tubes, you can imagine the thoughts going through the guys' heads," he said. "Will I hasten the death of my own airline? Will my buddies go down the tubes because of me?"

I walked out of the terminal, and the Maui night was warm, and a soft breeze blew on my face from the Pacific. The main reason I'd chosen 714 as a subject instead of a different L-1011 was that it was going to Maui. I'd figured in Maui I could go to the beach during the layover, eat grilled *ono*, drink mai tais, and do a little sightseeing before reboarding in the morning. Just like the other passengers. But now all I wanted was to sleep.

I boarded a van with the crew, for the trip to the Intercontinental. Captain Diehl was still complaining. Now it was pilot quality in the future he was worried about. With the military cutting back on pilots, airlines would have problems finding good ones, he said.

The two-lane highway was so black, Maui could have been Utah for all I knew. At the hotel Captain Diehl demanded that the clerk give me a room with an ocean view. The clerk said, "You're only going to sleep, aren't you?" Diehl leaned over the counter. "Ocean view!" he said.

He bought me a hamburger and a beer in the restaurant. He told stories about flying. Off duty, he reminded me of some lovable gruff character in a wagon-train movie, or of Wilford Brimley in *Cocoon*.

Upstairs I collapsed in bed and woke to an incredible picture-window view of ocean outside, thanks to Captain Diehl. It was everything you want to see when you look out a hotel window in Hawaii. The whole world was in tropical pastels, palm trees in the foreground, long, lavender cloud midway between pinkish ocean and rising sun. I wanted to spend the rest of the month in Maui. I did not want to get back on an airplane, never mind how much I liked 714. I couldn't believe I had to go back to the airport, where both the L-1011 and DC-10 would have spent the night having maintenance checkovers while the crew slept.

"We do a walkaround on the plane, and we check if the crew's written up problems on the way in," Gregory Koshi, lead mechanic for Aloha Airlines in Maui, had told me on my previous visit. Maui is such a small station for Delta that the company contracts light maintenance work out to the Aloha crews.

"We do the obvious check. We look for oil leaks," Koshi said. "Usually an L-1011 might come in with a coffeepot not working, or an audio out at one seat. If we find more serious problems, we call Atlanta. Sometimes Delta might send in mechanics from Honolulu. But usually the planes are in good shape."

Gregory's crew was probably doing the morning walkaround on the plane now, rechecking items they'd looked at last night. Tires. Brakes. They'd be eyeballing small appendages on the outside of the plane, like the long skinny tube, the diameter of a dime, that hung inside engines. They told the pilot how much thrust the engines were giving. The tubes worked using wind pressure. They have membranes inside; the wind pushes against the membranes in flight, and the pressure provides the thrust information. But if the tubes are clogged by ice or water or even insects that got inside overnight, the pilot gets wrong information. Which is what happened before the Air Florida crash in Washington in 1982, when the pilots taking off from National Airport cut power under the wrong impression that they were getting more thrust than they were. The plane hit the 14th Street bridge.

Mechanics and flight engineers always look inside the little tubes before takeoff.

Later, I planned to spend time with mechanics working on 714, both on overnight checks and big months-long overhauls. But now I went down to the Intercontinental lobby.

The only guests up at 5 A.M. were Delta cockpit and flight crew sleepily sipping coffee, or standing gazing out at sea, or sitting in a drowsy little group in the open-air lobby, waiting for the airport van to pick them up. Same flight attendants as yesterday. But different cockpit crew again. I met Capt. Steve Svoboda, a quiet, friendly man who was scheduled to fly 714 to Honolulu and L.A., and then ride as a passenger to its final destination, his home, Las Vegas. It would be a nice, easy day. I planned to hit the casinos during the layover tonight. Within hours 714's whole schedule would be different, but I didn't know that yet.

On the way to the airport, Maui tortured me with more beautiful sights: Windsurfers I wouldn't get to sail on, dormant volcano in the distance I wouldn't get to visit, ocean I wouldn't get to swim in. In the terminal the passengers seemed subdued. Their vacations were over, and 714 was taking them home.

Delta gate agents Rene Samuelson and Dennis Daly checked in arrivals. It was calm today, but I'd be at this airport at tenser times, when 714 was scheduled to head into Los Angeles during rioting that followed the Rodney King police trial. On that day, just out of the passenger's view over the ticket counter, below the smiling agents, telexes distributed to the Delta people would read, "JUST REPORTED—34 DEAD AND MORE THAN 1,200 INJURED SINCE THIS ALL BEGAN" . . . "COUNTRYWIDE LOOTING AND RIOTING OCCURRING / CITIES INVOLVED ARE LAS VEGAS / ATLANTA / TAMPA / SEATTLE / PITTSBURGH / BIRMINGHAM / SAN FRANCISCO . . ."

On that day, the tanned passengers, anxiously queuing up in front of the agents, would ask, "Any news? Is it safe to drive home in Los Angeles? Is the flight even going today?" I'd see how riot-ing, like bad weather or volcanoes or a closed airport, is incorpo-rated into a plane's schedule. And later, coming into Los Angeles, listening to the radio in the cockpit with the crew, waiting to see if we would be diverted, if there would be snipers shooting at in-coming planes, looking at the eerily empty freeways coming up ahead—carless during a curfew—scanning the city for the glow of fires, I would have the same thought.

But today, the mood was so comfortable, the number of passen-gers so few that ticket agents had time to call up little games on their computer screens, amusements provided by hotels or rental car agencies that want to make sure the agents keep them in mind. Ticket agents can arrange cars or hotels for passengers. Hertz was sponsoring a soap opera update on the computer. One agent called it up. Anyone watching him from across the terminal would see a man diligently reading his computer screen. But behind him, I read, "Monica becomes annoyed after finding Nikki snooping through her bathroom. The girl claims to have been merely search-ing for aspirin. . . . Holly fends off questions from her boss but is unable to resist the strains of a jukebox tune when Simon plays their song. . . ."

Out on the tarmac, 714 was boarding. Travelers trickled into the plane to a soothing recording of ukuleles playing "Little Grass Shack" and a video of Hawaiian rain forest, schools of fish in coral, hang gliders above Maui.

I fastened the seat belt, and as we pulled back from the gate, glanced over at the United DC-10. The winner of the battle. Scarcely any airlines still flew L-1011s in 1992, but lots of DC-10s were in service. Lockheed was out of the civilian aircraft market. Elliott Green hoped they'd get back in.

At the pushback we went into sterile cockpit. I watched the pineapple fields and ironwood trees fall away. Down on Hana High-way, a tiny yellow school bus crawled to a stop. Windsurfers skimmed seaward in a regatta of bright sails. A single white cloud floated ahead like a suspended island.

Maybe 714's predecessors had lost the fight with Douglas, but nobody at Delta regretted choosing the plane. In fact, in 1992,

Delta was still buying L-1011s, used ones from TWA and Air Canada, using some for parts, putting others into service, still loyal to their choice.

"Lockheed built the best cockpit in the world and put a plane around it," one Delta pilot told me.

Touchdown in Honolulu went smoothly. We taxied to the gate. The plug doors locked securely. The four hydraulic systems working smoothly. The autoland certified to land us if the captain chose. The Rolls-Royce engines throbbing. All the thousands of decisions that had been made twenty-four years earlier, all the test flights, all the bank deals, all the nights Elliott Green stood on top of the hanger in Palmdale, waiting for the new planes to come in . . . coalesced into a modern airliner. The flight attendants opened the exit door. Passengers terminating in Honolulu strolled out. Captain Svoboda stood by the door of the cockpit in his uniform, smiling, nodding at them as they left.

A woman looked up at him.

"Smooth flight," she said.

OVERSEERS

I didn't notice the men at first. They blended in too well in the terminal. Seven-fourteen had just landed. Passengers filed off, joined crowds heading for other flights, browsed for pineapples in gift shops, greeted friends.

Los Angeles-bound travelers read *Honolulu Record*s, waiting to board. But then I saw two men strolling the wrong way, trying to get into 714 while everyone else was getting out. Both oriental, in jeans, sneakers, and flower print shirts. The short one held a Nikon. The tall one shoved his hands in his pockets.

"Excuse me," Flight Attendant Frederika Chris told them, blocking their way. She'd been saying good-bye to passengers. "We haven't announced boarding yet."

The cameraman said, "Just one picture in the plane? Please?"

Frederika smiled. In nineteen years with Delta, she'd handled drunks, angry passengers, sick passengers, scared passengers.

I'm sorry, she said. But there was a rule. No one could get on until boarding was announced. And then only passengers.

The tall man shrugged. "Even for a second?"

"Take the picture from out here, can't you?" Frederika said.

The man with the camera reached into his back pocket, pulled out a badge, and his smile faded to a harder, official look. Maybe even a little disappointment. His ruse hadn't worked.

"FAA," he said. "You just saved Delta a $10,000 fine."

Frederika said, as they walked off, "The FAA's been getting on planes with phony badges. Sometimes the faces don't match the IDs. I caught one like that last month."

I ran after the inspectors, caught up. Could I interview them? No, they said. That would breach security.

As they mixed back into the crowd, I remembered reading that the Federal Aviation Agency had been created in 1958. It oversees aviation safety in the United States. Trains air traffic controllers. Certifies airplanes and crew. Licenses pilots. Sets security standards for airports and airlines. In 1988, the Aviation Safety Research Act ordered the FAA (by then the Federal Aviation Administration) to also do more research into aging aircraft, crashes, crew fatigue, workload management, and human factors.

No passengers had noticed the exchange between Frederika and the inspectors. But I realized that during my time with Delta I'd been surprised at the extent of the FAA's presence. Like many fliers, I'd always thought of the FAA as a bureaucratic, distant agency I never heard of unless it was investigating a crash—too late to stop it—or was being blamed for not instituting safety rules that might have prevented it.

At Delta the impression had changed. I'd toured maintenance hangers, and mechanics had instantly checked my ID, "in case the FAA is around." In cockpits, pilots had looked me over and said, eyeing my long hair, *You're* not FAA." They clearly expected inspections. I'd visited Delta's records office to read 714's files and watched three men at a table poring over folders. "They're FAA," a clerk had whispered.

"Are they looking for something special?"

"They're always here."

"*Every day?* You mean they come in and ask for any files they want? Do they make an appointment?"

The clerk had laughed. "They don't ask. They take what they want." And later, as I'd pored over microfilmed maintenance and repair records on 714, I'd seen dozens, even hundreds of cards describing standard work procedures, many stamped *FAA mandated*. Maintenance items. Inspection items. Procedures Delta might have instituted anyway, but no aircraft in the United States could fly unless they were done.

The FAA came up in every cockpit, simulator, meeting. Pilots complained of overzealous inspectors. Chief Pilot Reuben Black told me the FAA was requiring costly certification tests for the Pan Am pilots coming to Delta, even though they'd been tested at Pan Am. Vice-Pres. Harry Alger griped that Delta lobbyists in Washington had to fight FAA work-change proposals for flight attendants that would cost too much money. At a lunch for pilots, a speaker introduced herself as "Mother Malone. I deal with the FAA if you have a problem with them." Titters had broken out around the room. I'd thought there must be a lot of dealing with the FAA.

"From my standpoint they're like the cops," one pilot of 714 had told me. "It's like you go out with a state trooper in the car. And he says, 'I'll ride into town with you today and watch how you drive, take your license away if you break any laws.' But they've made this system the safest in the world."

I'd even gotten in trouble with the FAA myself. It happened one morning at an Air Traffic Control center thirty miles south of Atlanta, where I'd gone with agency PR representative Kathleen Bergen to watch controllers bring 714 in from New York. Up until then Kathleen had struck me as diligent, eager to please, coming up with ideas for interviews, going out of her way to phone FAA people in Washington for me, even suggesting things to do in Atlanta during my free time.

But the friendly mood had evaporated as we sat around with a superviser named Mike Ehrlich and I casually mentioned that I'd flown in the cockpit of 714.

Dead silence.

"You flew in the cockpit?" Kathleen said.

I changed the subject.

"You need FAA permission to fly in the cockpit," Kathleen persisted. "Did you fly in the cockpit?"

I had no idea if Delta had gotten permission. I asked Mike a question about radar, and the mood eased. But an hour later, driving back to Atlanta, in the middle of a conversation about bagels, Kathleen said, "You flew in the cockpit, didn't you? I'm going to have to report this. I wouldn't be doing my job if I didn't."

"Come on," I said. "I'm no security risk."

It turned out Delta hadn't gotten permission. But on this occasion there was no fine, since FAA inspectors decided it was an oversight. To them, it had not been a question of whether I was a risk. It had been a question of keeping the system intact so someone who *was* a risk would never get into a cockpit.

Whenever I flew in cockpits after that, Delta got permission.

Right now 714 was in the air again, over the Pacific, in calm, beautiful weather. I left the jump seat and strolled through First Class, where Frederika was serving breakfast. I smelled coffee, and sunlight streamed through the windows. The passengers were relaxed. I realized how much of the jet looked the way it did because of the FAA. The gold and aquamarine seat covers may have been designed by a decorator, but the fabric was flameproof because of the FAA. Forty percent of fire-related deaths on aircraft are caused by flammable cabin materials. Like foam padding inside seats.

The soft rows of emergency lighting on the floor were scarcely visible in the bright daylight, but in a fire, amid billowing smoke, they would point the way to exits.

Marketing people may have had a hand in determining the number of seats, but none was more than 60 feet from an exit because of the FAA. And the little airworthiness certificate displayed in a plastic pouch in the cockpit wouldn't be there at all if "passengers," in a test, hadn't been able to escape a TriStar in ninety seconds, with half the exits blocked.

The fire extinguishers on board, the smoke detectors in the lavatories, the breathing masks for flight attendants, for fighting an onboard fire, all were required by the FAA.

"We deal in safety," William Dubis had told me in Atlanta, sounding a little like a sheriff in an old Western movie.

Dubis headed a fourteen-person inspection team working full-time on Delta Air Lines. Each airline has an FAA team assigned to its home base. Dubis worked out of the FAA's red-brick Georgia Flight Standards Office near Hartsfield Airport. We'd met there on a hot March day.

"If Delta crashes a plane, my butt's on the line," he'd said.

"Ideally, our goals and theirs should be the same," he'd added. He was an ex-pilot in Vietnam, a colonel in the Air Force reserves who'd flown C-141s during the war with Iraq. "We look at that company from the top down. Training programs, manuals, equipment, simulators. Maintenance."

In fact, when Delta or any U.S. airline applies for landing rights at foreign airports, the FAA has to approve the company maintenance program there before the United States government gives permission to fly.

Dubis admitted that the agency lacks the manpower to check every flight, every plane, every maintenance procedure, and said oftentimes investigations are launched after the FAA receives letters from passengers. "You'd be surprised how many people know about aviation. They see something and write us. Or they hear a flight attendant say something like 'Boy, the captain saved everybody on board on that trip.'"

"If Delta and the FAA have the same goals, how would you characterize your relationship?" I'd asked.

Dubis had smiled combatively. "We agree to disagree.

"We don't always see eye to eye on the best way to maintain safety. Sometimes I have to threaten legal action before Delta complies with a request.

"Here's an example. The FAA sent out a guideline that evacuation cards in seat pockets should include information that, in a fire, exiting passengers should follow the lights on the floor to an exit," he said. Delta interpreted "should" as not meaning "must." They didn't redo their cards right away.

"Delta said to me, 'We'll make the change when we print up our next batch of cards.' I said, 'Do it now.'

"Look, the liability to them, if one person dies on an airplane as a result of not finding an exit, is much greater than the cost of printing up the cards."

"What's the bottom line?" I'd asked. "Compared to other airlines, how safe is Delta?"

"They set the standard for the industry. It's comparable to the military." He'd sighed. "I want to feel good about my wife getting on their planes or your wife. Now I do. But I'm not going to relax."

Talking airline safety always made me think of Captain X. He was a pilot and author who had written *Unfriendly Skies, Revelations of a Deregulated Airline Pilot.* All the pilots I flew with had heard of Captain X. But none knew who he was, or what airline he worked for. Kathleen Bergen at the FAA had even given me a copy of *Unfriendly Skies.*

"Captain X takes us behind the scenes into the cockpit to show us the good news *and* the bad news," the jacket said.

The bad news, Captain X charged, was that despite the efforts of the FAA, there were dangerous flaws in the way airlines operated. Of course William Dubis was going to say the FAA did a good job. Of course Delta people were going to praise their own company. But Captain X represented the worst fears of average passengers like myself. He was every scary news report about flying I'd ever seen. Every charge that airlines cut corners. He seemed to be an inside guy confirming the worst.

I wished I could find Captain X.

I asked William Dubis if he knew the identity of Captain X. "No."

And Paulette O'Donnell. "No."

I wanted to ask Captain X about quotes in his book, like "Pilots have learned to shut up even if it means endangering the flying public," or "During the happiest years we have too many drinking problems." I wanted to talk with him about "the erosion of the safety barrier," which he charged had happened under deregulation.

There was another big reason I'd hoped to find him too. I had a feeling he was a Delta pilot. His book had started with detailed descriptions of Hartsfield Airport, which Captain X said he'd been flying into for twenty years. And later, there were notably fewer references to Delta than to other airlines.

Finally, a pilot I met in a bar said he knew Captain X, and two weeks later my phone rang and a man's voice said, "I'm a friend of John Smith's [not the real name of the pilot in the bar]." Captain X wanted to talk about his book. He had no objection to being named, he said, but his airline had asked him to keep his identity secret. I promised to do the same thing.

"Do you mind if I mention the kind of plane you fly?" I'd asked. He'd laughed. "Lockheed 1011s."

"Do you mind if I say where you fly them?"

"I see what you're doing. Honolulu," he said.

I flew to the ski resort where Captain X lived. He arrived at his racket club in a silver Mercedes sports car, wearing fresh jeans, loafers and no socks, a Dunwoody monogrammed V-necked sweater, and rose-colored aviator glasses that accentuated his tan, even though it was winter.

We drank vodka and tonics in the bar. Captain X had just flown in from Honolulu last night. Okay, I figured, here comes dirt on the FAA.

But Captain X surprised me. For all the big talk in the book, he was embarrassed about the way it had been presented to the public, embarrassed that he might have increased anyone's fear of planes.

"What about your quote about pilots shutting up even if it means endangering the flying public?" I said.

"That was on the book jacket and a quote from an Eastern mechanic, not me," he said, backpedaling. The jacket had said nothing about any Eastern mechanic. "When that jacket came out, everyone said, 'Wow!' but I was thinking, Things are taking a turn I didn't anticipate. And then I was on a talk show defending that quote, and we cut away for a moment and I said," he shook his head, " 'I don't remember writing that.' I went back to the book, and *it wasn't there*. I called the publisher. 'You got me defending stuff I didn't write,' I said. They said, 'It must have been in an early draft.' I said, 'I don't care.' "

Captain X sounded whiny. "Things got twisted around," he said. "On one show I was talking about my point, in the book, that in the old days 70 percent of accidents were caused by mechanical problems. Now they've been reduced, and most problems are human factors. But that doesn't mean there are *more* human problems. Just that there are fewer mechanical ones. I tried to straighten this out, and the host said, 'I don't believe you. You guys are out there drinking.' I said, 'So *you* write a book' and got up and walked off the show."

Poor Captain X. I asked him, "What about your quote, 'Even in the happiest times we have too many drinking problems?' "

"We don't have drinking problems today. It's out of context."

"What about eroding the safety buffer?"

Captain X sipped his drink. We were sitting on tall stools at a circular table, and "Josie" blasted from the loudspeakers.

"I meant that in terms of airlines that didn't have funding to keep maintenance at proper levels," he said, referring to Eastern, implying that since the airline had closed, the problem was fixed.

"I landed up on one radio show with a stewardess from another airline. She said, 'Ninety percent of pilots use drugs.' I said, 'You're a damn liar!'"

Captain X and his coauthor had gotten $300,000 for *Unfriendly Skies*, he said. "My heart stopped when I saw that book jacket," he lamented. "*People* magazine scheduled a photo shoot with me at LaGuardia Airport. It turned out they wanted me to stand in the foreground while LaGuardia's regularly scheduled crash-and-rescue team practiced on an old fuselage they intentionally set on fire. They wanted to pick up on the line, 'Most accidents are caused by pilots.' I fought them," he said proudly. "Finally they said they'd cancel the whole spread if I didn't change my mind. I said fine. The publisher went crazy."

I'd asked Captain X, "After deregulation, is flying safer or not?"

"On balance, positive."

"So are you sorry you wrote the book?"

We'd been in the parking lot, ready to leave. Around us shiny BMWs and Mercedes had ski racks on their roofs. Captain X had stuck his hands in his jeans pockets. He'd made a face.

"I wish I'd done it better," he'd said.

William Dubis enforced the rules, but much of the work the FAA did before establishing them occurred in Oklahoma City. Air traffic controllers who guided 714 through the skies were trained there. So were the investigators who pored over 714's records, and security personnel prowling airports where we landed.

FAA scientists studying fatigue or effects of prescription drugs or sleeplessness on pilots worked in Oklahoma City too.

I'd flown to Oklahoma before my trip with 714, and driven past pumping oil wells on the airport grounds to the FAA's massive Mike Monroney Aeronautical Center, a 750-acre, fifty-building campus with labs, offices, mock-up air traffic control rooms, even plane wrecks that future investigators could study.

The wrecks lay in the "boneyard," a sad little museum of death I'd visited with Chief Investigator/Instructor Carl Borchers. We'd walked past smashed automobiles, since FAA investigators work on highway accidents too. Then came the planes. A crushed, battered Piper Cub. A ripped-apart light Soviet model that had crashed in an air show. A section of burned fuselage, this one crashed intentionally, so badly damaged it was impossible to imagine anyone surviving.

Borchers had been a short, wry man who pointed out "patterns of damage" in the wreckage. But I'd kept imagining the terror, the heat of the fires, the screams.

"When a plane crashes, it becomes the property of the federal government," Borchers said.

"See the heating here?" He picked up a heap of charred metal from a smashed prop plane, careful not to cut himself. Held out a section half the size of a Volkswagen Rabbit hood, cream colored where the original paint remained, dull and coppery where it had burned off.

"This was a fire from a fuel line that was loose, dumping fuel on the draw system until it burned the wing off."

Nearby, I looked over three seats that had been ripped from a plane on impact. And the Soviet SU-26, which had actually once had a pleasing symmetry, had been admired, sailing into the sky. What remained of the wing looked more like fiberglass, in shreds. Borchers said it was here to show future investigators how crafts built of "composites," in this case overlapping sections of graphite, came apart. He said composites are now included in planes like the MD-11, and Boeing 757 and 767.

Dented, dulled engine bits had lain in a wooden crate stamped U.S.S.R. Shelves in back of the room had been piled with parts from a crashed helicopter. But the most frightening exhibit had lain in the dirt outside, on its belly as if it had slid in a crash, broken into pieces, and come to rest where the students could conveniently visit it. Borchers had led the way into the crashed DC-8. The aluminum skin had buckled. Fire had melted the windows into a black popcorn mosaic so that they seemed never to have been windows at all. A humid, rubbery smell permeated the shell.

To Borchers, each smashup contained a lesson for students. Here were plywood sheets covering gaps in the plane's floors, because the metal had ripped apart on impact. Here were the fused, melted wires hanging from the ceiling. Here were the cockpit instruments, exploded or unreadable because they were so black. And here was the reason the FAA existed. Everything I would look at during my stay was designed to keep planes out of the boneyard.

Later I'd walked through the "protection and survival laboratory" with Charles B. Chittum, a researcher and self-described "old ramblin' hillbilly from the Blue Ridge of Virginia."

"The purpose of this lab is to get people out of an aircraft alive if they're involved in an accident," he said, his fixed smile never leaving his face, seeming out of place for this conversation.

"Ninety percent of injuries in accidents occur during evacuation. From fire. From smoke inhalation," he said as we strolled past a crash-dummy test where an engineer named Van Gawdry was checking the strength of cabin bulkheads—the front walls in a new private jet. Van Gawdry wanted to see how the bulkhead would withstand the impact of human bodies. In the huge room, rows of dummys sat on the sidelines in wooden pews, roped in place, wearing institutional blue clothing, looking like restrained mental patients or jurors, or British peers falling asleep during a speech.

As I watched, technicians working under floodlights strapped a man-sized dummy into a seat. The seat would be pulled back on a track, cocked, and shot forward. Closed circuit cameras recorded every move. The technicians pulled switches, and there was a humming noise, and the seat slid back about 60 feet. The body was set to hit the bulkhead sideways, the same way it would if the executive jet being tested crashed. Van Gawdry said the test would help determine if the FAA would issue an airworthiness certificate for the plane.

A radio in the background played a soft Beach Boys melody. With shocking swiftness the dummy shot forward, my heart lurching at the violence of it, and the seat stopped in front of the bulkhead but the body, straining against its straps, swung violently and crashed through the wall. It seemed human—half swung around, legs looking broken, one black rubber-soled shoe off. It had looked like a polite person before the crash, sitting nicely with its hands at its sides. Now it looked dead.

"Once the wall went, the restraints became a loop around the soft tissue of the abdomen," Van Gawdry said, looking down at the dummy. "We've been working with this manufacturer for six months. They're going to have to strengthen that wall."

Chittum and I walked into a back room, a locker room filled with more dummies, as if they actually drove to work and changed into those blue surgeons' clothes here. There was a skeleton of a dummy hanging from a wire, like a human skeleton in a doctor's office. The dummy skeleton had a steel skull, metallic ribs, black rubber fingers I moved up and down. Chittum pointed out a canvas sandbag on the floor, shaped like a child. No facial features. Little canvas arms and legs.

Chittum smiled. "Try to pick it up," he'd said.

I reached for the dummy child. I couldn't budge it.

"That's weighted so you can see what a two-year-old would weigh at 3 g's," he said. "In the Sioux City crash, one mother told us she was holding her infant tight, and it disappeared. Rescuers found it 150 feet away. Alive. But you can't hold a child in your arms, and protect it in a crash."

Next stop, a big room with a 30-foot-deep swimming pool, which, empty, looked more like a building foundation. "We don't get a lot of planes crashing in water," Chittum said. "But in a cold water study, we tested different kinds of life vests to see if they could help maintain a person's body temperature. We put subjects in 55 degrees of water for two hours, or until their body temperature went down to 95 degrees. We found that a little protective cover on the life vest kept the body temperature warmer."

"So the FAA requires the new kind of life vest," I said, assuming a new rule followed the findings.

"Ha, ha, ha. No."

"Why not?"

Chittum laughed. "You're trying to get me to talk about legislation," he said. "The FAA promotes air safety but also air commerce. To do both at the same time and keep everybody happy is difficult. We're not here to run carriers out of business from overregulation."

"Then why test the vests?" I said.

Chittum nodded. "Let's assume next year we have three accidents in oceans. And a third of the deaths turn out to be from hypothermia. Then we have the information from these tests to use."

"So *after* the accident the findings would be incorporated?"

"There's that possibility."

Chittum gave me a book listing more FAA safety studies. On success in air traffic controller school; flammability of lip, face, and hair cosmetics in rich oxygen; aging in aircraft crews; human survivability in impacts after free fall; decompression on pilots; and evaluations of airline seats in terms of the way they effect head and face injuries.

But Chittum wasn't finished; he had more to show me. We left the building and walked toward what looked like a Quonset hut behind a chain-link fence, only it turned out to be another fuselage section, this one intact, on hydraulic stilts. Later today, he said, volunteer AWAC crews from a nearby Air Force base would be doing evacuation tests under smoke conditions in the fuselage. Inside there were rows of seats. Overhead racks. Windows and lights and carpeting. Just like 714. Then Chittum pulled a curtain, and the cabin lost some light, and he pulled a switch and smoke began billowing, plunging us into the world of Charles Chittum. The dark shell of an aircraft filled with smoke, jolting side to side on hydraulic stilts. The lights flickering madly.

Day after day. With the smells and the heat and the nauseating rolling of the crashing mock-ups. Researching what can go wrong.

"See that necktie you're wearing?" Chittum said with his knowing smile. "I'd never wear that on a plane."

"Why not?"

"One time, during an evacuation here, in the dark, I was pulled out of the plane by my necktie. Somebody in front of me grabbed it. You can't see a thing with the smoke. Now," he said, removing his tie, "I wear clip-ons."

"The people who survive disasters are people who plan," he said. "How many seats between you and the exit? Right now. Did you count them?"

He stared at me. I hadn't counted the seats.

"Eight," he said. "I know I have to touch eight seat backs to get to the exit on this plane."

"When I go to a hotel, when I'm in a high-rise, the first thing I do when I get off the elevator is put my baggage down and count every door between mine and the exit. I go to the stairwell and count the stairs between floors."

We left the fuselage and walked upstairs to the FAA toxicology and accident research laboratories. What a way to live, I thought. Chittum swung toward me at the door.

"Did you count the steps when we came up here just now?"

"No."

He knew I'd not counted the steps.

I tried to imagine him on his way to an FAA convention. In his clip-on tie and less flammable clothing, counting the seats in the airplane, counting the doors in the hotel, walking up and down the staircase, memorizing.

"Thirteen steps up. Two sections of steps. Twenty-six all together," Chittum said.

What if? Always what if? They were funny labs, these FAA labs. Burnt fuselages. Empty swimming pools. Movable seats smashing into walls. In the toxicology lab, where Chittum left me, researchers had been looking at bulkhead walls, concluding that they should be weaker because passengers often sustain neck injuries hitting them.

"But downstairs, researchers in crash-dummy tests want bulkheads to be stronger," I said.

"Hmmmmmm."

Scientists in the lab also studied toxic properties of flammable cabin materials. They burned cabin components and pumped the smoke into little cages with white rats in them. The rats were on treadmills. When their gait faltered, the gasses were taking effect.

Finally, I met Dr. Stephen J. H. Veronneau, superviser of the FAA's aircraft accident research section, in his small office, which was plastered with polaroids of crashes. I saw photos of smashed US Air and Skywest planes damaged in a runway accident in Los Angeles in February 1991. And an Avianca jet that crashed on Long Island when it ran out of fuel.

Despite his gruesome gallery, Veronneau seemed a boyish, warm man with a slightly technical delivery that did not blunt a sensitivity that came through. To him, the pictures were mysteries he must solve if lives were to be saved in the future. Veronneau's work was to convert injury into statistics, chaos into law.

"Those Lockheed 1011s are extraordinary aircraft," he said when I told him about 714. "They have a reputation for airworthiness among inspectors."

Veronneau had a bad cold, but he'd come into work anyway because he'd been told I was coming, and he wanted to help. He said he usually flew to a crash site as soon as he heard of an accident. Just then he was working on a LaGuardia Airport tragedy, where a Dutch-built US Air Fokker F-28 jet, Cleveland-bound from New York, had skidded off a runway and plunged into Flushing Bay after an aborted 9:30 P.M. takeoff in a snowstorm. I'd seen the wreckage of the plane, still in the bay, while coming into LaGuardia a week before.

Investigators were theorizing that ice on the wing had caused the craft to become unstable on takeoff and crash. Ice affects planes that way because it changes the configuration of the wing, ruins the smoothness, and angles, changes the way air flows over it.

The crash had horrified New York. Rescue workers on the scene had found shrieking, dazed survivors wandering onto highways in shock. Bodies floated in the water. Police divers covered themselves with foam so they could enter the burning fuselage, where they groped their way forward, feeling for flesh.

Twenty-seven people died in the crash. Twenty-four survived.

"Every night I close my eyes and I keep seeing and hearing the people screaming," passenger Robert Main, Jr., told the *New York Times*. "I keep feeling the heat of the fire. I've washed my hair a thousand times, and it still smells of jet fuel."

Veronneau knew if he could figure out *why* the survivors lived, aircraft might be made safer in the future. His tables were covered with reports of the accident. There were stacks of autopsy reports from the New York medical examiner's office. Files from NASA, which has an anonymous tipster line for air crew members who want to tell the government about problems with their planes. "We requested information on all takeoff incidents for that type of aircraft. There have been parallels," he said.

He also had a black-and-white diagram of the assigned seating in the crashed Fokker, so he could look at the dead in terms of where they had been sitting.

"Pink shading in a square indicates that those individuals are deceased," he said in his technical jargon.

"People survived in little pockets," he said, leaning forward at the pictures. "All around them, people died. We'll try and unravel these mysteries. There may be an important lesson for the design of aircraft or the training of flight attendants. We'll group snapshots, section by section of the plane, reconstructing the intact Fokker."

On the table, he arranged before-and-after shots. On one side, brand-new seats, waiting for boarding passengers. On the other, smashed post-crash seats, ripped from the plane, on rocks by the bay. On one side, smiling flight attendant near a door. On the other, caved-in door. On one side, a brand-new Fokker, looking like US Air flight 405 at 9:25 P.M. on March 22, 1992. On the other, the ship after 9:35.

Veronneau stared at his clues, "Why, in the middle of pink squares, the death seats, are there two white ones? *Why?*" he repeated. "Were those people faster? Smarter? Did one of them manage to slip the seat belts off underwater? *Or was it the plane?* Something about *those* seats? *That* row? Something structural?"

There was a pause while he thought about it. Then he said another part of his job involved checking claims made by witnesses in accidents. For instance, crew members in planes often have a hard time seeing ice on wings from their cockpit vantage point. In the US Air incident, "The crew worked diligently to see if there was ice on the wing, but maybe their vantage point wasn't as good as the passengers'."

"Why not require crew to walk back and look at the wings before taking off under icy conditions?" I asked.

Veronneau laughed. We were driving to lunch at a country club near the airport. "That's a good question to ask the regulators."

Over potato soup and a buffet, I told Veronneau about Charles Chittum and the way he counted seats and steps and hotel doors. It seemed to me that Chittum went a little overboard, but Veronneau and the other two FAA people at the table just nodded.

"When you go on a plane, you should wear comfortable loose-fitting clothing," Veronneau said. "You don't want fabrics that are going to melt. People go so far as to wear their stetsons to prevent flaming debris from getting on them. Leather offers protection. I usually wear comfortable, flat shoes. Women shouldn't wear high heels."

"Do you count the rows of seats to the nearest exit?" I said.

They all nodded.

Then Veronneau said, "In the Los Angeles crash, I was investigating it, and I dreamed I was a passenger aft of the overwing exit. I went through the impact. Attempted to get out. It was a vision of fire and smoke." His voice got lower. It wasn't so technical anymore. "And then I woke up."

He went back to eating soup.

"How'd you feel when you woke up?" I asked.

Veronneau looked into the distance. "Unwell."

In the life of 714, the FAA had always been there. Looking over Delta's shoulder, nudging, irritating, infuriating when they got too bureaucratic.

Darrell Wiemers, whom I'd visited after Dr. Veronneau, was a severe-looking, bullnecked man who I would have guessed was a cop. He helped design the FAA's security classes for inspectors in the United States and abroad. Soothing classical music played incongruously from a small radio in his office, and little banners from countries he'd visited hung on the wall like pennants.

"We teach: Don't necessarily believe what you see," he said. "A well-dressed guy, walking into a screening, could be a terrorist. A terrorist looks like you or me. Don't assume the obvious."

And not only with a person, either. In baggage, for instance, "we teach about 'invisible bombs.' Bombs with wires strung along, say, the inside of an attaché case. A security scanner has to be attentive. You're talking about thousands of items going through airport X-ray machines, hour after hour. And the screener, in some countries he's sitting there for eight hours. But you can't see after thirty minutes. Sherlock Holmes said, 'Watson, you look but you don't see.'

"Like the Lockerbie flight," Wiemers said, referring to the ill-fated Pan Am clipper blown up by terrorists over Scotland. I blew out air. One of my high school friends had been on that flight.

"That Lockerbie device could have been detected," Wiemers said. "Every electronic device has a symmetry. A way it's built. One thing we do here is build those things on a computer. Security people have to study the symmetries. The Lockerbie device had wires incompatible with the symmetry.

"Or take a .45 pistol and put it on its side, any beginner would know what to look for on the scanner. But if I were to lay the pistol perpendicular to the X ray—it doesn't look like a gun anymore.

"We teach profiles of possible terrorists," he added. "Look at the person buying the ticket. Is he carrying baggage? Does he come in at the last minute and pay cash for a one-way ticket? *The last moment?* The guy is paying cash because there's no paper trail. He doesn't want anyone to check up on him. Terrorists will give off signals. Dilated pupils. Shortness of breath. Sweating. Fidgeting."

"Isn't that the same behavior that someone gives when he's afraid he'll miss his flight?" I said. "And doesn't he rush up at the last minute too?"

"It's some of the same symptoms but guilt- or defense-induced stress is different from tension stress."

Darrell Wiemers sounded as if he knew what he was talking about until I told him a story one TWA flight attendant told me about a flight to Paris she had worked five years earlier. The story had always made me nervous.

She'd said three men had boarded her plane, sat together in back, one clutching a heavy briefcase that would not fit under the seat. The men were Arabs, she'd said, and at the time Palestinian groups were claiming responsibility for other bombings of the same airline. In fact, part of her crew's recent security training had included a story about three Arabs sitting together in the back of the plane, who eventually hijacked it.

But none of these factors would have been suspicious without the next part of the story.

"You'll have to put that briefcase under your seat or in the overhead rack," another flight attendant had told the man holding it.

"No."

The flight attendant had reached for the briefcase. The man had grabbed her wrist.

"It's very delicate," he'd said.

At this point the attendant became suspicious. "What's in there anyway?" she'd said.

"A bomb."

The plane was still boarding. The flight attendant had rushed to the cockpit, told the captain what was happening. The captain had stomped down the aisle.

"See here," he told the men, "if you don't tell us what's in that briefcase, I'm going to call the police."

Listening to the story, I'd winced. Oh, you're going to call the police, huh? I thought. *Bam!*

It turned out the men were diplomats, who thought the flight attendant was picking on them because they were Arabs. And after the plane arrived in Paris, the captain came out of the cockpit and asked the flight attendants, "What was it those three guys told you?"

I asked Darrell Wiemers what he thought of the captain's behavior.

"Good, because it worked," he said.

"You thought it was *good*?"

"Well, maybe the captain should have told them, 'Saying it's a bomb is a federal crime,' " Wiemers said.

"What if it *was* a bomb?" I said. "Don't you think it was dumb not to take the guy seriously?"

"Well . . . yes," Wiemers said. And as a passenger, I suddenly felt less confident in the FAA training program.

The courtroom was small, and there was no jury, just Administrative Judge John Mathias presiding. The FAA attorneys sat on one side, more frugally dressed than the Delta attorney on the other. I was on the seventeenth floor of Atlanta's Peachtree Summit federal office building. And Mathias was one of four Department of Transportation administrative judges who travel the United States and territories, listening to civil cases against airlines, cases with maximum fines under $50,000.

There were three such cases against Delta on the docket the day I attended. Breach of security in Memphis. Captain flying with an expired medical certificate out of Dallas. Security matter so secret I couldn't watch.

"Given Delta's size, it's probably no better or worse than any other airline in terms of cases we bring against it," FAA southern region Assistant Chief Counsel Ron Haggadone told me.

Later I would think, when the two FAA inspectors tried to sneak onto 714 in Honolulu, that this is where the matter would have ended up if they'd succeeded. Until recently cases against airlines were tried by the Justice Department in federal district courts, but a congressional study showed too few of the cases ever reaching trial. "The DAs told congressional investigators, 'We're swamped with criminal cases. Dope and crooks. We don't have time for two-bit FAA cases,' " Haggadone said.

But the two-bit cases piled up. I sat in court and listened to the facts. Prodded by a Memphis reporter, a fired Delta employee had sneaked through company security at Memphis airport by flashing a retired military ID. Judge Mathias fined Delta a thousand dollars. "The real evidence barely outweighs the hearsay evidence," he said.

Next case. Delta Capt. Stanley Collins took the stand and admitted that in 1987, while piloting a Delta Boeing 727, he'd flown several legs carrying an expired medical examination certificate. He did not realize it had expired until there was an inspection spot check, because there had been a change in Delta's notification procedures, he said. He'd been distracted by illness in his family during that time. He had a spotless record otherwise. He'd immediately gotten the required checkup once he'd realized the problem.

Since the FAA had already decided not to fine the pilot and was trying the airline instead, the Delta attorney argued that neither should be penalized.

"What we have here is a technical violation and not a violation of substance," Delta's lawyer said that day, arguing that the company had corrected its notification procedure.

"This falls far down the line in seriousness," he said.

FAA lawyer Randy Hyman disagreed. "The certificate is a piece of paper, but it is the only way we know if a pilot is medically qualified to fly."

Collins had flown six legs with the expired certificate. Maximum penalty was $10,000 a leg. Hyman asked for $500 a leg. Three thousand dollars in all.

"We're not looking for a high penalty but a reaffirmation from the court of the regulations," she said.

Mathias fined Delta $3,000.

Everybody smiled at each other leaving the courtroom. Outside, I saw Collins talking on a street corner with Delta's attorney. Maybe the fine was small compared to the company's annual income. But

I remembered the stories at Delta about founder C. E. Woolman picking up paper clips in the office to save money. And Delta's hatred of waste. Collins did not look happy at all.

Now, in 714, watching the Pacific Coast of the United States get closer, I sensed the FAA as an invisible web around the aircraft, in its equipment, crew, procedures, future.

In 1992 the FAA was considering new additions to safety regulations. Ten years from now 714 might have a sprinkler system on the ceiling. The FAA was testing them at another complex in Atlantic City, New Jersey. The sprinklers might give passengers an extra two to three minutes of crucial escape time in a crash, officials said. But what if the system went off accidentally and damaged electronic equipment? What if it *caused* a crash? What if the water corroded parts of the plane? And what about cost? Carrying 2,000 pounds of water would mean cutting down on revenue-producing passengers and cargo, in the middle of a recession.

Or maybe 714 will be carrying nonflammable fuel. That was one possibility the FAA tried out recently, experimenting with a fuel that might not explode during a crash. The mix was tested in California. As a crowd of press and officials watched, a remote-controlled Boeing 720 jet came in for a crash landing, touched the ground, and blew up in a fireball. That was the end of research on nonflammable fuel.

Or perhaps in ten years 714 will carry baby seats. Or life jackets for over-water flights? Or really strong passenger seats that won't break away during impact. Some people had even suggested turning seats around so they face the back, lessening injuries from impact on crashes.

At the moment, though, I was looking forward to the next flight leg to Las Vegas and a night at the blackjack tables. Last night I'd missed my opportunity to enjoy Maui. I'd been too tired. But tonight would be different. I felt lucky. I would try the Golden Nugget first, then move to the MGM Grand. I would try a little craps. Couple of slot machines. Maybe catch a show. Ah, the life of a flier.

"Seven-fourteen's not going to Las Vegas anymore," Captain Svoboda told me.

"It isn't?"

"It got switched. From LA, you're going back to Honolulu. After an hour layover."

"Well, at least I'll get a night in Honolulu," I said.

"That's what you think. An hour layover. Then back to LA." He shrugged. "I'm getting off in Los Angeles. Have fun."

An airplane on the ground loses money. I could imagine Paulette O'Donnell in Atlanta, laughing. This is what she'd warned me would happen. "The plane'll never finish the rotation it starts," she'd said.

It was going to be a long night. We came in and touched down and rolled to the gate. The crew changed again. The passengers left. The cleaning crew tidied up, vacuumed. The food service people stocked more mai tais on board. The TriStar looked new again. Sparkly and clean again. The Muzak began playing. From the glass bubble, I could see out to the lounge, to the line of passengers starting to board. At least they looked like passengers. With their jeans and Nikons and suitcases. Then I remembered the two men who'd tried to sneak into the airplane. And remembered how Delta people always asked me if I worked for the government. And I wondered if anyone I was looking at out there was FAA.

FRENCHIE AND THE KID

I was so tired the cockpit seemed to shrink, become a little glass cubicle with the dusk sun blasting in. There might have been no passengers or cabin or airplane behind us. Capt. Jim Porter shook hands strongly. He'd slept this afternoon while I'd been in the air. He was fresh and clean-shaven, starting his workday.

Nightfall in Los Angeles was morning for him.

Two days of travel had left a tight feeling in my stomach. I watched the sun setting, but my body told me it was noon. I was hungry for dinner but stuffed from breakfast, eggs and bacon I'd eaten on the way in.

Ship 714 had flown almost 7,500 miles in the last twenty-six hours. "Your system doesn't know what hit it," Jim Porter said. It occurred to me that FAA researchers had missed an opportunity. If they wanted to study effects of time zone change, they should have hooked me to their electrodes. Never mind playing Ping-Pong with volunteers in Oklahoma, at 3 A.M., to keep them awake.

My disorientation made me doubly appreciate work rules for pilots, who could not fly for more than twelve hours at a stretch.

But then I started thinking about pilot fatigue. Surely captains boarded 714 when they were exhausted sometimes. Or distracted. Or hadn't slept the night before.

Even professionals have bad days. The "what ifs" started. What if a pilot had the flu? How did he give 100 percent? What if his prescription medicine caused drowsiness at high altitudes? What if someone in his family had died? What if he were in the middle of a divorce?

"It's really something you have to forget. It can distract you," Porter said.

More importantly, how did the system compensate for frailties? The constant checking and rechecking was one way. But now Porter said something that revealed another angle to the problem.

"I don't believe we've flown together," he told Copilot John Mrak and Engineer D. H. Goodhue. "How long have you been on an L-1011?"

"Eight months," Goodhue said.

What if? What if a crew was wide-awake and functioning, but working together for the first time? What if they came from backgrounds so varied that they used words in different ways? On the ground miscommunication is merely frustrating. You say something that someone else misinterprets. Ten minutes later you straighten it out. But in the sky, where split-second judgment is required, the wrong word can bring death, as it had for the crew and passengers of the Avianca jet on the wall in Stephen Veronneau's office. The copilot there had radioed he was "low" on fuel instead of "out of" it.

"If we have an emergency, you fly the plane," Porter told Mrak, who would be piloting this leg. Standard pretakeoff briefing. "Goodhue and I will try to figure out the problem. If it happens below 1,000 feet, bells or whistles, turn them off," he told Goodhue. "At 1,000 feet we'll deal with it."

At Delta, which was undergoing a massive expansion, the scene I was watching must be common enough. Pan Am pilots flying for the first time with Delta copilots. Engineers out of the Navy flying as commercial crew for the first time. Ex-Western people with ex-Pan Am people with ex-Northeast people with brand-new hirees.

For our next leg to Honolulu to go smoothly, Porter, Goodhue, and Mrak would have to instantly meld into a cohesive unit. Become interchangeable parts with the crews that had come before. Once we pushed back, there would be no practice period. No testing communication. No getting to know each other as 714 lifted into the sky.

"Standardization" would do it. I'd heard that word over and over in pilot training and at the FAA. Every crew must use the same procedures. Say the same words. Every crew must use the same checklist, the white four-page card D. H. Goodhue now held in his hand.

Once again I was amazed how a mundane-sounding item held a key to survival. The checklist codified 714. It was the crews' memory, tradition, even second chance. If a pilot forgot something, the checklist reminded him.

"The checklist is the heart of the airplane," Capt. Jack McMahan had told me in Atlanta. "In the old days, it was so simple, a pilot who had to use it didn't know his plane. Today, there are so many things to remember, you can't take your knowledge for granted. . . ."

"A TriStar is 4 million parts flyin' down the road," he said.

Every innovation found its way to the checklist. Every law, every backup system designed by engineers. Every safety lesson the FAA learned from a crash.

Without a checklist, death could come from misunderstanding. Suppose, for example, reading the list during taxi, a copilot said, "Flaps," meaning, "Did you position the flaps for takeoff?" Suppose, without the checklist to tell him how to reply, the captain answered, "Okay" instead of "checked." Suppose by "okay" he meant, "I'll do it in a second." Suppose the copilot thought he meant "I've positioned them now."

In fact, suppose the captain had been saying "okay" for years. It had never made a difference. But suppose tonight he got a call from the tower and forgot to position the flaps. Suppose tonight he'd learned his daughter had cancer. Or was distracted by a warning light or was paying attention to de-icing the plane or calming a distraught passenger or hurrying to lift off and avoid a delay.

Then tonight might be the night the crash happened. The one in a million fluke.

I did not want tonight to be that night. I remembered how at the FAA, Inspector William Dubis had said, "We kept Delta's feet to the fire" to get them to accept standardized language on checklists. I'd thought at the time, Big bureaucratic deal.

"Engine start panel," Mrak said, reading from the checklist. Porter replied, giving the exact response called for, "Checked."

"Standby flight instruments."

"Checked."

If the flight went well tonight, before we shut down in Honolulu, the crew would check through 232 items, all specifically listed for every flight. There was a "before pushback" checklist and a "start" list and "taxi" list. There was an "after takeoff" list and "climb," "descent," "approach" list. I was surprised at the number of checklists. There was a "shut down" list. A "termination" list.

"Landing gear," Mrak said.

"Down."

"Hydraulic systems."

"Checked. Pumps off."

I thought back to Captain McMahan's Atlanta living room, where the retired hero had walked me through what he called "killer items" on checklists, explaining how they'd caused accidents. I listened to Porter and Mrak doing the checklist, and heard Jack McMahan's warnings in my head.

"Stall warning," Mrak said.

"Checked," Porter said.

McMahan said, in my head, "These are lights that should be latched in before takeoff. They glow orange if the system's failed. If stall warning lights are on, you can't take off. There's probably an electrical or hydraulic problem. It's a 'no go' item."

"Antiskid," Mrak said.

"Checked. Off."

McMahan said, "That's a sensor on the brakes. If it senses a skid, the captain better back off on the brake. You don't want a skid with a 400,000-pound plane."

"Windshield heat," Mrak said.

"Idle. On."

McMahan said, "At high altitudes, even on a hot day, you need the windshield heated. It gives resiliency. At 35,000 feet, the temperature outside is about minus 55 degrees centigrade. Without heat the windshield could crack. It would surely crack if you hit a bird. By the way, items on the checklist should have been done earlier. The list is to make sure they've been done."

"Flaps. Slats," Mrak said.

"Checked."

McMahan, sitting in his French sitting-room style living room, surrounded by aviation books, charts he'd brought up from the basement, and photo albums, had said, "This is the most important item during takeoff. Slats are part of the leading edge on the wing. Flaps are on the trailing edge of the wing. On takeoff both should be down to increase the wing area and reduce the stall speed of the plane. Lots of accidents have happened because flaps weren't set right on takeoff."

"Fuel distribution!"

"Checked!"

McMahan: "You don't want 10,000 pounds more fuel in the left wing than the right. Think what that would do to balance."

Now I decided I would monitor the lists all the way to Honolulu, if I could keep awake. That seemed a good way to watch crucial items that came up during every flight.

But before taking off, we had a little dead time left on the ground. Work completed for the moment, Porter turned to me. He was a big man in silver aviator glasses, with an easygoing manner that conflicted with his hard nonstop gum chewing. He could pass for actor Christopher Walken's father, with his high cheekbones and round face.

Looking from him to Mrak to Goodhue, I had the impression, as often happened in cockpits, of a time line of age. The engineer so youthful I could see the shine from his shave, the razor lifting off his sideburns. Mrak slightly less firm with middle age. Porter silvery and distinguished in his uniform.

Cockpit joke: "What are the nine words you never want to hear in a cockpit?"

Answer: From the engineer, "In my experience . . ." From the copilot, "I've been thinking . . ." From the captain, "Hey, watch this!"

Porter showed his LA roots. "How's your screenplay coming?" he joked. "On Melrose Avenue they did a survey of people, walked up to them and asked, 'How's your screenplay coming?'" He laughed. "Seventy percent answered."

It turned out Porter had a screenplay idea himself. "I call it *Frenchie and the Kid*," he said.

It was about a couple of guys he'd met in Hawaii during a layover. There was Frenchie—the ex-Caribbean charter-boat captain, a real ladies man. He piled up a charter boat in Panama and was persona non grata in the Caribbean . . . hell . . . the *Atlantic*. And the kid. There was this dopey boat they have.

"The kid was in a motorcycle accident," Porter explained. "He got hit by a car while driving his girlfriend around. But he's a good guy, because even though he raised his leg away from the impact, he *put it back* when he saw his girlfriend's leg was exposed.

"So then he's in the hospital, and a lawyer walks in and next thing you know, *B-I-G* settlement. The kid spots this sailboat in the harbor, with a For Sale sign on it. But what does he know about boats? Nothing. That's where Frenchie comes in. The kid buys the boat, but it turns out to be the biggest headache he ever had—it's all rotted underneath—and in the end Frenchie and the kid are chartering it, and a big storm comes up, and the boat is going down, except just before it sinks, a yacht owned by a Japanese billionaire *cuts it in two!*"

Last scene, Porter said: The kid's back in the hospital. The lawyer walks back in.

Porter grinned, chewing gum.

"I got a beginning. I got an end. I need a middle," he said.

Porter and Mrak went back to the checklist. For some items two people did it. For specified items the list required all three.

"INS mode selectors," Mrak said.

"Nav," Porter said as he moved the switch from align to the nav position.

McMahan had explained, "They've already punched in the navigation systems into the computer, put in latitude and longitude. One guy did it while the other checked. Now they're checking that the information is *locked* in the computer. You have to do that before you move the plane. Otherwise, just by moving it, you throw the navigation system off."

"Anticollision," Mrak said.

"On," Porter said.

McMahan: "They're flashing red lights on top and bottom of the fuselage that let everyone on the ground know the engines are running. There's so much noise outside that ground crew can't rely on the noise of the engines to alert them that they're on. People have been sucked into engines."

The "before start" checklist was over. Seven-fourteen was ready to push back from the gate. It was time for the pushback/start checklist.

McMahan said, in my head—to Mrak's "pitot/alpha heat!"—"They're little tubes outside the engine. They tell you airspeed, altitude, and rate of climb. By heating them you make sure that any moisture that got inside doesn't freeze and block sensors. If that happened, you wouldn't have the proper air speed. Erratic or no altimeter. Erratic or no rate of climb. In Baltimore, a 727 was lost because of lack of pitot heat. Somehow, in winter, they forgot to turn the heat on. Then during climbout, at 20,000 feet, they started getting strange readings. They didn't know what the hell was going on. They stalled."

Seven-fourteen taxied along a row of jade-colored lights. I saw the red neon Hyatt Hotel sign and "Fly Delta." We would be lifting off to the west, into an intense violet glow suffusing the sky, punctured by bright white globules, which seemed to float gently down toward us and materialize into airplanes.

"Altimeters!"

McMahan: "There are three of them, on the instrument panels of the captain, copilot, and the center instrument panel. Just a little gauge within the altimeters should be set to the barometric pressure of the airport when you're on the ground. If the pilot doesn't know the pressure, he can't know the altitude. The altimeter *uses* barometric pressure to help calculate altitude.

"Eddie Rickenbacker, the old president of Eastern, was almost killed in the 1940s, one night in a rainstorm, when the DC-3 he was in had the altimeter set wrong. They thought they were at 2,000 feet, but they were at 1,000. They flew into the ground."

"Airspeed/EPR bugs!"

McMahan said, as if watching them from over my shoulder, "Airspeed bugs are set based on the aircraft's gross weight. You already know these are little markers the crew adjusts, to tell them, when they're going down the runway, the speed where they can still safely abort takeoff, the speed they need for rotating the nose off the ground and lifting off, and the safe climb speed. You need enough speed to climb even if you lose an engine.

"EPR bugs. Engine Pressure Ratio. The power the engines will use during takeoff. Each engine has an EPR gauge and adjustable markers that provide the pilot a quick reference for establishing his power settings.

"All the bugs are crucial. I remember the first passenger jet, the British Comet, crashed because they rotated too early, couldn't get airborne at that speed. Then another one had a late rotation and hit something at the end of the runway."

"Flight controls. Spoilers!" Mrak said.

In my head McMahan nodded, the old retired master pilot with his bullet head, sports shirt, his nonstop talk of aviation.

"They're checking to make sure the rudder, ailerons, elevators, stabilizers are free and working," he said. "A pilot can't see these surfaces from the cockpit, so he relies on the gauge. The pilot rolls to the right and the ailerons go up on the right side, down on the left. Spoilers come up on the right side, they stay down on the left. When you land later, the spoilers will help slow the plane on the runway."

To the blast of engines, an Alaska Air 757 took off in front of us, elevators rising while the nose rose, landing gear retracting, blue logo receding as the jet lifted away. Porter asked me to help the crew watch for other airplanes when our turn came. It was something pilots in Los Angeles always said. LAX was one of the less popular airports with pilots. They worried about all the private planes in the sky.

"This is Delta 157 heavy," Porter told Air Traffic Control. Takeoff went smoothly. D. H. Goodhue had the card in his hand as we rose. Time for the "after takeoff" checklist.

"Fuel panel!"

"Landing gear!"

"Radios!"

"Humidity control!"

"Altimeters," he said again, having moved to the "climb" checklist. McMahan's voice seemed to say, "Under 18,000 feet, I already told you they set the altimeter to the airport's barometric pressure. You have to know how high you are *from that airport*. Because all airports are at different heights. But after 18,000 feet, pilots reset it to standard barometric pressure. Because when altimeters in two planes say 20,000 feet, you want them both at the same height."

The Channel Islands flowed by below. The flight attendants brought us coffee. For the next four hours, until we began to descend, there would be no need for any checklist.

Porter relaxed. As we chatted, I realized he had the same gift as Captain McMahan. He could explain technical aspects of flight so they made sense to laymen. In the quiet cockpit, in the dark, with the instruments glowing soothingly orange and the moon up and the engines humming smoothly, it seemed like a good time to bring up questions I'd wondered about, since the night my wife and I almost went into the Atlantic on the Swissair jet.

I asked, *"How does this thing stay in the air anyway?"*

He nodded and chewed gum. "Did you ever stick your hand out the window of a car when it's going fast?" he asked. "You cup your hand to catch the wind. You play with different shapes, and the wind has more force against some than others. The wind hits your hand and pushes it up. The faster the car goes, the higher your hand goes. If the car went fast enough, you wouldn't be able to get your hand down.

"That's the principle of how a plane flies. Speed coupled with the shape of the wings. The wings are more curved at the top than at the bottom. It's called 'camber.' It means when air hits the wings it rushes past snugly against the bottom, and loops up over the top. It creates a partial vacuum above the wings, and a cushion for it underneath. If the plane is going fast enough, and the up elevator increases the angle of attack, raising the nose, the aircraft rises.

I asked, *"When the plane is on automatic pilot, or autoland, how does it know where it's going? And why doesn't it crash into the ground?"*

"A pilot can hook into autopilot several different ways. And each works on a different principle. The first is 'pilotage.' I put the plane on a heading, the altitude I want, climb or hold or descend at a certain speed, and the plane does it. The autopilot flies it how I set it. If I tell it to head south and descend at 500 feet a minute, it'll do that till I stop it.

"The next system is called 'VOR navigation.' We use it over the continental United States. I set the airplane up to fly to or from a radio beam from a government-owned radio station that only broadcasts navigational beams for airplanes. The autopilot is hooked into that beam.

"Then there's an 'INS' navigation system which is not dependent on anything outside the airplane. We use this over water. A gyroscope in the plane senses the movement of the plane. It can tell from the movement what direction we're going, and how fast. It knows where we were when we started, where we're going, and where we want to go. Using the gyroscopes, the computer automatically adjusts the plane to go where we want.

"But I'm not finished," Porter said. "Now we get to the landing system. The 'ILS' system uses a radio broadcasting at the end of the runway, so the plane can line up with the runway. A localizer beam enables the plane to line itself up. A glide slope beam gives the plane a 3 percent angle for descent, and the plane follows the beam down.

"When we land automatically, five miles out from the runway, we're 1,500 feet up and lined up at a 3-degree slope. As the airplane approaches the ground, at 1,000 feet, a radio altimeter (which bounces a beam up and down from the plane to tell the computer how high we are) activates and hooks into the autoland. At 50 feet the altimeter, hooked into the throttles, closes them and brings the nose up. And the airplane touches down."

I said, *"Pilots often define speed in terms of 'mach.' What does 'mach' mean?"*

"Mach one is the speed of sound. And the speed of sound varies with different temperatures. Get too close to the speed of sound, you can get 'mach buffet' and stall. The plane's computer figures out what percentage of mach you're going by taking weather information and combining it with speed. If the pilot knows his speed in terms of mach, he can avoid it. You don't buffet."

I said, *"I've also heard the term 'coffin corner' in relationship to mach. What is coffin corner?"*

Porter nodded and angled his hand into the air diagonally, like a plane taking off. "A plane has to go at a faster speed at a higher altitude to stay up. But you finally reach a certain height where, if you go that fast, you hit mach.

"Of course you don't want to hit mach, so you need to slow down. But the problem is, at that altitude, if you slow down too much you can also stall. Finally you reach a height where there might only be a 20-mile-an-hour difference between stalling from encountering mach buffet from going too fast, or from going too slow. That's coffin corner. The pilot is trapped. You don't want to go there."

I shuddered. I said, *"You keep talking about speed. But I'm curious how a plane knows how fast it's going. In a car, a speedometer is linked to turning wheels. But in a plane, which isn't touching earth, since speed varies with wind, height, temperature, and thrust, how does the plane figure it out?"*

"It calculates it. There are different kinds of speeds. Look at the instrument panel. You see the gauges for 'airspeed' and 'true airspeed' and 'ground speed'?"

Airspeed is the air pressure on a diaphragm in a tube outside the plane. *True airspeed* is when the computer combines that reading with altitude and temperature to determine how fast the plane would be going if you didn't factor in wind. *Ground speed* is true air speed plus or minus wind.

The reason we need to know these three kinds of speed is that each one serves a different purpose. Since stall is based on air pressure, we need to know airspeed to determine if we might stall. We need true airspeed in order to calculate ground speed. And we need ground speed to help us navigate. Ground speed would be equal to speed in a car. Miles per hour.

It sounded a little like the old Abbott and Costello routine, Who's on first? What's on second? Porter grinned and leaned back and chewed gum. He said he'd known he wanted to be a pilot since he was five, in Minneapolis, growing up with a Braniff captain across the street and a Northwest captain two houses down.

"Back then Delta was little. But those pilots said, if you get a chance, go with them," he said.

Unlike most Delta pilots, Porter wasn't ex-military. He'd gotten an instructional license while at the University of North Dakota, where he'd been a business major. Then he'd ferried airplanes for an airplane broker in Chicago. He'd started at Delta as an engineer on a DC-6.

"I loved 'em. They flew low. There was something to look at."

In the cockpit it was dark and peaceful, and the banks of instruments glowed with soothing orange light, and the moon seemed immense outside the glass ball. I think I dozed in my seat. It was almost time to descend, almost time for the checklists to start again when I woke up. I had one more question for Jim Porter.

"I'm always hearing about hydraulic controls on airplanes. What are they?"

Porter found a piece of scrap paper and sketched a crude drawing of what looked like a piston inside a cylinder.

"Simple. Hydraulic fluid, under pressure, floods the cylinder. The fluid pushes against the piston, moving it. The piston is attached to cables or actuating arms working the ailerons, landing gear or elevators. The pilot controls the flow of fluid, so he controls the plane. Simple."

"Altimeters!" Engineer D. H. Goodhue said. Seven-fourteen was beginning its descent into Honolulu.

"Checked!"

In my mind, I was back in Jack McMahan's living room, looking at the oil painting of McMahan in his captain's uniform, over the piano. We munched his wife's homemade raspberry muffins.

"How come Porter keeps resetting the altimeters?" I asked McMahan in my head.

"Remember I told you, at 18,000 feet, he set the altimeters at standard barometric pressure of 29.92 inches? Coming down, he has to reset it to the airport barometric pressure, which he gets over the radio. Then on the approach, the crew verifies they have the latest barometric pressure for the airport. If they don't, and it's cloudy, they can fly it into the ground."

"Airspeed! EPR bugs!" Goodhue said.

"Checked," everyone said.

McMahan, in my head, leaned back on the couch, comfortable in his short-sleeve sports shirt. He'd piled old looseleaf manuals and route maps on the table. He said, "The engineer sets the engine pressure ratio bugs for landing. He calculates 150 percent above stall speed. You always want to stay 50 percent above stall speed while maneuvering. When you start your approach, you'll want 140 percent above stall speed. When you come over the runway, about 130 percent. You don't want to go too slow and crash.

You'll touch down nose up, then spoilers up, slow it down, your wheels touch at about 120 percent."

"Hydraulic panel!"

"Checked!"

"Humidity control!"

"As required!"

"No smoking lights!"

"On!"

"Flight attendants!"

"Notified!"

Again, I barely felt 714 make contact with earth. Back in the cabin, the passengers were applauding. We headed down the middle of the runway. It seemed that Jack McMahan would have nodded, liking the landing. "It's easy to get complacent without the checklist. One time in Montreal, I remember the maintenance crew had shut off fuel to the engines. But enough remained in the fuel lines to start the plane. We could have run out of fuel in the air and crashed.

"My second officer messed up too. He didn't check the fuel tank valve switches. But I was lucky. I saw it on the checklist. And turned it on.

"Killer items," McMahan repeated, running his finger over black-rimmed items on the checklist. "They'll get you if they aren't set."

At the gate, Porter shut the plane down to the "Shutdown" checklist, seat belt lights off, anticollision lights off, electrical panel checked, air-conditioner off, standby power off.

McMahan said, "There was a DC-8 in Detroit. They came in with their stabilizer set wrong, and after landing, they forgot to put the stabilizer back to zero, which means they probably missed the after-landing checklist. And then they missed it again before taking off, which means they missed the before-takeoff checklist. And they crashed. Those checklists can save your life."

"Logbook write-ups," Goodhue said, meaning did Porter want Goodhue to jot down any problems 714 was experiencing for the next captain, who would be piloting 136 passengers on the Honolulu to Los Angeles red-eye, Delta flight 1566, due to take off in one hour.

There were no write-ups. A little gas up, and ship 714 would be ready to go. It was 7:30 P.M. in Honolulu.

Porter and crew finished the "termination" checklist. Nav systems off. Emergency lights off. Master radios off. Radar off. He would spend the night in Honolulu. Down in the flight office, Delta Capt. James V. Cagle and his crew of Copilot Joe Turner and Second Officer Gary Hammerman were picking up their flight plan, which told them 714 should burn 83,380 pounds of fuel back across the Pacific. That it would carry 114,000 pounds to be safe. That Hilo, Hawaii, and San Francisco would be our alternate airports. That in Los Angeles, runway 25R was closed.

Jim Porter had never met James V. Cagle. Porter was from LA, and Cagle lived in Vicksburg, Mississippi. Porter was technically minded. Cagle was a musician who'd written the official song of his hometown. Porter wanted to write a screenplay. Cagle had written a children's book. They had different rhythms. Different styles. Different personalities. But they piloted the same plane.

Standardization was the key to safety. The checklist was the key to standardization. Porter left the cockpit, and the new crew appeared, hung their jackets up, stowed their fat black briefcases by their seats, ordered coffee from the flight attendants, read the log to see if there were any problems with the plane.

Gary Hammerman picked up the little white card. The checklist card. The crew was totally absorbed in working from the card.

"Circuit breakers!"

"Checked!"

"Oxygen mask!"

"Checked!"

"Voice recorder!"

"Checked!"

"Engine bleed controls!"

GHOST STORY

I first heard of the Ghost of Flight 401 years before I set foot on a Delta plane. My wife, the ex-stewardess, told me about it. She always told stories of the super-natural: one about an Athens hotel wing closed because of ghosts, one about how the face of Jesus appeared on a tortilla in New Mex-ico, a story of boys in Prague who said the Virgin Mary appeared to them.

One day she told me about an airplane—famous in the airline world, she said—that had crashed back in the 1970s, and whose flight crew kept materializing on other planes, showing themselves to crew or passengers, disappearing again.

The crashed plane had been an Eastern plane, she said. And she added that after many more incidents, the airline discovered that parts of the crashed plane—still usable items like ovens—had been installed in the planes where the sightings had taken place.

True or not, it was a great story. I forgot about it until my first cockpit flight on a Delta TriStar, from Atlanta to Salt Lake City. That morning, over Utah, Copilot Pete Hayden asked me if I'd ever heard of Eastern flight 401. It was a Lockheed 1011 that had crashed in Florida in 1972. He started elaborating, and I realized he was telling the same story as my wife.

Pete reached into his black travel case and pulled out a paper-back book, *The Ghost of Flight 401* by John G. Fuller.

He had an impish expression on his face.

"I carry these and give them to flight attendants," he said. "It scares them." He looked like a happy kid on Halloween. "Ghosts."

I scanned the book. There was a picture of an L-1011 on the cover, superimposed over a ghostly, half-materialized man in a captain's uniform, except the man showed no pupils in his eyes, only eerie whites.

"Excuse me," I said, "but I don't understand why even a superstitious Delta flight attendant would get scared reading this. Flight 401 was Eastern. And so were the planes where the ghosts were seen. Eastern, not Delta."

"Don't you get it?" Hayden said, the grin widening. "They *used* to be Eastern planes. Delta bought them."

"Now they're our planes," he said.

Three o'clock in the morning is the time for ghost stories. I was so tired I didn't know what watches were showing in this particular time zone, but for me it was three o'clock. I made my way from the cockpit to First Class, found an open seat and pushed it back. I closed my eyes. Drifting, I thought back to John Fuller's book and what I'd read in it.

I saw flight 401, a TriStar, just like 714. Flying that clear, calm December night from New York to Miami. The scene on board probably the same. Maybe the clothes a little different, the hairstyles a little longer, but the ship cruising smoothly, like 714 was now. The engines whispering quietly, like 714's were now. The flight attendants serving beverages. The passengers like the ones around me. Vacationers. Businessmen. Children and adults. There had been a french poodle in the luggage bin that night, in a little cage.

Flight 401 had been Eastern's designated ship 310, a jet only five months old that night. It had only a thousand hours of flying time. Eastern called their TriStars Whisperliners, and ship 310 would have the unfortunate distinction of being the first TriStar to crash. It would go down because of a combination of little factors unforeseen by the engineers who had spent so much time designing it, and the airline people looking over their shoulders the whole time.

The flight was almost over when things began going wrong for ship 310. As it came in for a landing, while doing the checklist, Capt. Bob Loft, First Engineer Albert Stockstill, and Second Officer Don Repo, all veteran fliers, noticed only two of the three landing-gear lights were on. Which could mean only two of the three gear were down.

"No nose gear," investigators later heard Stockstill say on the cockpit recorder.

"I gotta raise it back up," Loft said. "Goddamn it."

Loft took the plane back up to 2,000 feet. He was annoyed because although it was possible the landing gear was broken, the probability was that just the $12 warning light was out. But there was no way to check without visually looking at the landing gear or changing the bulb and seeing if the new one worked.

"Put the damn thing on autopilot," Loft told Stockstill. "See if you can get that light out."

As the men began trying to get the bulb out, Flight 401 left the more lighted airspace over Miami and began flying over the Everglades, which were dark, a crucial factor in the crash. Stockstill had trouble twisting the bulb out. Loft said, "You got it turned sideways."

The bulb still wouldn't come out. While Stockstill wrestled with it, Second Officer Don Repo left his station to climb down into the "hell hole," the electronics room beneath the cockpit that I had seen on ship 714. The only way to check the landing gear visually was to squeeze past the rows of electronic equipment down there, come to a small periscope, and look out. If the gear were down, Repo would see two red marks lined up outside.

But now things really began to go wrong. And unbeknownst to the pilots, it would be a safety feature on the plane that launched the next tragic chain of events. Safety-conscious engineers designing TriStars had built into the autopilot an escape valve—a real pilot could disengage it instantly by applying 15 to 20 pounds of pressure on the control column. In an emergency he would have no trouble taking command back from the plane.

But what wasn't clear at the time was that someone accidentally bumping against the column could disengage the system too. Loft, leaning forward, nudged the column.

The autopilot went off, but neither pilot knew it.

Ship 310 began a slow glide down toward the pitch-black Everglades. Because the angle was so slight, and there were no lights below, nobody realized the plane was descending.

"You got a handkerchief or something so I can get a better grip on this?" Stockstill asked Loft, still fighting the bulb.

Down in the avionics compartment, Don Repo reached the periscope, except when he looked out it was too dark to see whether the red marks were lined up. He needed light, and the switch was back in the cockpit, not down in the hold.

As Repo strained to see better, and the plane eased below 1,700 feet, a soft altitude warning bell sounded, except it lasted only half a second, and it was located on Repo's engineer panel. Repo, down in the hellhole, couldn't hear it. And investigators listening to the black box later heard Loft and Stockstill talking when the soft chime sounded. Nobody heard it.

At 900 feet Flight 401 got one last chance to survive. An air traffic controller in Miami noticed the plane at the wrong altitude. On the radio he asked how things were going. Loft replied, "Okay." Since momentary deviations on radar screens were common, the controller decided to wait for another radar pass to see if the problem would correct itself, John G. Fuller wrote.

Ship 310 was fifteen miles west of Miami International Airport now.

Just after 11:42, Stockstill's voice on the recorder said, "We did something to the altitude."

"Hey, what's happening here?" Loft said.

That was the end of the recording.

As the sun rose over the Everglades the next morning, Eastern ship 310 lay in pieces over a 1,600-foot area. Miraculously, although the crash was classified as "nonsurvivable" by the FAA, thanks to the sturdiness of the TriStar, seventy-four passengers lived. But Loft died in the cockpit. So did Stockstill. Repo was pulled in agony from the hellhole and brought by helicopter to Hialeah Hospital, where he died a few hours later.

Soldiers bagging bodies found dismembered limbs and naked passengers whose clothes had been ripped from them during impact. Many bodies were covered by long lacerations, cuts from swamp sawgrass.

In the end, the nose wheel was found locked in place. Ship 310 could have landed safely. It was the $12 bulb that had broken.

"The cumulative result of several minor deviations from operating procedure triggered . . . disastrous results," the National Transportation Safety Board reported. They faulted the crew for failing to monitor flight instruments during the last four minutes of the flight. Recommended that in the future the hellhole have a light switch. Recommended that cockpits be equipped with a flashing light to warn if planes deviated from the altitude the autopilot was supposed to be flying. And recommended that air traffic controllers learn new procedures for instantly warning planes that deviate from flight paths.

The NTSB ordered that special radar be installed in airliners enabling crews to monitor terrain.

So far the aftermath had followed a grim but familiar scenario. Investigation. Recommendation. Painful fading from immediate memory. But the story of flight 310 was not over. A few months later, two flight attendants and an engineer of Eastern ship 318 reported an astounding incident. It seemed one of the attendants, down in the galley, opened an oven and was terrified to see what seemed to be an apparition of a man's head inside it. She saw the face. The features. The hair. She called another attendant, who said she saw the apparition too. The skeptical flight engineer was called down. He reported that the vision spoke to him, and warned him the plane would catch on fire.

Shortly after that one of 318's engines caught on fire. The crew landed it safely.

Another incident occurred in Newark, New Jersey. Ship 318 was preparing to leave the gate for a flight to Miami, when a flight attendant noticed during a routine head count that there was an extra passenger in First Class. The addition was explained by the presence of an Eastern captain, in uniform, in one of the seats.

It was quite common for an off-duty captain to fly in First Class, but when the flight attendant asked the captain about his travel plans, he wouldn't answer. The attendant called the engineer, who tried to talk to the captain too, without success.

Finally, as First Class passengers got a little anxious, the pilot was called and came down the aisle. He leaned over to talk to the passenger/captain, recoiled and said, "My God, it's Bob Loft!"

In front of all of them, the mystery figure disappeared.

More reports began spreading through the company. A woman

passenger on 318 began screaming during a flight. She said a man had materialized beside her in the empty seat and vanished. A passenger in a window seat called the flight attendant to report a strange cloud shape hovering over a wing. Instead of falling back as the plane moved forward, this shape moved right along with it. During turbulence, it drifted down and touched the wing, and buffeting would stop. When the ride was smooth, it lifted away. The flight attendant and the ship's engineer both said they'd seen the cloud.

Many stories centered around the galley. Flight attendants reported the galley getting cold, reported an odd man-shaped cloud, reported feeling a "presence." Some Eastern employees began to avoid flying on ship 318, but many others sought it out, believing the figure, who had now been identified by many witnesses as Don Repo, to be benevolent.

Eastern Airlines sent anyone who reported sightings to a company psychiatrist.

But reports kept mounting. Then Eastern leased some TriStars to TWA, a standard practice in the industry, and the stories started there too. A woman began screaming at the gate in Phoenix. She said a man had materialized in the seat beside her and disappeared.

Author John Fuller, investigating the stories, found that some parts of crashed ship 310 had been installed in 318. Eastern began removing them. The oven was taken out. The voice recorder was replaced after the flight to Mexico City when one of the plane's engines had caught on fire.

"I can't help feeling," Fuller wrote after competing his investigation, "that Don Repo will turn into a gentle and benign legend that will benevolently haunt the airways for a long time to come."

Over the next twenty years after flight 401 went down, five more L-1011s met tragic ends.

On April 14, 1974, a TWA TriStar parked and locked for the night at its gate at Boston's Logan Airport suddenly caught on fire in the rear fuselage. All engines were off at the time. Nobody was on board. The craft was unsalvageable. Investigators never determined how the fire started, but Lockheed representative Dave Columbus, whom I spoke to about it, said arson was suspected.

On August 19, 1980, a Saudia Airlines TriStar, carrying Muslim pilgrims to Mecca from Karachi, India, was over Saudi Arabia, eighty miles from Riyadh, when a fire broke out in the rear cargo compartment and began spreading. The captain wasted five minutes continuing away from Riyadh while the crew investigated the fire. Then he turned the plane around but did not declare an emergency.

Coming in, the captain began singing in Arabic. He wouldn't answer other crew members when they asked about evacuation. He told Air Traffic Control to "stand by" when they asked if the plane needed assistance. He refused to turn off the fuel valves during the landing checklist. By doing that, he caused pressurization in the cabin to build to the point that the doors became impossible to open.

When rescuers finally got in, they found bodies stacked around the exits and in the cockpit, which passengers had burst into in a frantic effort to escape. There were no survivors.

The next TriStar to die was a Delta plane. On August 2, 1985, Delta flight 191 was heading for Dallas/Fort Worth Airport from Fort Lauderdale during a rainstorm, with 152 passengers and eleven crew on board.

At 5:59, with flight 191 starting to come in, the local controller told American Airlines flight 539, two planes ahead, "There's a little bitty thunderstorm sitting on the final, it looks like a little rain shower." The Delta crew did not hear the advisory because it had not been switched over to the airport frequency yet.

Next plane to land was a small Lear jet, which came in safely, but its pilot experienced wind shear—a marked fluctuation in wind—during landing. He later said he did not report it because he "had his hands full" during the approach, and had not yet cleared the runway when the Delta plane crashed.

So the Delta crew had no idea they were flying into one of the most severe sorts of wind shear, a "microburst." An inverted mushroom-shaped explosion of wind that blasts down on the earth, lasts seconds, and is capable of splitting trees open. If a plane manages to bull its way through the *down*draft, the center of the microburst, it immediately hits a powerful *up*draft of wind and water bouncing off the earth on the edges.

At 6:03, the time when the Delta plane was handed off to local controllers, according to the cockpit voice recorder, Capt. Edward Connors said, "Tower, Delta one ninety-one heavy out here in the rain, feels good."

At 6:04 and eighteen seconds, the transcript read:

FIRST OFFICER: Lightning coming out of that one.
CAPTAIN: What?
FIRST OFFICER: Lightning coming out of that one.
CAPTAIN: Where?
FIRST OFFICER: Right ahead of us.
　At 6:05 and nineteen seconds:
CAPTAIN: Watch your speed. (Sound of rain begins.)
　At 6:05 and twenty-one seconds:
CAPTAIN: You're gonna lose it all of a sudden. There it is.
CAPTAIN: Push it up, push it way up. Way up.
ENGINEER: Way up.
CAPTAIN: Way up. (Sound of engines at high RPM.)
　At 6:05 and thirty seconds:
CAPTAIN: That's it.
CAPTAIN: Hang on to the . . .
FIRST OFFICER: What's Vref?
　At 6:05 and forty-four seconds:
AUTOMATIC VOICE: Whoop! whoop! pull up!
UNKNOWN VOICE: Push it way up!
AUTOMATIC VOICE: Whoop! whoop! pull up!
AUTOMATIC VOICE: Whoop! whoop! pull up!
UNKNOWN VOICE: Oh shit.

　Delta flight 191 emerged from the rain cloud, touched down in a field, cutting grooves in it, bounced off highway 114, hit a car and smashed a second, killing its driver, and as the pilot applied full throttle, still trying to control it, it veered toward water towers dead ahead and slammed into them. One hundred and thirty-seven people died.

　In five seconds, the crew had had to cope with a head wind of 10 knots going to 27 knots. Then a sudden tailwind of 40 knots. The plane got through the downdraft. It had been the updraft it had not survived.

The National Transportation Safety Board ruled that the crew was negligent in attempting to land in a thunderstorm, that Delta's training in wind-shear avoidance was lax but not negligent, that the air traffic controllers breached their duties by not reporting indications of dangerous weather to the plane, that a National Weather Service meteorologist at the airport had breached his duty by taking a dinner break without making sure someone watched his radar for him, and that the weather coordinator at the airport should have maintained a continuous weather watch during the meteorologist's absence.

At Delta, more wind-shear training became required for pilots.

At the federal level, Secretary of Transportation Jim Burnley announced a new rule requiring commercial airliners to carry equipment to warn pilots encountering unexpected low-altitude wind-shear conditions. By 1992, when I boarded ship 714, every plane would be equipped with it.

But the next TriStar loss occurred in May 1986 when an Air Lanka jet was bombed by terrorists while on the ground in Colombo, Sri Lanka. Sixteen passengers were killed and forty-one injured.

Finally, in August 1992, the final TriStar to be destroyed as of this writing became a TWA L-1011 which developed an engine fire while taking off for San Francisco from New York's Kennedy Airport. The pilot safely landed the plane, and the crew evacuated all passengers, but fire engulfed the jet shortly afterward.

No one was killed. And none of these other TriStar tragedies gave rise to ghost stories. Only flight 401 had sent its apparitions out into the world. Some Eastern crew members even tried to exorcize the ghost.

John Fuller reported one second officer, Dick Manning, who went down to the galley with a Bible and holy water.

"The moment I got down there," Fuller wrote that Manning said, "the lights started flickering on and off. I sanctified the galley with a cup of water, which was symbolic of the blood of Christ, and I sprinkled it around and around. As I did, a wind started blowing down there, all over the place. It was like a 30-knot wind."

Manning said a figure of Repo materialized in the galley, flickering in and out.

"I said to him, 'Don't you know you are dead? You are dead. You have lost your life. Your spirit remains here, but you have not taken to your rightful place, where you belong.' "

Manning told Fuller the figure disappeared.

I don't know if I believe in ghosts or not. I've never seen a ghost. One time, when I was driving my Volkswagen Rabbit in Washington D.C., the oddest feeling came over me. I became convinced that my dead grandfather Willie was trying to tell me the car was dangerous. Nothing like this had ever happened. I didn't think about my grandfather often. And I had never thought any dead person was trying to communicate with me.

But the feeling lasted two days, kept getting stronger the whole time, and then an electrical fire started under the dashboard. I never had that feeling again.

I hoped that Don Repo was at rest. But what I didn't know yet, half dozing in 714, was that the stories still hadn't stopped. Within a day I'd know otherwise.

Because twenty-four hours later, at 3 A.M. in Atlanta airport, I'd be going over ship 714 with mechanics, watching them fix the plane, and one of them would say to me, "You know about the ghost, don't you?"

"What ghost?" I'd say, surprised.

"We got some planes from Eastern," he'd say, "and the mechanics were working on them, getting them ready, and suddenly two of the mechanics ran out and wouldn't come back. They were contract guys, from California. They said they saw something, a figure, in the plane. It terrified them. They got sent home."

And even later, I'd hear the stories from cockpit crews at Delta. Mechanics had seen a ghost, they'd say. I'd ask flight attendants about the rumors. And get a phone call from Paulette O'Donnell, in Atlanta.

"You're in trouble, Bob," she'd say.

"How come?" I'd say.

"We got a complaint about you. Were you asking flight attendants about a plane that crashed?"

"That was an Eastern plane," I'd say. "And it crashed years ago."

"Bob, were you asking if parts from that crashed plane were on a Delta plane?"

"Paulette, what *were* these complaints?" I'd say.

"I don't think I can tell you that."

"Who made them?"

"I don't think it would be right to tell you that. But you're not going to be able to fly in our cockpits anymore, at least for awhile."

So *is* there a ghost? Is Don Repo still there? *Is* there a benevolent presence haunting the Eastern ovens I'd seen in Delta planes?

I looked out the window. It was dark outside. I could see the wing, and I strained to see if there was a little cloud over it, a shape that kept pace with the plane, that hovered above it, that settled protectively onto the wing if turbulence occurred. But there was nothing. Only the stars. And the night.

The ghost had never visited 714 anyway. At least I thought it hadn't.

I slept.

THE TWO TINAS

T ina Clark* washed out on radar, just couldn't get the hang of it and lost her air traffic controller post. Tina Crocker* passed training and guided airplanes, 714 among them, over the southeast United States. Tina Clark told me she was transferred to a less busy airport, Palmdale, California, where she worked with planes on the ground, never in the air. Tina Crocker, signing off with pilots, often heard them sing, cheerily, "Thanks, Betty," joking about her name, thinking they were the first to say it.

Both air controllers were in their twenties. Both blond. Both single. At the moment Tina Clark occupied the jump seat of 714 on our way to Dallas. Tina Crocker was back in Hampton, Georgia, where I'd met her, on the early morning shift. Perhaps, in a few hours, I would hear her on the radio.

I was in the rearmost cockpit seat, and Captain Cagle flew this leg from Los Angeles to Dallas. A hundred and forty-two passengers on board. I had to stand up to see outside. Below, the Colorado River was a black jagged thread wriggling through the Arizona desert. Just looking down made me hot. I saw no towns, no roads, not even any cactus. It looked like nothing had grown down there in 10 million years.

"We deal in voices," Tina Clark said.

*Names changed by request.

Voices. And stress. Both Tinas and the other 18,000 air traffic controllers in the United States work in one of the most anxiety ridden occupations, according to reports and articles I'd read. I told Tina Clark about them.

"A controller has to make thousands of life and death decisions," one FAA official told *Smithsonian* magazine. "All we require is that he make the right one every time."

"We must recruit constantly. The job has received a great deal of negative publicity, particularly with regard to stress," an FAA report said.

"At 1,000 mph, jetliners pass within 1½ miles," read *USA Today*. "The FAA is investigating why there were communications problems between the jets and controllers."

Was there really so much stress in air traffic control? Stress so high it might endanger passengers? Or was it just one more instance of the central paradox of aviation manifesting itself? A safe system kept that way because everyone in it never stopped talking about the worst.

That certainly seemed to be the way FAA researchers viewed it. Their report, *Stress, Anxiety and the Air Traffic Control Specialist . . . A Decade of Research*, said 92 percent of controllers answering their questions reported liking the job. And even claimed their favorite part of it was working heavy traffic. Light traffic bored them. Controllers tended to be personality types who liked the challenge of busy work.

Then again, what about the controllers who had not chosen to answer the questions?

Tina Clark had not been surveyed. Off duty at the moment, she looked uncontrollerlike to me in candy pink plastic sunglasses, deep purple velvet pants and felt boots, a knit sweater with a patch design in gold, aquamarine, crimson, magenta. She'd seemed shy when she'd boarded, and I couldn't see her eyes. Her hair fell over her face when she leaned forward. She was pale and thin in a Sissy Spacek way.

She said nervously, "You have so many things to do on the job. You have to make split-second decisions. An airplane doesn't stop flying because you say hold it."

Now, she was using one of her nine "familiarization trips"—jump

seat rides air traffic controllers get each year on domestic airlines—
"to get to my grandfather's ninetieth birthday party."

"You want to know what being an air traffic controller is like?"
she said while the cockpit crew listened. "Imagine 200 blind two-
year-olds wandering around on an interstate, and you're driving 100
miles an hour and trying not to hit them."

"If you don't like being a controller so much, why don't you quit?"
I asked.

Tina Clark sighed. She looked up from making her grandfather's
present, gold foil covered chocolate candies shaped like coins,
which she was tying into mesh bags with ribbons.

"I have to pay rent. Buy food. I have nothing lined up," she said.
"But if I'd known how much grief I'd get on this job, I wouldn't have
taken it."

Statistically, Tina Clark is typical of air traffic controllers. Her age,
twenty-six, is median. It's a young person's job. She didn't finish
college. She had no aviation experience before joining the FAA.
Then again, tests show neither educational background nor flying
experience influence the quality of a controller.

What does make a difference, FAA experts say, is how cool,
forceful, and quick on his or her feet an applicant is. How well a
controller can visualize space with twenty-five planes crammed in
it, flying in different directions. How well they can determine
which 600-mile-an-hour craft might hit another one.

Controllers also have to deal with pilots who argue over instructions. They clear packed skies during airport closures. Block off
sections of atmosphere when the military needs it. Coordinate
search and rescue flights after crashes. And rush in patients to airports when they need emergency medical care.

Air traffic controllers man 403 control towers and 23 en route
centers in the United States, but since there are 17,000 airports including small ones, tens of thousands of private planes are in the
air in addition to the 449 million passengers flying each year in
commercial airlines.

That's stress. In just 1987 over 1,000 near misses were reported
between controlled airplanes. In 1989, at Washington D.C.'s en
route center, a computer refused to take handoffs as planes ap-

proached the capital, and frantic controllers called each other on phones. Another time, in Dallas, a computer scattered false airplanes all over the radar screen. And then there are the times the screens go blank.

Against this barrage of technological difficulty and the waves of flights overhead, controllers have only a few tools at their disposal. They can order changes in speed, direction, and altitude. Delay takeoffs and reroute flights. Or put planes in holding patterns, providing the pilots listen.

But their main aids are imaginary boxes. Just as airlines see the sky as a series of highways, controllers grid it into boxes, each with its team watching over the traffic inside, "handing off" planes to the next box, receiving new flights from the boxes around them.

"You want to see what the atmosphere looks like to us?" Stan Ensley had told me. He was the manager of the Hampton, Georgia, en route center, thirty miles from Atlanta. He'd picked a little wooden jigsaw puzzle off his desk. Taken apart the puzzle until I saw a second layer of pieces underneath. Then a third.

"This is the area we control," he said. "The bottom layer is 0–23,000 feet, then 23,000–33,000, then the ultra-high level, 33 and above. And each section has a team of controllers on it."

Thanks to the box system, every plane in the air at any given time is supposed to be on some controller's radar screen.

Take 714. Just an hour ago, Captain Cagle had needed route and gate clearance from a "clearance delivery controller" before we could back away from the gate. Then a "ground controller" had directed us on the taxiway to the runway. A "local controller" up in the tower guided the takeoff until we were five miles out. A "departure control" controller deeper inside the tower, in a windowless radar room, had talked us through the maze of low flying planes until we neared 14,000 feet, roughly fifty miles east of the airport.

Crisp voice after voice, like a bucket brigade passing 714 across the country. As we'd closed on 14,000 feet the departure controller had initiated an electronic signal, and 60 miles away, at the Los Angeles en route center, a little block of information had begun flashing on *another* controller's screen, which meant we were about to arrive at his airspace. No little World War II-style blips on the screens by 1992. Instead, the flight's number, destination, company, make.

If everything went well on this leg, we would be handed off from box to box all the way to Dallas, with the takeoff procedure reversing itself when we reached 14,000 feet, fifty miles from that airport.

Tina Clark, still tying the tiny little presents, said, "Actually, I do learn a lot when I fly in the cockpits. I'm not a pilot, and when I'm working, I don't realize what they go through when we talk to them. Controllers will give several instructions—altitude, heading, and frequency—quickly. But up here I realize it's easier to say it than remember it and put it in the computers at the same time. It's safer for controllers not to give too much information at once."

As she spoke we passed over the Gila Bend Mountain Range in southwest Arizona, Delta flight 1566 to controllers, just north of Mexico. We'd fly over New Mexico to El Paso and then be in Texas the rest of the way. Wagon trains had needed months to make this trip.

Tina Clark said when she used to work in Los Angeles, she'd been nervous all the time. "I realized it was real people up there, who could die," she said.

"But at Palmdale you feel comfortable?"

She stiffened. I had the feeling she would be haunted by fear as long as she was with the FAA. "It's less stressful, but when I hear about an accident in the news, I feel concerned for the controllers. People carry it around in their minds. I hear stories. Controllers walking around, thinking, I could have done something. I heard the story about one controller who went off the deep end. He was never the same after that."

No air traffic controllers existed when commercial airliners started flying passengers in the United States. Pilots flew where they wanted, and company radio operators advised them on weather or landing conditions. By 1930 the skies around big cities were getting so crowded, Cleveland Airport hired the first controller, who used radio to direct planes.

Other airports followed, but there was no central authority overseeing the work, Carl Solberg wrote in *Conquest of the Skies*. And each airport had its own procedures. At Chicago's Midway Airport in 1932, the chief traffic control clerk gave three approaching pilots their landing sequence. Immediately the pilot scheduled to come in second yelled, "I'm only two miles away. I'm first!" The pilot scheduled third shouted, "I've passed the Maywood tank. *I'm* first!" The disgusted controller growled, "Nuts to you. You're on your own. I'm going downstairs for a cup of coffee." Then he left.

Four years later the first systematized air traffic control was established, but airlines formed it, not the government. The six biggest companies created Air Traffic Control, Inc., at Newark Airport, the busiest facility in the world. Controllers couldn't talk to planes directly. They had to go through company operators, who relayed instructions to pilots.

"Landing four planes an hour was pretty good," one controller said.

In 1936 the federal government finally took over, putting the Bureau of Lighthouses in charge of Air Traffic Control.

Controllers were finally talking directly to pilots. They mapped planes on charts by hand because there was no radar yet. They operated red and green lights by runways to let pilots know if it was safe to land. In some airports they complained about having to carry baggage, sell tickets, and answer phones. One reporter visiting National Airport in 1937 found the chief controller looking out the window, holding three microphones while ten loudspeakers blared.

There were still no highways in the sky. Pilots asked permission to go where they wanted, and if another plane wasn't there, controllers said okay. Radar arrived in the 1950s. But it was a primitive kind, and in order to know which blips on the screen represented which planes, controllers pushed little blocks of information, "shrimp boats," across the flat screens as the blips moved.

With the 1970s came digitized radar. Then "highways in the sky" in 1981. That year Pres. Ronald Reagan fired all controllers participating in a strike, decimating controller ranks by two thirds.

Suddenly inexperienced hirees or military controllers or supervisers were guiding commercial flights. And it was easier for the new people to keep track of them if they kept to predetermined routes.

It would be years before the number of controllers even approached prestrike levels. By 1989, when Tina Clark decided to try to become an air traffic controller, the FAA was still replacing the people who had been fired. It was a four-year process to achieve full status on the job.

"I was twenty-three. Living in Inyokern, California, working in a dry cleaner's and living with my mother. It was a low point," she said. "In my floundering around, a guy I was dating, a mechanic, told me about the Air Traffic Control test. I said I'd take it to humor him."

Tina took a standardized written test designed to measure memory, math ability, and ability to visualize objects.

"They showed pictures of aircraft, gave the speed and altitude, and asked, which will be within a thousand feet of each other in three minutes. They showed a series of geometric patterns and codes. We had to figure out the relationship."

Passing score was 70 percent. Tina got 100 percent. But she'd only completed the easy part. Next step was the ten-week FAA screening program at the Air Traffic Control Academy in Oklahoma City, which critics have called boot camp.

"I never want to go through anything like that again," she said.

She wasn't alone in criticizing the harshness of the program. "We've known for a long time the way we recruit, train and screen controllers is counterproductive," acting FAA administrator Barry Harris told *USA Today* in 1992, when the agency was on the verge of changing the system. "The instructor screeners are there to wash you out, not to help you make it. The process produces an employee who is in conflict with management from the day he or she starts."

"The screening program, I didn't even like walking around here when we had it," one instructor-supervisor told me at the academy after it was changed. "You'd have these egomaniacs instructing. They'd take a cigarette lighter and two strips of paper, and let's say some candidate made a mistake, two airplanes got together. They'd scream, 'You just killed everybody on those airlines!' And burn the strips up! Ridiculous! I'd see grown men cry. Stupid. And why? We weren't supposed to be teaching them to kill someone. We're teaching them not to."

The instructor shook his head. It wasn't that he didn't appreciate the gravity of the job. In his own days as a controller, he'd lost two planes, had gone through horrible nightmares about it. But he felt that hysteria was not the best way to teach. "Oh, the screamin' and hollerin'," he said. "Once, I heard an instructor shout at a student, 'That's not the fuckin' way I told you to do it!' I said to him, 'You're outta my classroom.'"

The changes would come too late for Tina. She went through two months at the academy, knowing with the other candidates that only half of them would pass, doubly scary to the ones who had quit their jobs to try to become controllers.

In Oklahoma City, Tina memorized aviation laws, navigation, communication. She spent three weeks in a "tower controller lab," a classroom with a toy airport on a table. Students took turns "controlling" traffic from a booth while classmates in contact with them by headset moved the plastic airplanes by hand, during timed scenarios.

"It's a good place to get practice and phraseology, to learn how the tower works, to learn to relate to each other," said Steve Atkinson, who designs courses for the academy.

In their rented apartments, at night, trainees tacked maps of imaginary airways to walls, ceilings, laundry rooms. They had to memorize them. Because what if radar failed?

In the "radar simulation room" they sat before radar screens, which looked real but worked more like video games, since the "planes" on them were not real. They were imaginary ones operated by other people in the room. Trainees had to "control" the imaginary planes, which moved slowly at first, then faster and faster. Instructors sat at their shoulders, looking on.

"Some candidates left little pools of sweat on their seats afterward," Tina said.

"We had to apply the letter of the law," she remembered. "If there was a requirement that planes had to be separated by ten miles, and we deviated by even a fraction, or gave them *more* than ten miles to be safe, the instructors would assume we didn't know it, and we'd fail. They'd give us twenty different aircraft to manage, no picture in front of us, no map. We'd have to make decisions instantly.

"Your mind would play tricks on you. You'd think you told a pilot something but you didn't."

Final grade was based on lab problems and written tests. Tina passed and was sent to the Los Angeles en route center for field training. No radar work for her yet, no guiding planes in the air. She started out as a "strip puller," an assistant controller helping a veteran team by providing them with information on planes approaching their sector—strips of information a computer prints out.

Then she graduated to radar. Then she washed out.

"I have to admit, in a way, it was a relief."

Tina Crocker, on the other hand, was a full-fledged air traffic controller earning $60,000 a year bringing in planes. To meet her I'd gone to Atlanta's en route center, in Hampton, Georgia, thirty miles from Hartsfield Airport. Like most centers it was built during the Cold War, and situated far from an airport so if there was a nuclear strike on the city, the en route center would survive. Which would mean so would any planes in the air during the outbreak of war.

Boston's center is in Nashua, New Hampshire. Washington, D.C.'s, in Leesburg, Virginia. New York's in Islip, Long Island. Cleveland's in Oberlin, Ohio.

A hard windy rainstorm fell that morning, creating havoc for earthbound and air traffic alike, the storm battering the fine old houses and golf course near Emory University, where I stayed, the ribbon of interstates carrying rush-hour traffic past the red "Fly Delta Jets" sign downtown, the squarish FAA building near the airport where I'd hooked up with PR escort Kathleen Bergen, the roads south into the country, more rain hitting the strip malls, and signs saying "Clayton Detention Facility," "Matt Thompson Taxidermy," "Tara Baptist Church," "Hot Boiled Peanuts."

We'd parked in a lot filled with pickup trucks, in front of a large windowless building that looked more like a warehouse, except for the derrick shaped microwave towers outside.

"Last year we ran 2,200,000 airplanes through here," manager Stan Ensley told me inside. He was a brisk, businesslike man who called airlines "customers." A stocky, energetic talker. He said the center watches over airspace over parts of Alabama, Georgia, South

Carolina, Tennessee, Kentucky, Virginia, and North Carolina. Atlanta center is the second busiest in the world, after Chicago.

At Hampton there was even an underground facility for taking control of all FAA activities if Washington was destroyed.

"Right now we've probably got four planes going to Charlotte, four to Chicago, four to Miami, four to Birmingham, four to New York, four to Fort Lauderdale, four to Dallas, and all those suckers pass over here in an hour, so even at high altitudes our routes are crowded.

"Thousands of planes and millions of lives are on these guys' shoulders," he said.

I went downstairs, stood on a mezzanine catwalk and looked down on the main control room, two aisles lined with glowing radar screens, air traffic control stations, forty-five of them, mirror images of each other, manned by three-person teams of controllers. The casual dress on some people—rolled-up sleeves and jeans and sneakers—clashed with the somber air with which they talked into headsets, stared at screens, jotted flight information on little strips of paper.

There was also a weather section and a "flow control" where controllers maintained contact with Washington, D.C., coordinating Atlanta-bound departures from other airports during the storm, keeping planes in other cities on the ground so they wouldn't stack up over Hartsfield.

Tina Crocker was working the northeast sector, from where 714 would be arriving that day. A push was on so the screens were particularly busy. Plus, because of the storm pilots had a mile and a half visibility, they would only see the runways during the last thirty seconds of landing.

"Delta 157 heavy, turn right, heading two, six, five, radar vectors for spacing," she said into a microphone.

She seemed perky, professional, and feminine in a pink cashmere sweater, tight jeans, and white tennis sneakers. She had unusually beautiful light green eyes.

"Delta 157 heavy, right, heading two, six, five," the pilot repeated.

On her screen, pulsating like heartbeats on a monitor, the little blocks of information, each representing one plane, fanned in from all directions, converging into a funnel shape that narrowed as they jerked toward the airport. One block of information included the letters *RW*. "Coca Cola company jet," she said. One said, *G227*. "Ground speed 227 knots." *MU2R*. "Mitsubishi twin-engine turboprop," she said.

It was clear why the original test air traffic controllers take gauges their ability to decode information.

L: "Lifeguard. Sick patient coming in," she said.

"When I was being trained my boss used to cover the strip and say, 'What kind of plane is it?' " Tina said. "If I didn't know, he'd say, 'Why didn't you check when he called in? Why didn't you memorize it?' "

"What difference does it make if you know what kind of plane it is?" I said. "You give it the same orders, right?"

"Different planes perform differently. If you know what type it is, you know what kind of climb or descent it will give you."

The push ended, and we sat around during a break. If air traffic control was as stressful as critics charged, today had to be an example of it at its worst, with the winds still rising over Atlanta, the twenty-mile separation between planes instead of five, the barrage of incoming pilots wanting to land.

"When you look at the screen, do you see those blocks of information as airplanes?" I said.

She leaned back in a swivel chair. We were a few feet behind the team that had replaced her during the break. The screens showed far fewer blips now. "It's just a data block to me."

"Do you think of yourself as having a relationship with an airplane?"

"None of us do. Some guys look at it like it's a video game, but I hate video games. To me, I'm talking to a target on a scope. Two voices. A pilot and copilot. A blip on the screen, and all blips look the same. The only time I think of it as a plane is when I go to the airport and see all those people and get on a plane myself. Then I think, Holy shit."

Tina seemed calm talking about it. I guessed that you got used to controlling planes after a while. She said, "I used to see airplanes flying in my mind, every which way, when I first went into training. I used to dream of planes every night. Yeah, it was stressful then. But my instructor in Oklahoma City said, 'When you plug in that jack you have to be an asshole.' Now I just bark it out.

"I feel my personality change when I plug in that jack."

The life of an air traffic controller. She was a divorced mother with two kids. On weekends she hiked with the kids and the dog. Each day at seven, when she started her eight-hour shift, she checked the wind with pilots to make sure the weather report she had was right. In winter, she worked planes a little harder, since she knew they could climb faster in the cold. She'd memorized the terrain beneath her airspace, because it affected weather. "I've got mountains, so it's turbulent in the east departure sector."

Pilots knew her voice.

"One guy calls me Happy Voice," she laughed. Another, taken with her voice, had come to the center to meet her and ask her on a date.

I was thinking that the system seemed to have worked. Tina Clark, anxious over the job, had been reassigned to an easier position. Tina Crocker, cool on the radio, had stayed at her center.

But then what about personal stress? I wondered. Even a top controller must have times when home life is shaky. How does a controller pay 100 percent attention to the planes then?

Tina Crocker and I went to dinner to talk about it. She chose the Lone Star Restaurant, a country-western place near her home in Georgia. "The armpit of Atlanta," she said. An area of small homes and ugly strip malls and massage parlors and pawn shops.

"You want to know about my life?" she said with the same upbeat tone, which belied what she was about to say. "Believe me, it's been no Betty Crocker life for me."

Where should we start? she said. The father who molested her? The husband who hit her? The lover who'd left her when she got pregnant?

I was taken aback. "My father was Air Force," she said. "When I was eight, living in Idaho, he used to come in my bedroom and stick his penis in my mouth. The room would start spinning. He would say, 'You want this real bad.' I wanted to scream, but he told me I couldn't. He called me a whore and stuff."

She spoke easily, matter-of-factly. This had all come out in therapy over the last three years, she said.

She said her dad had laughed at her, when, as a teenager, she told him she wanted to be an air traffic controller.

"He said girls can't do that," she said.

She forgot about it and went to college in management and dropped out when she met her Tunisian husband. "He married me because he wanted to stay in the United States."

The story got worse. There was the move with her husband to New York. The clerk job in a cheap Manhattan hotel that she hated. The horrible air traffic controller screen in Oklahoma City. The first days on the job, working all night, taking care of two kids all day while her husband did nothing.

"I was losing my mind, working full time, keeping house full time. I went to a shrink, and found out I was doing the job to prove to my dad I did have control. A woman could do it. At New York they were all military, all old-timers, like a multitude of my father, all over again, driving me crazy, and there was depression and pressure."

Tina moved to Atlanta Center. She started an affair with another controller.

"It's like Peyton Place here," she said.

At the Lone Star, a country-western band played a Doc Watson tune and lines of single women in tight jeans and high-heeled boots two-stepped on the dance floor while the singer wagged his tongue at them.

"He hit me, and I sent him to prison for a night," she said, meaning her husband, talking about the end of the marriage. "I took him to court. He wasn't allowed to come to the house. He broke into the garage. Put sugar in my gas tank. He used to park across the field and watch us. He turned off the security light in back. He took the dog."

"Were you working during this period, bringing in planes?"

"Sure," she said, as if it was an odd question.

"I took the kids to a shelter. I didn't have any clothes. I had no money to pay bills. *He* had the checking account. He threatened to take the kids to Tunisia."

"You were bringing in planes during this?"

"Right."

The waitress brought burgers and beer. After the divorce, she said, she moved in with the other controller, got pregnant and had an abortion. They split up. He immediately started another affair.

"I'd come home and cry every night," she said. "Just sit on the floor and cry." She nodded before I even asked the question. "Yes, I was bringing in planes then."

We switched to a happier subject for her, former lives she said she'd had. She had known her controller-lover, Ed, and her husband in several of them.

"In ancient Spain, Ed and I were married. I was a man and he was a woman. We were wine makers. That was a happy life.

"In another life I was a slave. My husband was the master. As I turned into a young woman, he started having sex with me. Ed was the old black man, the overseer of the slaves, the only one who could talk to the master.

"I was an American Indian in Montana. I was a respected healer of the tribe. That was a very rough life, but interesting."

The whole time we talked, I kept thinking, I'm a passenger on 714. I'm coming into Atlanta on the northeast sector. I'm flying through Tina Crocker's airspace as she talks to the pilot, with twenty other planes nearby. It's raining. She had a fight with her ex-husband that morning. She stayed up crying last night. She thinks she used to be a slave.

We left the Lone Star and drove back to the house Tina shared with her two sons. Ford pickup in the driveway. Sticker reading "World Peace" in the living room. Moroccan glasswork atop a wall unit containing books like *Back to Eden*, *Crystal Gem and Metal Magic*, *The Oracle Within*.

When I offered to drive her babysitter home, Tina wasn't sure if she should trust a man, any man, with a teenage girl.

I told Tina that anyone reading about her might have the same questions I did. They might be nervous when they read the part about working while going through all the personal stress. I asked her if she thought her abilities as a controller had gone down during that period.

In an instant her face changed from vulnerabe to cool and professional. It was like she'd become another person. The transformation was amazing. I knew what she was going to say before she said it. And I believed her when she did.

"I told you. When I plug in that jack, I change."

I kept thinking about Tina Crocker. I imagined her driving to work in her pickup, on a day when her husband had broken the light again. I saw her falling asleep crying, at home, then going in to work to watch the little planes crowd her screen. In the end I asked Steve Atkinson about Tina. He was an ex-marine and ex-controller who designed courses at the FAA Academy in Oklahoma City. Which meant essentially he helped determine the criteria of who makes a good controller.

He was a friendly, helpful man who called me Babe. He'd gone through some tough moments himself. "In Charleston we had a fellow run out of fuel on final. His wife was with him, and his children. He survived but they died, and it was tough on all of us. I didn't sleep very well. I—I don't want to sound melodramatic," he said sheepishly, "but I felt like there was somebody in my bedroom. I don't mean a ghost or spirit . . . just an odd feeling. . . . I called in sick the next day. But you know the saying, you fall off a horse and you get back on."

Another time, in the Marines, he said, he was controlling a jet where the pilot jettisoned onto a runway and died.

It was clear, when I walked around the FAA campus with Atkinson, that he had great sympathy for the candidates walking past us, young men and women carrying books, sitting on the grass quizzing each other, gathered nervously in a hallway waiting for their turn in the radar lab.

"Sometimes it scares me to see us send people out of the academy to the New York center. Or San Francisco or Chicago. Some people do very well. But they have absolutely no idea what they're facing. It. Is. Scary. I was an air traffic controller for ten years before I went to the New York training center. And when I went in there and looked at the radar scope, it was glowing, literally shining from the number of planes on it.

"Someone who wants to be an air traffic controller should expect to be overwhelmed. To feel like they've been dropped in the middle of the ocean and told to swim home. All controllers have had those feelings, I don't care if they tell you otherwise. I don't care if it's level 1 or level 5. They better be ready to deal with losing the picture and getting it back. They better be ready for anything. I've been shot at, and that's what it felt like when I lost the picture on level 5."

That was when I told him about Tina Crocker, to see what he would say. To see if he'd be worried. But instead he nodded while I talked, and straightened and even, strangely, began to smile.

We were alone in the training lab, standing by the little plastic airplanes and toy runway, with photos of airliners like the L-1011 on the wall around us.

"I'm proud of her. P-r-o-u-d. That's typical of controllers," said Atkinson, thirty-nine, a high school dropout who got his high school equivalency diploma in the Marines. "An absolute separation of personal and professional. You handle it. That's all there is to it."

Atkinson ran his hand over the table. He wore a linen jacket with a black-and-white pattern, and too wide a tie. "I'll tell you something even management might not know. We have a way of helping each other. Someone's having stress at home, we let 'em take a break during heavy traffic. Put 'em on flight data instead of bringing in planes. You know, it got so bad at the New York center when I was there, people snapping at each other, hollering, almost fistfights, that the controllers started telling each other, 'I'm gonna call in sick tomorrow. I need a day off.' Helping each other. Never mind management."

"What happens if you can't give someone a break? If traffic's too heavy?" I said.

Atkinson got the same hard look on his face Tina Crocker had had. "Then they handle it.

"Oh, man. I used to just perspire. I had to have a cigarette. I'd get to work an hour early, to get into the flow, to get myself ready. Walk into a lunchroom at any air traffic facility, and you'll see people pacing. People standing up eating their lunch. People walking up and down the hall. *Burning off the adrenaline.* I started lifting weights and jogging to burn it off. So I wouldn't snap at my wife."

"Excuse me," I said, "but at the same time you're telling me all this stressful stuff, you seem to be getting excited, remembering it. Is that right? Like some action junkie? Or am I wrong?"

Atkinson blushed. "You hit the nail on the head," he said. "You put me on the spot, babe. The dread to do it, and then you get there, and there's an adrenaline rush." His eyes started shining. "Totally opposite feelings minutes apart. Not even wanting to go to work. Feeling sick. And then you get there, and you do the first couple of transitions." His eyes glowed.

"Hey! Give me more," he said.

Tina Clark wiped hair from her eyes, and on the radio, we were being handed to Dallas/Fort Worth center as ship 714 approached 14,000 feet. Below, the white, parched desert had given way to brown flat panhandle.

"Delta 1562 heavy, descend and maintain one four thousand. Dallas/Fort Worth altimeter. Two niner niner four," a controller's voice said. I thought, Twenty years from now pilots may never hear a controller's voice.

By then, Stan Ensley told me, computers will automatically communicate ground to air, so controllers don't waste time, seconds which become more precious with each new plane that takes to the air.

"Right now a controller is limited by how many words he can say in a minute and how many words the pilot repeats back to him. Everything we do is verbal. Every clearance. Every direction. But under a new system, controllers will be able to keyboard, transmit and receive data, rather than be verbal. It'll be a lot quicker because the controller can key something in, key something else in, key something else in without having to wait for a response."

In fact, FAA officials told me, in the future the controller's job will involve less hands-on activity all around. "The controller's participation may evolve from an active manager to a more passive system monitor," said the FAA report, *Selection of Air Traffic Controllers for Automated Systems.*

"As the job itself changes, questions arise as to how long a selection system based on the current selection criteria will be effective," wrote Carol Manning, a researcher with the FAA.

"The thrill of expectation might be gone," she told me.

In other words, twenty years from now, air traffic controller stress might come from too little to do, not too much.

At the moment, though, at least the dreaded screening program was gone, replaced by a five-day version, which Steve Atkinson said would be equally accurate in identifying qualified candidates for controller.

"Our average time to become fully trained will fall from about a little over four years to probably two and a half years," Barry Harris told *USA Today*.

Another change at the academy since Tina Clark's days involved the installation of a $10.5 million simulator for controller students. A three-sided glass "tower" where instructors electronically simulate and mix nine basic scenarios in the "airport" outside, a cartoon view of a runway, cornfield, circling or landing planes.

"One controller works all traffic on the ground, one works runways and air within five miles, just like real life," Atkinson said.

On the day I visited the simulator, instructors showed me planes landing in fog and snow, at night, in rain, in broad daylight. Students manned the controller positions with the instructors behind them running emergencies like cockpit smoke, rough-running engines, no radio, no gear.

Atkinson said sometimes instructors have planes purposefully ignore instructions, just the way, in radar lab, they read back instructions wrong to see if the students catch them.

I asked one of the instructors to crash two planes. A United Airlines jet and a small twin-engine private plane approached on the runway, the bigger jet creeping up on the little one, and my stomach tightened, and I realized the instructors had grown very quiet, since they were all ex-controllers, and the impending collision was no game to them. The two images merged on screen, a red ball erupted, and then there was nothing where the craft had been.

I heard Steve Atkinson let out a long, shaky sigh.

He seemed to speak for Tina Clark and Tina Crocker. And 18,000 other voices pilots hear as they fly. He seemed to speak for all the crisp, competent voices I heard when I flew in the cockpit of 714, guiding us through weather, landing us, warning us, signing off with cheery good-byes.

"I don't like to see that, even in pretend."

SHEER COMPLICATION

Packed with 302 passengers, ship 714 rolled toward takeoff along the east side of Dallas/Fort Worth airport, one more plane in an endless line of jets crawling through each other's tail washes. The runway was nowhere in sight, neither was the terminal. The taxiway went on so long it felt more like an interstate. The flat gray vista merged with the sky and magnified the sense of mechanicalness characterizing mass travel today.

Wing after wing, rudder after rudder. An infinitesimal parade of like images. Dallas airport's primary value seemed to be that it marked a spot on the way to somewhere else. I remembered reading that some travelers—people prone to emotional stress—actually went into depressions here. The sprawl of the airport brought on anxiety in them. At the time, the notion that mere space could depress someone seemed farfetched to me. After an hour here I knew what the writer meant.

I'd been in 714 three days now, flown to Utah, California, Hawaii, and what had I really seen? A cockpit? Airline food? The same movies I could watch at home? Trapped in the line of planes, 714 seemed more like a bus at the Port Authority.

Not a magic craft anymore. The ultimate in American rootlessness.

Boy, was Dallas depressing. Perhaps in the old days travel had been harder, but its reward lay in the immersion in other cultures which the difficulty entailed. In 714's vacuum-packed world, everything came in foil, from the peanuts to the passengers.

We inched closer to takeoff. I remembered Manhattan parties I'd been to, businessmen or artists talking about travel as if it had broadened them, when in fact the constant movement had done nothing more than enable them to ignore their personal lives, which were usually a mess.

"In Mexico City there's this great restaurant. . . . I had the shirt made in Hong Kong. . . ."

Two weeks earlier, I remembered, I'd been on the number 3 subway in Manhattan, and a man and woman had gotten on at Wall Street, bankers or brokers from their expensive clothes. In voices loud enough to carry through the car—which meant they were practically screaming considering the noise level in New York, they'd kept up a conversation like this.

"On Tuesday I have to be in Rio because the Lima meeting is Friday and after that, Vancouver, oh, God, but at least Frank will be in Belgium until Monday when we have to meet up for dinner in Prague. But don't worry, the Budapest thing isn't until after Istanbul, which gives me time to scoot to Milano. Paris is what I need after an Eastern European jaunt."

"Assholes," a woman next to me said when they left.

I felt relieved when 714 finally lumbered down the runway and took to the air, fighting its way into the by now oppressively familiar pollution haze that blanketed the continent. I wished politicians would look out the window when they flew. No one who did that could fail to be alarmed by the deteriorating atmosphere.

Get me out of here, quick. Below, outlying Dallas showed itself as rows of boxy houses. Then we were over fields, chugging through the dirty brown mass toward predicted turbulence over the Delta country, the company birthplace, the one-room ruin in the Louisiana woods.

Seven fourteen was retracing the earliest Delta route, Dallas to Atlanta.

Back in the 1930s passengers flying this trip would board planes at 9:20 A.M. and arrive in Atlanta at 5:30 after making six stops, never flying higher than 7,000 feet. A one-way ticket cost $38.50. There were no stewardesses. Copilots carried baggage and served box lunches. Delta had only twenty-seven stockholders. All employees knew each other.

At the moment, 714 carried more passengers than a whole year's roster back then. In fact, passengers throughout the industry were so scarce in the early years I'd been amazed to learn what airline personnel did to get them on planes.

Take Oscar Bergstrom, Delta's Atlanta district traffic manager from 1935 to 1937. He promoted ticket sales, did public relations, handled promotion and advertising. He visited civic clubs to drum up business. Once he read in the society pages that socialite Jeanette Farmer of LaGrange, Georgia, was to leave for San Francisco to begin a world cruise. He wrote her, offering to come to LaGrange to help her with itineraries.

He visited fan dancer Sally Rand at a nude ranch near Fort Worth to help promote business.

In another story, wrote W. David Lewis and Wesley Phillips Newton in *Delta: The History of an Airline*, an Atlanta passenger demanded that Bergstrom's people wake him at his hotel before his flight and ready him for the bus ride to the airport. Delta operators called, but he was in the hotel restaurant. Delta paged the man a few minutes later. He demanded that he finish breakfast before the bus left. And when the bus left without him, he kept calling, demanding a ride to the airport. Finally the Delta operator told him the bus would return for him. The passenger demanded a taxi, at Delta's expense.

Bergstrom provided one.

Not exactly the service passengers got in 1992.

In 1992 Delta employed 77,000 people to look after 550 planes. All the manpower, money, focus, finance, all the lobbying in Washington, all the legal maneuvering, all the mind-boggling complication was concentrated on 550 planes. On the fleet and its queens, the L-1011s.

All those planes weren't even in the sky at the same time. Some were in maintenance. Or at gates. Or sitting idle, spares to be used if other planes broke down. Eleven and a half billion dollars in operating costs in 1992 for 550 planes. The levels of complexity here would probably have been inconceivable to Oscar Bergstrom when

Delta headquarters occupied the little building in Monroe, Louisiana.

Every aspect of this flight from Dallas to Atlanta had its own bureaucracy, rules, schedule. Down to a specification on how many seconds to cook a chicken.

For 714 to be over Mississippi at this moment, on time, with passengers on board, a thousand holy standardized details had been packed into those immense looseleaf manuals everyone in the company seemed to carry. Had been drilled into 77,000 heads.

I'd spent days visiting the battalions of support personnel in Atlanta. Hundreds of people in tiny partitioned cubicles or little offices, each a human extension of the flying machines, monitoring the computers, wooing customers on phones, babying the fleet.

That an L-1011, any L-1011, would be flying this route today had been decided six months ago by Mike Bell's "schedule development" department. Bell's analysts matched planes with route combinations. It was more than a question of whimsy. The difference between flying a 767 and an L-1011 on the Salt Lake City to Anchorage route, just for one day, could cost Delta $5,000.

"We redo the schedule twice a year," said Bell, a shy, tall, balding man who'd averted his eyes while he talked about "fleet optimization" and "spilled revenue." That's profit lost on legs where the plane is too small to carry all passengers who want to fly. But sometimes, Bell said, you have to schedule a smaller plane on that flight anyway. Otherwise the company loses more revenue on the flights preceding or following it, where only a handful of passengers are booked. Why waste all that fuel cost on few fliers?

"We look at individual flight segments, historical demand for seats. It's a juggling job. And a seasonal one. You might want an L-1011 on a segment in summer, but in the winter the demand may change."

Once Delta's computer matches a plane to a rotation, analysts fine-tune the schedule. Make sure there's parking space at that particular airport for that size plane. And runway space. And special widebody container loaders for L-1011s.

After talking to Bell, I visited the glassed-in "equipment control" office, where staff assign specific planes specific rotations six days before flights. And monitor the assignments as flight time approaches, watching maintenance needs, equipment breakdowns, and orders from flight control, which wants a plane somewhere else.

"Every passenger waiting for a plane is going to have one show up," said equipment analyst Bill Settles. He said, on the day of the flight, "flight control" takes over.

And all those people just worked on scheduling machines. Two more departments priced tickets, again starting the process months before a flight.

"We know 338 days in advance what the projected prices will be on any flight," Revenue Control Analyst Linda Bennett told me in Atlanta.

We sat in her little cubicle, looking over printouts. Bennett and other analysts break down, on every flight, what percentage of passengers will probably be business travelers, what percentage military, retired, vacationers, children.

"We look over historical load patterns, factor in the time of day, the season, if it's a holiday. We make educated guesses how many seats to sell at full fare, how many at a discount.

"Once a price is fixed, it may never change, or it may change a dozen times as flight day approaches," said Bennett, an ex-teacher and social worker and mother of two. She said during the months before a flight, analysts keep a check on bookings, offering fewer cheaper seats to customers on a flight that's filling up fast and more discounted tickets on one that's oddly empty. They also calculate what percentage of passengers won't show up, and gamble how much a flight can be overbooked.

"Every flight has a certain percentage of no-shows, but exactly how many overbookings can we make without having to turn away passengers," she said, "is the guess.

"We can overbook 5 percent or as high as 30 percent. We want to fill the flight, but we want to make money doing it," said Bennett. "This might sound corny, but this is my livelihood, and I don't want it to go away."

Every ticket, every bit of space in 714 quantified. Every aspect of flight broken into even more components. Linda Bennett might determine how many seats to offer at a discount, but *how much* of a discount? *How much* for full fare? *How much* to match rival airline prices during price wars?

Just to reduce the price of every Delta seat by one dollar a year would mean a $77 million loss for the company. Price wars can ravage an airline. Fill up seats but lose billions at the same time.

I visited Andy Scantlebury, a pricing analyst, during a fare war. At the time TWA and US Air were lowering fares. So was Northwest. American had announced it was going to charge only four basic, unchangeable fares, but the new system was breaking down already.

Scantlebury's job was to make short- and long-range forecasts and recommendations to marketing, to squeeze the best profit from each seat without losing customers.

And customers baffled him. It amazed him that passengers expected to be able to fly from coast to coast for $99 and felt overcharged if they couldn't. They seemed to apply a different standard of value to flying than to other products they bought. The whole way they thought lacked common sense. The other day he'd been in a hardware store, he said, and the clerk had said something about the unfair price of tickets, and the whole store had stopped while Scantlebury explained the basics of profits at airlines.

"Fare wars create unreasonable expectations in people," he said.

"I keep a low profile at parties," he added.

When I met him at 8 A.M. one Tuesday, fifteen minutes into his shift, he was studying another one of those massive printouts. It was as thick as a New York phone book, and it showed fare changes the day before.

"Yesterday was slow. American Airlines only made 669 domestic fare changes. Continental made 10,438. Delta, 7,418," said the Boston native, baseball-statistics fan, ex-philosophy major at Notre Dame, and, as usual, a complexity junkie. He was an eager man who asked me as many questions as I asked him. A man curious about the world around him.

"That's slow?" I said.

"Domestic fares can change 250,000 times a day," he said. "You should see it when it's busy."

Analysts worked by geographic area, and Scantlebury concentrated on the rich route from the northeast United States to Florida. Yesterday ship 714 had flown from Boston to Orlando, and I asked Scantlebury what changes had happened just on that route yesterday and so far today. He studied the printout like a horse player eyeing a racing form.

"Hmmm," he said. "Northwest did something to their fares."

He had to call details up on the computer, from a service airlines subscribe to, where they list price changes on a daily basis. Watching the numbers come up, Scantlebury frowned.

"Northwest's low discount fare today is $225," he said. "One way coach, immediate purchase. But tomorrow it will be $260."

How to decipher this? Scantlebury forgot me for the moment. In the middle of a price war, when everyone else was lowering fares, Northwest was *raising* one. "Why did they do this?" he said. "I can't phone them and ask them. It's against the law. I have to conjecture. Let's see."

Scantlebury called up the accompanying restrictions on the new fare. How many days' advance purchase was necessary? How many days was the offer good for? What did Northwest intend to charge for a ticket on the same route a few days after the new fare was announced?

He sat back, and blew out air. "This may be more serious than I thought.

"The question is," he said, "will this increase be across the board, or just here. One price change on one fare is small. Multiply that by 1,000 cities, it's significant."

Scantlebury sighed. To marketing, he lamented, whatever price recommendations he came up with were always too low. To passengers, too high.

"You never get a call from people saying 'Hey! Great fare!'" he said.

Then we stopped talking as the analysts were summoned to their regular 10:30 briefing, an update on the industry this morning. Similar scenes were probably going on at American and TWA and United and US Air. Hundreds of men and women emerging from little cubicles to stand in corridors and try to figure out what their counterparts were doing to woo those fickle passengers into seats. All of them, at every company, keenly aware of the airlines that had gone out of business, of the analysts at Pan Am and Midway and Eastern who didn't have jobs anymore, or salaries or pension plans or health plans. Everyone I met at Delta, mechanics, ticket agents, flight attendants, and financiers, had their eyes on the balance sheet all the time.

Linda Bennett had said, "This may sound corny, but it's our livelihood, the health of this company."

And the bottom line for Delta was the cost of Scantlebury's seats.

I felt like I was at a meeting of CIA analysts listening in on Radio Beijing, trying to figure out what news broadcasts mean in communist China, trying to see beneath the surface and guess what decisions had been made in the enemy camp.

"TWA has Charlotte introductory fares today. Pass it up the line," a supervisor said. The analysts stood at the entrances of their cubicles, nodding. This was bad news. An enemy advance. Or as Scantlebury, who liked baseball metaphors would say, a base hit.

"US Air is changing the prices to Columbus. In Omaha marketing has reported our loads dropping, but rising on TWA."

A discontented murmur rippled down the corridor. "Hasn't TWA hit Omaha lots of times?" one analyst asked. He referred to one- or two-day special promotional fares that airlines sometimes offered.

"*Lots* of times," the supervisor said disapprovingly while the analysts nodded some more, disturbed, frustrated, taking it personally, actually not understanding, in their loyalty to Delta, how passengers could choose seats on the basis merely of cheaper fares.

"I don't think in terms of higher fares. I think of them as more reasonable fares," Scantlebury had said.

Now he asked the supervisor, "How far can we go when it comes to matching these fares?"

It was the question of the day. The analysts argued about the TWA action.

"If TWA goes down the tubes, they'll have the highest liability," one said, meaning, What about all those stranded passengers?

"But their load factors are the highest in the industry," another person said.

"So what? Eastern's were too. TWA isn't making money."

"But they're still taking away our passengers."

"Are they? Those passengers may not have flown on Delta. Maybe TWA's taking passengers away from Greyhound."

Around and around. How to respond to TWA. How much to

lower the price of seats, which at some point will transform into substantially less profit, smaller raises, unhappy stockholders, and maybe—in the worst-case scenario, but one which has happened time and time again in the industry—real financial trouble. Not now, but later. Up the line.

The mood was, Damn TWA.

In the end, the supervisor said the analysts should "use their judgment." And in the end, Scantlebury decided to alert marketing to the Northwest fare change, but recommend no action at least for today, while he monitored the market closely.

After talking to Scantlebury, I walked over to reservations, where just the Atlanta office gets 34,500 calls a day, and needs 500 people to handle them. I walked through room after room divided into "bays" filled with desks, each seat occupied by an operator, each operator on the phone, looking at a computer screen, as more phones lit up. So this was the room I reached when I called for information or a reservation.

There was an "international section" for foreign tickets. A special desk where operators speak Japanese. A department just for particularly complicated tickets.

"There's a 'tip line' where our agents receive tips from employees on potential customers," said Glenda Stock, manager of the office. "There's one room where agents negotiate fares for groups of ten or more, their travel agents or even with the people themselves. We have one section to deal with travel agencies who give Delta over a million dollars of business a year. Just in 1991, that office handled 1,634,067 calls."

I watched Delta Meeting Network Sales agents handle conventions. A dentist group, 3,000 of them, were going to Acapulco, probably writing it off on their taxes. Three thousand soft drink manufacturers were going to Dallas. Good luck in the airport, I thought. Three thousand researchers were heading for Mexico to view a total eclipse. The National Rabbit Breeders' Group wanted transportation for their rabbits. McDonald's wanted Delta to transport ground beef, as well as people, to their convention.

Every detail, planned and researched. Salesmen visited corporations to solicit business. Delta sent orchids to secretaries who booked their bosses on airplanes. Nothing seemed left to chance.

Once again I had the thought that aviation had to be the most regulated form of complexity on the planet.

"Our agents have a very structured approach to callers," said Glenda Stock, a Dallas native, a thirteen-year veteran in the department, a pleasant, perky woman in a shark-tooth jacket and brooch fastening the white lace collar of her blouse. We sat in her office near Renoir prints.

"Our agents have specific questions to ask. They're told to avoid yes/no questions. Not to say, 'Do you want to take that flight?' Instead to say, 'We have been able to confirm you. What is the spelling of your last name?' "

Every passenger who flew on 714 was booked or serviced or monitored by these people. And there was still more, another staff of 210, in another office, just to deal with Delta's 12 million frequent fliers.

"American and United started these programs. Delta was one of the last carriers to institute it," said Joyce Fisher, who managed the department. "But it builds tremendous brand loyalty. And prior to having this kind of program, airlines didn't know their best customers."

That was the plus part. The negative was, "It's a monster. Trying to end it would be like trying to take a bone away from a Doberman."

Not that anybody wants to end it. In addition to sending out 6,000 free certificates a day, and 7,000 letters to frequent fliers, the office works with Delta marketing, targeting frequent fliers for special promotions.

"We might spend $500,000 for postage just to send out one mailing," Joyce Fisher said.

Twelve million frequent fliers? It was a long way from the days when Delta ran itself from the little brick building. From the early days when airline ticket agents hung out in bars trying to scrounge up business. Drove drunk passengers to airports to make sure they'd board planes. A long way from the days when Colonial Airlines, in a promotional, offered free tickets to wives who would travel with their businessman husbands. A long way from the days when Al Capone and four bodyguards appeared at Pan Am's ticket counter in Miami, bought five tickets to Havana, where Capone probably had rum runner business, and advised the agent, "Better see it's a safe plane—if anything happens to us, it won't be so healthy for you."

A long way from the days when a passenger complaint might be, "We had to land because of weather, and I had to take the train."

These days there was a whole complaint department, ninety-three more people. I remembered excerpts from the letters I'd read.

Dear Delta:

- My husband had physical contact with a Delta stewardess at the downtown Hyatt in Chicago, Illinois. My husband contacted a social disease from her. If she is unaware of it and spreads it around, I would not want another family to go through what we have. . . .
- MY NAME IS JERRY. I AM 9 YEARS OLD. I LIKE AIRPLANES. SO TRY NOT TO FUCK UP THE LANDING.
- The man in the seat was stiff as a board leaning back and fastened to the seat belt. His head was very visible above his seat. He was wrinkled and had age spots on the top of his bald head, with grey hair on the side. Everyone walked by in shock, thinking he was dead, and/or was a taxidermic.

  The question I want answered truthfully is, Was the man real and dead or was this just an excellent job of a wax figure?
- I saw Reagan and Gorbachev walking on the water of the Potomac River. We have had many flights, but this was the greatest.
- Now, and this next thing is very *important. Everybody* down to the last young lady was polite. *Everybody* said, "I'm doing the best I can. " *Everybody* said, "Don't worry about a thing." This naturally makes you feel lousy.
- In March I shipped a goat on Delta and upon arrival the goat was noted to have chocolate all over its mouth! Somewhere along the line someone fed that animal a candy bar! Any change in a goat's diet can give it enterotox and kill it!
- The nonrevenue [company employee] passenger did not behave quite according to guidelines. She told several passengers in the gate area that she was the president of Delta Air Lines, and to go on board and not worry about their tickets. She also told a passenger, "What the fuck do you want to change your seat for?"

- I have closterphobia real bad.
- How about a *soft* toilet seat like we buy at K-Mart?
- . . . then the attendant told the wheelchair patient, "The flight will leave in five minutes, but if you run you can make it."
- During dinner service on flight 850 from San Francisco to Cincinnati an impatient stewardess spilled a cup of hot tea on my pants and burned my penis.
- While boarding a member of my family in Orlando, the L-1011 TriStar was parked just outside the terminal. While the first officer was going through the checklist, the captain was dead asleep at the wheel, mouth open and all. The baggage and food service was loaded, the gate ramp pulled away, the airplane was backed away from the terminal, and your captain was still dead to the world.
- Please don't hurt my mommy and daddy, my grandma and gramp, my Aunt Rose, Uncle Bill, and my cousins, because they all fly on your airplanes.

"This is the sorriest department in Delta," said Fred Eisberry, who was nevertheless a jovial man in charge of complaints, and who clearly sympathized with most people who contacted the department.

"Usually there's something we could have done better," he said. "If we see there's room for that, in addition to the explanation we give them, we might send a credit they can use on the next trip, $50, as much as $200. We have a lot of latitude."

Like Andy Scantlebury, Eisberry said he doesn't tell people his job at parties. Even some members of his own family don't know what he does.

"Once we got a complaint from my sister," he said. "She didn't send it to me, she didn't know I work in this department. One of the staff saw the name and showed it to me."

Funny complaints aside, Delta's reputation with fliers is one of the best in the business. The U.S. Department of Transportation ranked Delta second best in passenger complaints per 100,000 fliers in 1992, after Southwest Airlines. TWA came in last. The National Institute for Aviation Research ranked Delta third, after American and Southwest, based on safety, on-time performance, baggage handling, and general consumer issues. The Department of Transportation said Delta had the lowest number of bumped passengers in the industry in 1992. And *Consumer Reports* ranked Delta second after Alaska Airlines in overall flying in 1991.

"Delta must be pretty confident about themselves if they let you see complaint letters," my wife said when I told her about Fred Eisberry and the funny-letter file.

And in the end, airline people probably complained about passengers as much as the other way around. I heard about children or old people shunted around from family to family, city to city, on planes. About drunks who threaten to kill the pilot or strip in the aisle. During a delay one day in Cincinnati caused by a fire on a runway at LaGuardia Airport, I got a Delta eye view of one obnoxious passenger while I stood behind the Delta service desk and one New York-bound man kept marching back every ten minutes, yelling at the clearly overworked and sympathetic attendant, "Are you lying about when the plane will take off? You're lying, aren't you? They tell you to lie."

But my favorite obnoxious passenger story involved a bank robber in Greensboro, North Carolina, who took hostages in town, ordered a car from police, and told them he was going to hijack a plane. Police alerted the airport as the robber headed for it.

"I closed our office, took everyone in the back office, ticket agents, ramp service people, told 'em what was going on, then I called the flight dispatch office in Atlanta," said Bob Thompson, Delta's manager in Greensboro at the time. "We had two planes due in. We held one in Raleigh and sent the other one to Charlotte. The other airlines did the same. When the hijacker got to the airport, he couldn't find anybody. No people. No planes. Nothing.

"So he left."

The turbulence never materialized over Louisiana. Seven-fourteen passed over Mississippi and Alabama, on the old route. Below, the Chattahoochee River marked the Georgia border, vivid blue against the brown and early green of the Georgia scrub woods in March. I imagined Union soldiers rampaging down there. We were descending toward Atlanta, at 14,000 feet, 250 miles an hour air speed, on the final leg of the 731-mile flight.

As we approached the airport, I knew a whole other level of sup-

port services would be readying for 714. To bring her to the right
gate at the right moment. To groom and stock her with food and
gasoline and magazines and orange juice. To make sure she was
functioning mechanically. To get the right passengers in the right
seats. To get 714 back on the taxiway, away from the gate, fully
functioning, in less than forty minutes.

As we approached, at the Dobbs kitchen, on the east side of the
airport, operators would be monitoring small black Infax machines,
television monitors listing incoming flights. Dobbs's 126,000-
square-foot kitchen prepared 30,000 meals a day. "We do everything but intravenous," operations manager Dave Figel had told me
when I'd visited.

"We're a private service serving twenty-one airlines. A factory of
sorts. We do 5.5 million meals a month, out of 170 locations."

I'd eaten plenty of those airline food meals. Delta staff bragged
about the quality of the food, but I kept remembering the time I'd
flown with Vice President Harry Alger to New Orleans, and Alger
had invited me to Delta's annual awards banquet for personnel with
many years of service.

"It's catered," he'd bragged.

"By Dobbs?" I'd said.

Alger snorted. "No."

In the regulated Delta world, as with everything else, Dobbs's
meals were prepared according to company rules. "Surface fat is
not to exceed one quarter inch in depth," I'd read in the Domestic
Service Guide, "the bible," Dave Figel said, which I'd been allowed
to see only after a ten-minute battle with Delta's food service liaison, who was afraid competitors would find out recipes if I saw
them.

> Place on charbroiler. Sear for three minutes each side. Place on
> wire rack after cooking so excess blood fat drips. Then put in quick
> chill cooler 40–42 degrees. After that move to reach-in cooler in the
> "hot belt" department.

Ah, ha. So that's how all those steaks had been prepared. Figel
had walked me through the kitchen, past what seemed like miles
of hairnetted workers at conveyer belts, scooping little gobs of

potato salad onto leafs of lettuce, putting strawberries in fruit salad, putting maraschino cherries on top, arranging salads in trays.

On one line the first woman lined a paper cup with lettuce, the next put a little turkey sandwich on, the next put pasta salad in a paper cup, the next one wrapped the whole thing in plastic wrap.

"Evening snack. Tourist class," Dave said.

In the "cold belt," an enormous walk-in freezer, workers prepared the evening meals for L-1011 flight 688, leaving in seven hours, the food coded by meal, class, flight. Four kinds of menus for each kind of flight, so frequent fliers wouldn't get the same meal all the time.

In a test kitchen I watched chefs in white hats trying to come up with a new meal for charter flights, experimenting with different combinations of cantaloupes, melons, pineapple wedges, spaghetti salad, brown rice salad, marinated cucumbers, shrimp, chicken and lettuce, putting the meals in blue boxes.

Then I watched about 10,000 chickens roasting in giant ovens, dripping, getting brown.

"The Dodgers don't take any liquor when they charter," Dave said. "Don Shula of the Miami Dolphins always gets a crab claw meal. One guy always has us board an extra meal for Elvis Presley, in case he shows up."

But Dobbs was only one of many support crews watching the Infax machine for incoming flights. In maintenance shops scattered around the concourses and baggage offices, supervisors monitored the boxes, readied crews to handle flights.

Cabin Services, underneath B Concourse, occupied a huge basement warehouse piled with thousands of cans or packages or boxes of Donald Duck Orange Juice, LaCroix mineral water, Dr. Pepper, cocktail napkins, decaf coffee, peanuts, Mr. & Mrs. T Bloody Mary Mix, Campbell's Tomato Juice, hot towels, olives, playing cards, Pawberry Punch, tonic water, Lipton tea bags, corkscrews, Mickey Mouse ears for kids, diapers, *Premiere* and *Field & Stream* and *Connoisseur* and *People* magazines.

And, in a fenced-in, locked-off area, miniature bottles of J&B Scotch, Courvoisier, Smirnoff vodka, Bacardi rum, Bailey's Irish Cream, Campari, and other liquors were shipped out to planes in special kits to cut down on pilferage, ninety bottles to a kit.

"When a short-haul plane comes in, say from Washington, D.C., we have fifteen minutes to stock it and clean it," said Ray Studle, who was in charge of the 150-person shift when I visited. "On a long-haul flight, we might have forty minutes. Might have thirty to forty planes on the ground at one time."

Military precision. As 714 came into Atlanta range, all these ground activities would be coordinated from the five-story Delta company airport tower, over Concourse A.

I'd visited that too, a big square room that looked like the Air Traffic Control tower, except it was shorter, and staffed only by Delta people. As each "push" occurred, the massive coordinated fleet arrivals and departures, Delta staff in the tower monitored incoming flights to alert other departments of their arrival, passed along special requests or problems, coordinated all the minute by minute airport activities, from assigning gates to updating the crucial Infax machines, to alerting the company if they monitored the captain radioing the FAA tower with an emergency. The Delta tower could call cockpits on a separate frequency, but they weren't allowed to break in on control tower transmissions.

The Delta ramp tower had been the busiest place I visited during my months with Delta, when it always seemed to be raining at the airport during tours, and the staff was always operating under pressure. That morning, during a push, the tower coordinators were barraged by a series of minute by minute problems. Planes late. Planes breaking down. Teletype machines machine-gunning equipment changes, gate changes. Two planes aborted takeoffs and needed to return to the gate, but which gate, since they were all occupied? A Delta captain, hearing that he would have two extra passengers on board, refused to take off until the company computed whether the extra weight kept his plane safe. Another captain was ready to go but Catering hadn't stocked the plane yet, and the passengers were getting angry.

A flight due in from Miami was delayed in Florida because of engine trouble, so at least that gate could be used for another plane, except then the Miami plane would be coming in when all the gates were full.

"As bad as it is now, it's going to get worse later," said one coordinator, meaning that delays have a ripple effect on pushes later in the day. He was right. Problems kept multiplying. Radar was out at O'Hare Airport, and everything was late taking off there. None of the passengers on a 727 inbound to Atlanta from Chicago would make their connections. The tower had to relay this information to Delta agents at the gate. A plane was late taking off because of a bad oven. The weather was worsening over Texas.

Throughout it all, the problems were handled, business as usual. The tower reminded me of a newspaper city room where the reporters worked on deadline, talking low and fast, getting things done but having no time for anything else. Each man or woman at his station. One coordinating maintenance, one food and cleaning. One talking to gate agents, advising them of schedule changes. One monitoring incoming cruise ships out of San Juan or Miami, making sure passengers made their airline connections. Another calling up an aerial computer depiction of the airport, with little glowing planes on the screen at gates, showing the type of plane, the size, the time of departure.

That planes actually flew according to schedules sometimes astounded me.

Weird delay department. "Baggage people opened the back cargo bin one time, and a chimpanzee got out of a cage back there," Mark Gunthorpe told me, while he worked monitoring the gate planning computer. "It tore up the plane. We tried to board with a tranquilizer gun, and somehow the chimp got hold of the gun. Everyone ran out. It was in there for hours, running around with the tranquilizer gun.

"Another time, one morning, a plane was ready to go and someone saw a duck stuck to the wing. Nobody knew how it got there. It was alive. But stuck. Maybe it froze on the wing. It took forty minutes to get it unstuck, and then it flew away."

I thought of all those passengers sitting around the waiting lounge, reading magazines, getting impatient, asking the smiling gate agent why the plane was delayed, having no idea a chimpanzee with a tranquilizer gun was rampaging down the aisles.

"How about you?" I asked. "Any difference between a chimp and a mechanical delay?"

He laughed. "A delay's a delay."

• • •

We came in smoothly and touched down and reached the gate on schedule. I could see the welcome towers of downtown Atlanta. The new captain, Fred Gordon, got on and gave me his card. It had a steer on it. Fred Gordon owned a ranch near Atlanta, he said.

In an hour we'd be lifting off again, heading south this time, along the busy southeastern corridor to Florida.

I thought back to that ruin in the Louisiana woods, the old Delta headquarters, and a black and white picture I'd seen of it. In the photo, the building looked about as big as a small one-story house, with its arched doorways, four windows, and a man in a white shirt and tie standing outside, hands in his pockets, gazing off in the distance, clearly having nothing to do. A small sign near the building said, "Danger, beware of propeller." The planes parked that close to the building. There was no push going on, like there was now. No Dobbs Food Service and maintenance workers with radios and Infax machines and Delta tower. The man in the white shirt looked like the TV Maytag repairman. The loneliest guy in town.

I remembered another photo I'd seen showing all the pilots and mechanics and Mr. C. E. Woolman—always Mister—standing in front of a plane. A dozen men in a semicircle, on a field of dirt, in 1929. The whole staff.

I left the cockpit and joined the stream of departing passengers heading out into the terminal, going home on a Friday night. A businessman in a blue cotton suit met by his redheaded wife and little girl in the waiting area. A college-age boy with a small knapsack, treading off alone toward the baggage carousel. Two elderly women, traveling companions, sitting down to wait for the next leg, on their way to Fort Lauderdale.

But mostly my attention was caught by a sour-faced man in a beret, standing beside a woman, looking disapprovingly from his watch to the clock in the terminal. Clearly something that had happened on ship 714 had distressed the passenger. I moved closer to see if I could hear what he was saying. But I was still astounded by all the incredible coordinated complexity that had gone into the flight.

The man frowned.

"Six minutes late," he said.

GRITS MEETS SUSHI

Back on the night before I visited Delta for the first time, I'd had dinner in an Atlanta restaurant with a lawyer friend who asked, over Budweisers, "What do you think will happen on your first day there?"

I rolled my eyes. "The PR people will take me to lunch," I said. "And?"

"There will be two of them. After a while one will start looking solemn and say," I said, leaning forward, parodying it, "Bob, I have to tell you something. I mean it. This is a greeeeat company."

The lawyer laughed. I said, "And the other one will say, '*really* great.' The first one will say, 'The people here are fan-tastic. My boss is terrrrrrific.' "

The lawyer laughed harder. "The other one will say, '*Really* terrific,' " I said.

"That's what happens every time you have lunch with PR people," I said. "Then you meet them a year later, and they say, 'I quit that place. It was full of jerks.' "

The next day I went to lunch with Paulette O'Donnell and her boss, PR Vice Pres. Bill Berry. We had fried chicken and cole slaw and sweet tea from mason jars at a truck stop near the airport. When dessert came, apple pie, Paulette said, "Bob, I have to tell you something. I mean it. Delta is a great company."

"Really great," Bill said.

"Our chairman, Ron Allen, is terrific."

"Ter-rific," Bill nodded.

"*Really* terrific," Paulette said.

I kept eating. I thought, I hate this. In the days that followed it didn't stop. Paulette drummed the message in daily. Delta was "special." Delta employees loved the company. They stayed for years. They were unbelievably loyal. She read me a magazine story referring to a "typical Delta love-in." Delta was a "family." Delta was "people."

Finally I couldn't stand it anymore. We were driving through downtown Buckhead, an Atlanta suburb, heading for a luncheon meeting of retired pilots, and Paulette, steering her black Lexus through about the six hundreth street I'd seen with the name of Peachtree, was waxing eloquent again about the special relationship management and employees had at Delta.

People company? I told her. Give me a break. That's the biggest lie in the vocabulary. Every company says they're a people company. You ever see those TWA commercials with smiling workers? Carl Icahn fired all his striking flight attendants. Hitler probably said, "This is a people Reich."

Paulette looked shocked.

I told Paulette about a magazine story I'd just finished writing. It was about South Africa, where I'd been sent by *Outside* magazine. Just before I'd flown to Johannesburg, the South African tourist board had given me a video so I could get a "feel" for the country. The tape had shown smiling face after face; black people, white people, Asian people, while a Teutonic-accented voice announced, "South Africa is *people*."

Then I'd gone to South Africa and visited the shantytowns and almost been machine-gunned in a riot and read notices on my hotel door saying, "Don't give black employees liquor." I'd watched friends of mine, white homeowners in Capetown, lock each room in their house, backing out of it and setting different alarms just to go to a restaurant. They were terrified of the "people." Other whites had warned me, each time I left any hotel, "Don't take the train to Johannesburg. People have been hacked to death." "Don't drive into the townships. People have been burned to death." "Don't pick up hitchhikers. People have been knifed to death."

People? I said to Paulette. Every heartless MBA in the world, every Detroit CEO firing employees while giving himself a raise, every shlocky commercial I see on television says, "This is a people airline. A people bank. A people computer company. And meanwhile everyone in the home office is at each other's throats."

Only when it came to Delta, I turned out to be wrong.

Now 714 was in the air again. Over southern Georgia with 302 more passengers. On time again. Fully stocked again. Up at 33,000 feet over clear skies, on the Friday night leg to Fort Lauderdale. Businessmen relaxing in back after a hard week. Couples sipping drinks or holding hands, on their way south for a weekend. The mood friendly, relaxed.

I realized, as usual, that the crew was also in good spirits. Watching Capt. Fred Gordon joking with the flight attendants who brought us coffee, I remembered how the mechanics I'd spent shifts with, the baggage handlers, the company operators in the ramp towers, the ticket agents, the flight attendants, the market analysts, had always seemed to like their work. That there had been a lack of even mild forms of labor/management friction that existed in many companies.

"Think about the mood at the home office when you walk through the corridors," Pilot Jack Saux, an ALPA union representative at Delta, had told me. "Nobody rushes. Everyone says hello. People walk around with smiles on their faces. Do you really think it's like that at other airlines?"

He was right. And it couldn't be underestimated. In defining the reasons behind Delta's surge from a regional carrier to a global one, and its prosperity during a time when other airlines were going out of business, I'd left out a key component in the company's success. A big reason why 714 was filled with passengers tonight instead of flying, half-empty, along the same route.

All the wonderful scheduling and equipment and clever marketing in the world couldn't save an airline if labor relations were wrecking it from the inside.

And at Delta, pilots and dispatchers aside, employees didn't even belong to unions. Whenever unions tried to organize them, employees voted them down.

The *Financial Times* put it this way:

> Delta is an unusually cheery place considering the airline indus-
> try is still trying to recover from its worst slump in 40 years. . . . Delta
> commands perhaps more corporate loyalty among its employees than
> any other US concern. Its paternalistic style of management is a
> blend of its own Deep South American roots, with its old conserva-
> tive values, and of the Japanese corporate ethos in which, without
> unions, jobs are guaranteed, pay levels are above average and work-
> ers, in return, are expected to put the company first.

Now I remembered how, shortly after I'd arrived at Delta I'd attended a retirement party for lead mechanic Jerry Ramsey in a bar
near the airport, buy-one-get-one-free-night, and met him for
breakfast at Shoney's and a golf game the next day. Ramsey had
worked on the big international L-1011s for over eighteen years. I'd
figured that now that he was retired he'd be more open about
gripes he had with the company. I knew he was only one person
out of 77,000, but I'd learn that his attitude was representative.

Ramsey had been a solid looking man with a flattop haircut, out
of World War II. He looked like the character Maurice, actor Barry
Corbin, on the television hit "Northern Exposure." Over bacon and
eggs we talked about the Pan Am acquisition, the debt load Delta
carried, the new routes to Europe. I was impressed with his knowledge, and later I would realize every Delta employee knew company finances, strategy, logistics—much more than just their job.

I'd asked Ramsey if during his thirty years as a mechanic he'd
missed having unions. He'd shaken his head.

"Didn't you ever worry about losing your job?" I said.

"Nope."

"Or health benefits or salary? What about if you had an argument
with management?"

"You can always talk to management. And whenever other airlines got raises, so did we. Our management is smart. When the pilots get anything, we come in under it. Look at other companies,"
said Ramsey, shaking his head. "The mechanic opens the engine.
Then the electrician has to pull out the wire. I don't need those
stupid rules. I don't need an electrician to do that. I *want* to do
that."

Another time, flying from LaGuardia to Atlanta, I'd sat beside a former Pan Am baggage supervisor who worked for Delta now. He didn't want to be named.

"At Delta, management tells us *why* they do things," he said. "That makes a difference. At Pan Am they never told us anything. Then again," he laughed, "they were stealing everything, so I guess they didn't want to tell us. At Delta, if you do your work, you're well rewarded. If you don't, there's accountability. If just one bag is left behind when the plane leaves, they want to know why. You better not pass the buck. At Pan Am guys would leave bags. At Delta, forget it," he said, shaking his head. "They'll say, you saw it, didn't you? Why didn't you do something about it? You can't get away with 'It isn't my job.'"

Pretty different from Eastern, Pan Am, TWA. Eastern had bought modern equipment and L-1011s, just like Delta. They'd used new computers, just like Delta. They'd organized a complex schedule as well as Delta. But bad morale and labor trouble had helped destroy the company.

"The unions ended up losing over 40,000 jobs at Eastern," wrote Jack E. Robinson in *Free Fall*. "The individuals who lost these jobs also lost a way of life, perhaps needlessly. Charlie Bryan, Eastern's IAM leader, more than anyone else involved, lost credibility. His positions on wages in the early 1980s, his intransigence, which led to the sale to Texas Air in 1986, his determination to strike at any cost, which led to the bankruptcy filing in 1989, all, when taken as a whole, caused more trouble at Eastern than any other single action or event."

At TWA, bankrupt as of this writing, flight attendants struck when Carl Icahn took over the company, and ordered massive pay cuts and work rule changes. TWA flight attendants I knew hated striking. They hated getting up at 4 A.M. on winter mornings and walking with picket signs in the cold. They hated the lack of a paycheck. They missed working. In the end they lost their jobs and future at the company when they were fired. As of this writing, the union and company were still fighting it out in court, five years later.

At US Air, mechanics and flight attendants were out on strike as I wrote this chapter.

But at Delta, no full-time employee had been laid off, even during recessions, since 1957. Grateful employees had even chipped in and bought the company a new Boeing 767 to thank management.

The *Financial Times* said:

> Delta management philosophy underscores the theory that offering job security to employees creates loyalty to the company, confidence in its management and reduces staff resistance to change. In turn, good employee relations enhances productivity and profits, and in the case of airlines, leads to better customer service and satisfaction.
>
> It is no coincidence that Delta has for the 17th consecutive year led all the other big US Airlines with the lowest rate of consumer complaints to the US Department of Transport.

By the time I would finish this book, though, Delta would be furloughing pilots.

Now 714 passed over the Georgia/Florida border, cruising south at 570 miles an hour. The sun blazed in the west, turned the sky purple. Towns below were lit up. The sky misted over and the towns disappeared. We flew through a white mass, which occasionally thinned enough to see vague glows, Florida towns below. They looked other-worldly, ethereal through the fog.

Thinking about labor questions, I remembered Carla Sutera, a baggage handler I'd spent a shift with in Salt Lake City on a cool spring day. Once she'd worked at Western, before Delta absorbed it, as a union member. Now, at Delta, no union protected her.

I pictured the short, dirty-blond twenty-nine-year-old, wearing dark sunglasses against the desert glare, a hooded blue Delta sweatshirt over a black-and-white striped workshirt. And black rubber-soled shoes to help her walk up the slippery ramp loaders into baggage compartments. She carried a radio strapped to her back so she could talk to the main office as pushes came in and out. Small yellow foam earplugs hung on blue plastic wire around her neck.

"I like working big planes," she'd said. "It's a challenge to get them out on time. More passengers. More baggage.

"I remember when Western ended," she said quietly. She was a shy, private person, and we talked in the landing area, between pushes. "We read in the newspaper there was going to be a merger.

Management didn't tell us. No one was certain what that meant. Everyone talked about it in the lunchroom. Then these Delta bigwigs came in from Atlanta, and one by one we went in to meet with them. We were guaranteed a job. They said, 'You can take the job at this salary or not. If you want to sign on the line, fine.' If not, their legal obligation was over. They offered me the same position, at lower pay than handlers who'd started at Delta, but each month the Western people got a little more until we were the same.

"I felt weird. Scared. Like starting a new job all over. Most of us didn't like it at first. Delta was more image-conscious than Western. We couldn't wear color T-shirts under our uniforms anymore. We had to wear white. The men couldn't have beards. But finally we realized we would get a paycheck twice a month. We wouldn't have to worry about it."

"Do you miss the union?"

Carla shook her head. "Our medical benefits are comparable or better to other companies. Our salaries are high. You have to screw up a lot to get fired at Delta. And they expect us to have high standards. That's fine with me. Also, people extend themselves more here. Mechanics or pilots help with bags."

"Did that happen at Western?"

She laughed. "No."

We stopped as ship 715 came in from Atlanta, bound for Los Angeles and Honolulu. Carla drove a ramp loader to the rear baggage door. She coordinated the workers bringing baggage carts to the belly of the L-1011. She crab-walked up a ramp and crouched, entering the forward compartment, to move luggage from the plane. First off the jet was a mesh cage with a shivering German shepherd inside named Heidi. Animals coming out of baggage compartments were always quaking with fear. I thought I'd never send an animal on any airplane if I could avoid it.

"I talk to all the animals," she said.

Swiftly, Carla sent down boxes, duffel bags, golf clubs, and a box of fruit. Following color-coded stickers on the baggage, workers placed them on appropriate carts, to be loaded on other planes.

An eight-foot-long white cardboard box stenciled "Extreme Care," came down the ramp. The words "Containers, Incorporated," on the side, meant it was a coffin. Carla said. "It's a corpse."

It was going home to Bozeman, Montana. Baggage loaders drew blue curtains around it on its cart, its airport hearse.

"You learn to ignore them," she said. But she said, "It's so sad when it's a child."

Down came a blue knapsack going to Bozeman. A gym bag in candy pink. A mauve cosmetic case. A raspberry-colored canvas, strapless suitcase. There was a wooden box from a pet shop in Huntington, New York, stenciled "Live Tropical Fish" with a manifest on the side:

> Contents: twelve Colombian boas, two black pine snakes, 2 New Guinea viper boas, one African house snake, two Solomon Island ground boas, one ambon amethystine python, four green iguanas.

"Gives me the heebie-jeebies," said Carla, who was working her fourth push of the shift. Average day for Carla Sutera. She would work at least three more pushes today. Then she would attend a Little League game her stepson was playing in, make dinner for her stepsons and baggage-handler husband, read an installment of *The Firm*, and be asleep by ten.

"We move mail," she said. "And material going to Alaska for the pipeline. Flowers, all over the place. Penguins going to zoos. Miniature horses. I had three reindeer on a flight not long ago. Sometimes I think, watching the bags, that these are pieces of peoples' lives. I look at the flowers and think, Someone will be lucky to get these. The bags are like a puzzle, going from place to place. Boxes of pineapples from Hawaii. You know someone had a good time, on vacation. Battered bags that look like they've been around the world. You wonder where they're going. Where they've been."

"Do you fly overseas a lot? You can go for free," I said.

She blushed. "I never did." She was a nervous flier.

I went into the cinder-block station just off the loading area, where company printouts taped to the wall gave handlers the latest corporate financial news: big loss this quarter. There I met Tom Brothers, another baggage loader who'd been in the union back at Western.

He was a handsome man, who'd had a chance to play pro football, he said. He'd been with the Cleveland Browns for a week, injured his wrist, wrecked any chance of being a professional athlete, and gone to work for Western a few days later.

"I never liked the union. Why should I pay dues to protect someone who's a fake?" he said. "Delta's a family. I didn't believe that when I first heard it. But there's no need for a union here. The company addresses problems. I remember when Delta first came here, they were going to eliminate our 2:30 shifts. We were upset about it. A couple of the old guys, with their union attitudes, said, We're gonna start a petition. And they did. And got several hundred names on it. When management got wind of it, they said, Whoa, let's take care of it locally. They called a meeting of all the handlers, which had never happened before. They said, This is why we want to eliminate the shift. But we want to hear from you. Why are you angry? Why do you want to *keep* the shift?

"We were surprised because management was listening to us without our having to go through the union. I mean, when you have management and union, there's always friction. In the end Delta didn't eliminate the 2:30 shift. And those guys who started the petition never started another one."

"The Western way was, if you had a problem, you went to the union man. The Delta way is, go through your supervisor. If that doesn't work, you can go to his boss. You can even go through *his* boss."

I went back to Carla Sutera. She was working a 727, during another push. As she helped load bags on carts, she said that in summer, coming soon, loads would be down. In the heavy air, planes needed to be lighter to take off. There would be less work for baggage people.

"For every degree the temperature goes up, there's something like 1,700 less pounds we can carry in the planes," she said.

I said, watching how hard she worked, "I guess you're looking forward to summer."

Carla looked surprised. "Are you kidding?" she said. "Work's my job security. I hate to see a big plane go out carrying only 100 bags."

Maurice Worth, senior vice president of personnel, had been at the meetings with the Western baggage handlers too. He'd been the Delta management representative present, the liaison between

Delta and Western, in Salt Lake City to help the merger go smoothly. He'd done the same thing at Northeast.

"We met with every shift," said Worth, a silver-haired, heavyset, amiable man in aviator glasses and a red-and-white striped shirt. "I remember when I mentioned to the management staff there that we were going to do that, the head of labor relations laughed at me. 'They'll eat your lunch,' he told me. 'I'll give you three days.' He didn't come to the meetings."

Maurice's wall in his Atlanta office featured big black-and-white photographs of Delta personnel: a smiling baggage handler, a flight attendant bending to serve a passenger with a tray, two pilots walking toward an airplane.

"We met in the baggage room," he said. "There were about seventy-five people there. They were quiet, standing in back, some tough-looking characters. They didn't know what to make of this kind of meeting. I was used to it, but I was nervous. You don't know if someone will go for your throat. The first thing anyone said was, 'This bag room stinks. It smells like fish.'

"And I answered, 'We're experts in running an airline, not dead fish.' They laughed. I said, 'What do you think about it?' The ice was broken. Later I ran into the manager who had told me I'd never survive in there. He looked pretty sheepish.

"Look," Worth said, leaning forward, "there's a certain amount of pride in wanting to make things right. You have to face these people at meetings once a year. Or they show up in my office. I can't ask a manager to explain something to them that I don't believe in. On a day-to-day basis, we have personnel representatives in key cities. Their phone numbers are published. Workers are encouraged to go to them. Sometimes they go to them instead of their manager. Like a buffer.

"So far it's working," he said.

Part of the reason management at Delta seemed sensitive to labor was the company's practice of promoting from within. Worth had started out as a ramp service agent in Dallas. Ron Allen, Delta's chairman of the board, began as a part-time analyst. David Garrett, the chairman before him, started as a reservations clerk. Whitley Hawkins, the president of Delta, worked gates at the Lexington, Kentucky, airport. Harry Alger, senior vice president of operations, was a flight engineer on Delta planes and later a pilot.

On a more local level, one of Carla Sutera's supervisors at Salt Lake City, Shan Larson, started as a reservations clerk.

She told me, "That makes all the difference in the world. It gives you empathy for what people are doing, and they know it. Say I'm talking to someone about a disciplinary problem. They didn't follow safety rules, and they're trying to tell me it wasn't necessary. They drive a forklift, and they're not supposed to take it under the wing of an airplane, but they did. They tell me, 'It's the only way to get it lined up to load the plane.' Well," she said, "I drove a forklift. I know it's not true. There is another way.

"They respect you for it."

Middle management had the same gratefulness to be at the company that their staffs did. And they paid attention to little details too. I sat around with Portland acting Station Manager George Marks one day and watched him fill out an employee commendation for a baggage handler.

"What did he do?" I said.

"Helped someone fix a car."

"A passenger in the airport?"

"No, on his way home. Not a passenger. Some woman's car broke down, and he fixed it."

"Wait a minute," I said. "The company's giving him a commendation for helping someone when he was off duty? Helping someone who wasn't even a passenger?"

"Well, he had his Delta shirt on, and she saw it, and wrote us. That kind of publicity is priceless."

William Felker, another Delta station manager in New Orleans, had been an intense-looking, short, dark, jowly man who told me, at a retirement party for a Delta pilot, "I started out eighteen years ago out of high school. I had no education. Delta Air Lines educated me and gave me a livelihood. Gave me an opportunity to be perceived as the most successful person in my family. There are hundreds of people like me out there. Do you know that Delta just gave us a 7 percent raise? In the middle of a recession, a 7 percent raise? I went to a meeting of station managers, and there was a financial guy there and he said, 'It's a bad idea, the raise.' But they gave it to us. That raise costs $120 million a year. Do you realize how much senior management has faith in us, that we'll go out there and find a way to make up that shortfall?"

He leaned closer. His face was flushed. He said, practically gripping my sleeve, "We'll find a way. To get the passengers. To get the $120 million, and that's $120 million a year, not just for one year. But senior management knows we're good for it. *We'll make it up!*"

Finally I went back to Paulette O'Donnell and told her I'd been wrong. Delta really did seem to be a "family." Sometimes the togetherness drove me crazy. Like when I wanted to interview one person, and a committee would show up. I'd schedule a meeting with a pilot, and he'd say, when four of them arrived, "I thought Joe would want to talk to you, and Sam and Eddie and Fred." I'd call to ask to speak with a retiree, and three would be there when I arrived at Paulette's office.

First I thought it was a fluke, then I saw it was a habit. Once, when I was touring the reservations department, every time I walked into a room, supervisors would call clerks over to talk to me. Each clerk would give a little speech he'd prepared. How the department operated. What they did. It was clear they'd been told I was coming. It was irritating because for months I kept telling Paulette, when she arranged visits, that I wanted to talk to one person at a time, not twenty. Then I realized the lengths management had gone to, to make the clerks feel involved in the project. Other times, in different departments, I was asked, Do you mind telling everyone here what you're doing? Giving a little talk?

And then there were the meetings. Regularly scheduled gripe sessions, in every department, between management and labor. Annual sessions between top management and anyone who wanted to come. Visits to outlying stations. Closed-door free-for-alls with baggage handlers, flight attendants, clerks. There was the sense that at Delta, everybody, from the CEO to the maintenance crew, had to account for their actions sooner or later.

Again, the notion that senior management would actually sit still and be grilled by lower employees had seemed farfetched to me until the senior vice president of operations, Harry Alger, asked me if I wanted to fly to New Orleans with him to watch him address a meeting of Delta pilot union (ALPA) representatives. And later attend an "in command seminar," a question-and-answer session between him and Chairman Ron Allen, and new pilots. Alger said the questions could get pretty blunt at times.

The New Orleans meeting took place in the French Quarter at the Bourbon Orleans Hotel. Alger faced a ballroom-sized horse-shoe-shaped table of union representatives from a podium. The mood was cordial, with the reps chuckling good-naturedly when New Orleans representative Jack Saux jokingly called union members communists. Everyone wore ties and jackets. Outside, the sun was dazzling on the cobblestones and balconies, and the air smelled of raspberry-flavored coffee from a shop across the street.

Alger opened the meeting with his standard speech about needed cutbacks in an age of austerity. "Your company is under the burden of several billion dollars in lawsuits. Business as usual?" he said, using the line I'd heard him say at other speeches. "Hell no!" But at a union meeting, that could be inflammatory. At other airlines austerity had meant salary cuts, work rule changes, strikes. It was clear from Alger's words that in the not-too-distant future, Delta employees would be called on to make sacrifices too.

"Revenues from fares are down," Alger said. "If we continue to lose money in the magnitude and scope we are now, and we continue to invest in new airplanes and facilities, that equals increased borrowing, increased interest. The situation is 'significant.'"

But the pilots basically accepted the analysis, at least for the moment, trusting it, and the questions, when they came, seemed more cooperative than antagonistic. The reps were more like members of a team acquiring information than antagonists preparing for battle. Would "globalization" of the air industry mean Delta would have to deal with lots of little competitors like Air Florida and People Express, low-priced airlines, springing up all over the planet? Could Delta help the U.S. government become more "machismo" in the way they thwarted foreign airline demands for access to U.S. markets, instead of caving in to them? Would Delta's new long-haul MD-11s be equipped with bunks for crew members on the Asia runs? Wasn't the company wrong in opposing federal legislation to improve work rules for flight attendants, since the proposed legislation would hurt low-budget airlines more?

What about the quality of hotels during layovers? Was Delta doing anything to improve them?

The relationship between Alger and the pilots seemed as much defined by the respectful mood as the inquiries themselves. Yes, the company was looking into hotels, Alger said. No, it would be better to fight flight attendant work-rule proposals because they would cost Delta millions. And Delta flight attendants themselves were helping to lobby against them in Washington. Yes, Delta was trying to strengthen the government's position in keeping foreign airlines out of U.S. domestic markets.

At the in-command seminar, which occurred two weeks later, the questions got rougher. We were in another hotel, this time near Hartsfield Airport. This time it was Alger and Ron Allen at a table in front of another group of pilots.

Both executives looked natty in well-cut suits. Allen was a big man, balding in a way that accentuated dignity rather than detracted from it, wearing a blue-and-white striped shirt and a tie with a maroon pattern matching the linen bunting hanging from the table.

The pilots, in ties and jackets, were all ages, since the occasion marked graduation to flying all kinds of Delta planes.

"Do you think we're visible enough in Europe?" one pilot demanded. Allen admitted better marketing was necessary. "A few years ago we were doing generic advertising for all countries. That didn't get the job done. Now we're targeting country by country," he said.

The pilot pushed harder. "Well, what about group tours and packaging. Are we doing that?"

Yes. But it needs a lot of work.

"I don't disagree with you," the pilot said.

"Is Douglas helping us with the icing problem on the MD-88?" someone asked. Yes, Alger said.

"How susceptible are we to computer viruses?"

This was a big question since the planes use computers in flight. "We had a virus in a few computers on the ground. We hired someone to check it," Allen said.

When the subject of lobbying in Washington came up, one pilot asked pointedly if Delta's team was effective there. "We were surprised to learn Pan Am's liaison wasn't known in Washington," he said. "Is ours?"

Allen said, "He works with legislative aides. He used to be a legislative aide. We have good relationships with both the Senate and House chairpersons of the aviations subcommittees. We have a very effective relationship with the FAA."

The pilot seemed doubtful, and Allen unperturbed. After the meeting, he came over to ask me how the book was coming. I told him I was surprised at the candor of the meeting. Allen shrugged. It was no big deal to him. That's the way things are around here, he said.

The first major labor dispute in aviation occurred in 1919, when airmail pilots walked off the job. The reason was fog. The instigator was pilot Leon Smith, nicknamed "Bonehead" because he once walked into a whirling propeller and survived.

Bonehead was supposed to lift off from Belmont field on Long Island that day and carry sacks of mail to Washington, but he refused. In the last two weeks, fifteen airmail planes had crashed in fog. Of all weather problems experienced by early pilots, fog was the most deadly. Pilots could see thunderstorms and fly below or around them. In heavy winds they could set the planes down in fields. But in fog they couldn't tell where land was, could fly into trees thinking they were fields. On that morning, the fog was so thick Leon Smith couldn't even see the end of the landing field. When he wouldn't take off, he was fired.

The backup pilot refused too. And was fired.

The pilots struck. They were sick of nonfliers telling them to go up in hazardous weather. "We will insist that the man who risks his own life be the judge—not somebody who stays on the ground and risks other peoples' lives," a pilots' manifesto read.

Four days later they got their way. From then on, in bad weather, pilots would not have to fly unless field managers, who would also be pilots, went up to check the skies.

By the early 1930s the Air Lines Pilot Association (ALPA) had formed, but it was a weak organization, and airlines suspecting that one of their pilots had joined it frequently moved them to another city.

ALPA pushed for better pay, fewer hours, and safer equipment for pilots. Average pay rose from $250 a month to $600. When Century Airlines Chief E. L. Cord, the Frank Lorenzo of the 1930s, cut the pay to $150, pilots struck and hired planes to fly alongside Cord's airliners, painted "Century is unfair to pilots" on the side.

Airlines wanted pilots to fly 140 hours a month. ALPA got the number reduced to eighty-five hours. It's seventy-five hours at Delta now. And also had a hand in introducing the bidding system and the seniority system by which pilots, and later other airline personnel, request jobs and shifts on a monthly basis.

ALPA opened a permanent Washington office. The organization is active today in lobbying for safety, antiterrorism measures, and in safeguarding pilots' work rules in airlines.

Delta pilots joined ALPA in 1935, and promptly aroused the ire of Mister C. P. Woolman by intervening in Washington when precious airmail route 24 came up for renewal, until Woolman granted a pay raise. Charles Dolson, the pilot who brought ALPA into Delta, said Woolman never forgave him, but nonetheless kept advancing him through the company. In 1970 he became chairman of the board.

Delta's mechanics were unionized in 1936, and stayed that way until 1947, when the United Auto Workers (UAW-CIO) and the International Association of Machinists were battling to represent them. Delta hesitated to give mechanics a pay raise, and the UAW-CIO called a wildcat strike.

But some mechanics kept working. Then the Fulton County Superior Court issued a restraining order against picketers, limiting the number of pickets the union could have to two. Then a companywide pay raise took the wind out of the union sails. The mechanics' contract expired and was not renewed. The union was out. In 1949, some mechanics began a campaign to bring in another union, and it was voted down.

That's the way it's been since.

At Delta, the importance of all the basic communication could not be underestimated. One Atlanta management consultant told me a story about a company he advised to talk to workers and find out what they wanted. Management refused to talk to them itself.

"Delta does it every day," he said, "without paying an outsider."

Another time, after listening to an ex-Pan Am baggage supervisor go on for half an hour about the way Delta management talks to workers, I said, "It sounds kind of basic to me."

"Yeah," he'd said. "But Pan Am didn't do it."

And I remembered another corporate consultant, who works with Japanese companies in New York, who had asked me my impressions of Delta. I'd told him about flying to New Orleans with Harry Alger and the "in command seminar."

"Sounds Japanese," he'd said.

In the end I understood why Paulette O'Donnell told me all those stories about the Delta "family." Why she got this weird Moonie expression on her face whenever the subject came up. Why flight attendants on the Honolulu leg had asked me, concern on their faces, "You're not going to write something bad about Delta, are you?" Why a gate agent in Cincinnati had said, "This is my job, and I want to do it right." Why the chief of the ramp tower in Salt Lake City had told me, "I'm lucky to work here." Why pilot after pilot I flew with said, "Delta was my first choice." Why mechanics I met on the midnight shift told me, "I love it." Why even the L-1011 pilot who called me at home one day to gripe about the company said, when I asked him if he'd rather work somewhere else, "Are you crazy?"

Okay, Paulette, you win. Delta is a people company.

Ship 714 descended through thick clouds toward Fort Lauderdale's airport—at least that was what the altimeter said, since I couldn't see land. Capt. Fred Gordon worked the controls. He was a bearish, friendly, deep-voiced man with a hint of sadness in his expression. He invited me out to his cattle ranch near Atlanta, to visit and look at the Georgia countryside with him.

The clouds were no problem for 714, although they were the kind of obstacle that had caused that first pilot's strike in 1919. We banked left, our floodlights forming tunnels through the moving mist ahead, then shining back in our eyes, the mist rushing toward me so fast I had to avert my head because it seemed like the glass bubble would collide with it.

Then we broke from the cloud bank, into a luminous dusk sky studded with bright stars. Seven-fourteen was over the Atlantic, I saw Fort Lauderdale all lit up ahead. By a trick of light, I thought another plane headed toward us, but it turned out to be a ship below. And I understood why pilots said at dusk, when the boundary between earth and sky merged, you could lose your bearings.

It was hard for me to believe 714 had now flown over 15,000 miles in less than seventy-two hours. Had carried, so far on this rotation, roughly 2,200 passengers since I'd boarded it.

The airport grew larger. We touched down smoothly, and I heard clapping in back. We rolled to the terminal, on time again. Captain Gordon would take us back to Atlanta, on the last leg of this rotation before I got off. I felt as if I had been in the plane for weeks.

Fred Gordon unstrapped himself and got up and walked to the doorway. His uniform was immaculate. His cap was in place. He stood by the doorway smiling at the departing passengers, the symbol of the Delta family to them. "Thanks," they were saying. "Thanks for the flight." "Nice flight." "Thank you." "Good-bye."

Fred Gordon smiled back at them and said thank-you too. He was the image they'd take home with them from the flight. Harry Alger had told the pilots at the "in command seminar," "I want to thank you for the job you do. There are many things you do, little routines, but they really stand out as different. One thing you do is come out of that cockpit and thank our passengers for flying with Delta. And that little gesture on your part does more . . . I get more of my business friends who fly Delta, Oh, by the way, they say, that captain was standing by the door. When you can make that kind of contact with the passengers, and with fellow employees, help them out, thank them for a job well done, answer questions, you don't know the impact that has."

Fred Gordon grinned and nodded and said, "Thanks." "Thanks for flying with us." "Thanks." "Thanks." A soothing image. A friendly image. A family image. And more than just an image. I'm starting to sound as sappy as Paulette O'Donnell. He was another Delta employee happy in his work.

COFFEE? TEA? ME?

As desperate as airlines were in their early days to attract passengers, it never occurred to them to hire flight attendants, women who would pamper customers and serve as examples of calm when flights got rough.

Airlines thought of offering special prices as incentives to fliers. They invented credit cards. They gave out certificates certifying First Class fliers as "admirals" in the fleet. They ferried passengers to airfields in luxury coaches. Their representatives spoke at civic clubs on the advantages of air travel. Their station managers hung out in bars to drum up business.

On board, copilots served box lunches to the handful of travelers brave enough to risk the bumpy, uncertain rides. And since copilots and pilots were both gun toting, mail-guarding, seat-of-the-pants type fliers, they may not have been the image airlines wanted to project. Passengers preferred to see Jimmy Stewart at the controls. Not Jack Palance.

The idea of including women in the crew never came up.

Steve Simpson, the manager of Boeing Air Transport's San Francisco office, proposed a small change. He suggested hiring stewards, Filipinos, small men who would move around easily in the cramped cabins, attendants like those serving U.S. Navy ships. Simpson figured the cheerful faces would keep passengers' spirits up on rocky rides.

Then Ellen Church walked into his office. The San Francisco

nurse was a flying enthusiast who, like other aviation pioneers, had become interested in flight at early air shows. She'd thrilled to stunt flier Ruth Law, doing loops at a Midwest fair.

Church proposed that Simpson hire women flight attendants. Nurses who would come in handy when passengers became airsick.

Simpson shot off a memo to the home office when she left. Quoted in *Conquest of the Skies*, it read:

> It strikes me that there would be great psychological punch to having young women stewardesses or couriers or whatever you want to call them. . . . I have in mind a couple of graduate nurses that would make exceptional stewardesses. Of course it would be distinctly understood that there would be no reference to their hospital training or nursing experience, but it would be a mighty fine thing to have this available, sub rosa, if necessary for airsickness.
>
> Imagine the psychology of having young women as regular members of the crew. Imagine the national publicity we could get from it, and the tremendous effect it would have on the travelling public. Also, imagine the value they would be to us not only in the neater and nicer method of serving food but looking out for the passenger's welfare.

Not to mention that attractive flight attendants would give passengers something better to look at than baggage.

Boeing senior management immediately saw the advantages of the idea.

So Ellen Church became the first chief stewardess. She and the other seven nurse/flight attendants Boeing hired had to be under twenty-five years old, weigh under 115 pounds, and stand under 5 feet 4 inches tall. They wore uniforms of green twill: double breasted jackets and skirts, a cape for outdoors, chunky-heeled lace-up shoes, and a beretlike hat.

They served the same meal, morning, noon, and night. Coffee, fruit cocktail, rolls, and fried chicken from steam chests. Once one of the attendants' planes ran out of gas and landed in a wheatfield in Wyoming. The attendant told Carl Solberg, "People came in wagons and on horseback to see the plane. They'd never seen one before. They wanted to touch it and touch me."

If no seats were available on a flight, attendants sat on mail sacks. If the planes weighed too much to climb over mountains, pilots landed, put off an attendant or two, and took off again. One big job the new employees had was to make sure passengers on their way to the bathroom didn't accidentally open the exit door instead.

In the generally masculine world of flight, pilots resented having women crew members. And their wives liked it less. But passengers loved it. TWA surveyed their customers to find out if they wanted women flight attendants. Respondents said "no" but TWA's passengers defected to United at a brisk pace.

American added stewardesses in 1933, TWA in 1935. Eastern hired nurses too but switched to male stewards until World War II, when the able-bodied men were all drafted, and airline President Eddie Rickenbacker bowed to the inevitable.

Stewardesses passed out chewing gum to help equalize pressure on passengers' ears. As planes got bigger, on long sleeper flights to Florida or the West Coast, or the Pan Am Clippers to Hawaii, they turned down bunks, roused passengers, handed out morning orange juice, and arranged tables for breakfast.

Delta, conservative as usual, inaugurated female flight attendant service in 1940, on DC-2 planes, between Atlanta and Dallas/Fort Worth. Birdie Perkins, a flight attendant on that first day, came to the company from an Alabama hospital where she had been assistant night supervisor of nurses. Her $60 a month salary as a nurse jumped to $110 at Delta. Her mother begged her not to go. It was dangerous, she said. Her two-week training included courses in food service, ticketing, scheduling, and meteorology. She was required, on paper, to be able to make an instrument landing of the plane.

Birdie and other Delta attendants were warned that passenger complaints would mean instant dismissal. They wore navy blue uniforms in winter, beige in summer. On longer flights they served ham, potato soufflé and thermoses of coffee. But what they didn't do, what no airline did in the 1930s, was serve liquor. European airlines had long been serving alcohol. Pan Am provided overseas passengers with wine and hard drinks. It wasn't until the 1950s, when most states had finally repealed their prohibition laws, that Colonial Airlines began serving liquor on flights to Bermuda. The response was so enthusiastic TWA and American put drinks on too. Delta, with its large number of Bible Belt passengers, held out. So did United, where Pat Patterson, who had been the first airline executive to approve stewardesses on planes, now had a daughter at American serving drinks. He objected to that. As if she were some lowly barmaid.

But drinking on planes was much too popular. Patterson relented in 1955.

By the early 1960s, when my wife was a little girl watching jets overhead from her front yard in New England, being a stewardess was the most glamorous job she and a whole generation of future flight attendants could imagine.

"They looked so beautiful in those hats and gloves," she said.

Long before I met anyone at Delta, I'd been hearing stewardess stories from my wife. At parties, at business meetings, at dinners, people always asked her, "What's it really like to be a stewardess?" And often there was an odd mixture of fascination and disdain in their voices.

Sometimes she told a story about a man who'd asked her out on a date, become obnoxious on it, and when she turned down another invitation, shouted at the street, *I dated a stewardess!*"

She told more stories, about days off in Greece, London, Zurich, Cairo. She'd flown all over the world for free during her off-time.

"What about sex on planes?" people would eventually ask. And she'd tell my favorite story, about one kind of jet that had an elevator in it and a galley under the cabin. Stewards and stewardesses would go down in the elevator and have sex during flights, she said. In fact, on her first day working that plane a male attendant had asked her, "Want to see the galley?"

"When I got down there he'd set up music, and blacklight posters. He wanted to have sex," she said.

"Did you do it?"

"No."

"What kind of plane was this?" people asked.

"A Lockheed 1011."

One time she phoned me from an airplane, and as we talked, I heard a passenger come up and say, "Hey! Baby! You? Me? Paris? Dinner? Tonight?"

"No thanks."

"No thanks?" the man said. "Well—uh, then—uh, can I have a Coke?"

Later my wife left her job and became a successful business-woman. Interviewers seemed amazed that a flight attendant could do that.

Snobs.

And now, as a Delta gate agent in Fort Lauderdale announced boarding for ship 714's last flight of this rotation, its return trip to Atlanta, inside the plane chief flight attendant Marvin Scott took his station by the door to greet the handful of passengers trickling on.

Watching the easy exchanges between crew and customer, it struck me how inconceivable it would be to passengers getting on a plane to see *no* flight attendants. Unnerving. That's what it would be. With the cockpit door closed, sealing off the flight crew, and the ground soon to be 29,000 feet away, Scott and the other 17,500 Delta flight attendants had become the symbol of the company to the public, the contact point between flier and corporation. A visible touchstone of safety and poise.

On a plane passengers could hear a pilot on the intercom, but they rarely spoke to one. The mechanics and food service and cabin people were strangers on the tarmac, viewed through windows. The chairman of the board was a name in a newspaper. But flight attendants were in the same cabin as you.

One Atlanta frequent flier had told me, "You know what's scary about flying? It's the sense, once you strap yourself in, of putting yourself in strangers' hands. Flight attendants give the strangers a face."

It made me think of all those passengers—corporate presidents, diplomats, doctors, professors—clapping when a plane touches down. If flying is a constant battle inside a passenger between two parts of himself—a caveman looking out the window and scream-ing, "*Get me out of here!*" who wouldn't be surprised to find a witch doctor running the cockpit instead of a captain, and an allegedly sophisticated modern human who could plan dinner in London at lunchtime in New York—then Marvin Scott the professional flight attendant weighed in on the side of the sophisticate.

Now Marvin told a weary businessman walking in at the end of a long week. "Twenty A? Down this aisle, sir."

Marvin Scott, human face of airline magic, stood six feet tall, a big reason he liked working roomier planes like the L-1011. On 714 he was head waiter, head nurse, maître d', public relations man, smiling in his navy blue jacket and slacks, gold-plated fifteen-year wings on left breast pocket, conservative Delta tie; red background with blue royalty crests. No facial hair allowed. Short hair close cut on the side. Brown eyes and black skin.

"We used to have more options in the uniform, but the FAA felt that in emergencies passengers might not readily recognize attendants," Scott said. "In the old days you could get on an L-1011, and there would literally be no two flight attendants dressed alike. So the rule changed."

Scott got on the intercom and announced the flight number and destination. "You'd be surprised how many people get on the wrong plane. They come tearing to the front after the announcement," he said.

He and other attendants closed and latched the doors, and engaged a mechanism to ensure life rafts would automatically inflate in an emergency. He made sure passengers were seated. He helped a woman lift a bulky carry-on bag into the overhead rack. He handed a blue Delta blanket to a man in 4D.

Scott told Captain Gordon that everyone was down, which meant the plane could be moved.

At the very least this evening, if the flight was uneventful, Scott would direct the crew serving drinks. He would note passengers' moods, chatting with them if they looked lonely or scared. He would, just by being there, reassure customers.

If emergencies arose, he'd been trained to handle them. If a businessman had a heart attack, Scott would try to save his life. If the plane ditched in the ocean, Scott would be in charge of getting passengers safely out of it. If someone went berserk on board, which had happened to him, he would have to restrain him.

"I'm going to ask you something people used to ask my wife," I said. "I don't think this, but aren't you just a glorified waiter?"

Scott shrugged. "A person's job is the integrity with which he performs it," he said. "And anyway, being a waiter is not negative to me. And someone *did* say that to me once. A man doing my taxes. We'd been talking about my job. How much time off I get. How much money I make. I could see him thinking, 'This guy's living a great life, and making money doing it.'

"He was jealous," Marvin Scott said.

It isn't easy to be accepted into Delta flight attendant school. Eighteen hundred applicants went through training in 1991, out of 40,000 who applied.

"And everyone who gets in doesn't get through," Marvin Scott said. "People wash out."

At the school, where I'd attended classes, Scott the individual had been molded into Scott "the Deltoid," as Atlantans affectionately call Delta employees. He'd learned company ways. Had been taught how he treated passengers could be a big reason they come back. If one of Delta's strengths is service, as industry analysts say, then in a world where dozens of airlines reach the same cities, on the same schedules, with similar safety records, and often at lower fares than Delta, Marvin Scott could make the difference.

To qualify for training, applicants have to be at least twenty years old, between 5 foot 1 and 6 feet tall, have weight in proportion to height, and decent vision. It's a plus for an applicant to have experience serving the public. Delta wants some college or equivalent training.

"That says you have dedication, commitment," said Debi Hamby, a former attendant and current manager of flight attendant training, whom I met in Atlanta.

The course lasts five weeks, six days a week, at corporate headquarters. Students can live at home if they're locals, or choose dormitory housing at the school. Instructors are current or former attendants.

Debi walked me through the school before I went to class. She was a petite, perky woman with a flight attendant's smile, which could harden into something more corporate when it was time for me to go. And the Delta Ground Training Center had looked like the rest of headquarters—boringly functional. Bare walls. No-frills capitalism. The ghost of frugal Mr. Woolman seemed to have directed the architects, and saved money that had gone toward higher salaries, better health benefits, keeping employees on the payroll during cutback times.

"In classrooms," Debi had told me as we paused outside the Image Center, "students study FAA emergency procedures, plane operations, serving customers. They learn about pressurization, first aid. Can they work equipment requiring lots of steps? How are their hand-motor skills? Their hand-eye coordination? Can they handle a stress-related problem? A physical handicap?

"We sprinkle proficiency tests through the curriculum to find out if their performance remains consistent.

"In flying," she said, "you don't get many chances."

In the Image Center, where Estee Lauder beauty consultants advise future flight attendants on appearance, I looked into a long mirror ringed by bulbs, dressing-room style, reflecting silver-colored manikins in a corner: one a woman in a flight attendant uniform, gazing into the distance; the other a naked man, a coathanger over one wrist with a uniform jacket on it, someone's joke.

There was a collection of Estee Lauder products in glass cases. Private Collection Body Lotion. Beautiful.

There was a little hair salon where an Atlanta beauty studio came in to do hair. And shaving, nails, and hair for men.

There was a board where, under a sign warning "Unauthorized Accessories," I saw a blue banana-shaped hairclip. "Banana clip is wrong color blue," read its tag. A black bow tie. "Fabric is too shiny." Silver earrings. "They dangle." A barrette. "Too ornate."

And, on an adjacent board, accessories that fit the carefully cultivated Delta image. "Three rings are permissible. No more than two rings may be worn on one hand," said one notice.

"Stud earring. Gold, silver, pearl, or color-coordinated studs on gemstones. Cannot exceed the size of a quarter in circumference."

"One moderate-sized black or navy bow tie not to exceed 5 inches in width used to secure hair is acceptable."

The specifications seemed comically rigid at first, posted up in black and white, but then I remembered comments Atlanta friends had made when I'd told them I would be spending time with flight attendants.

"They're always so perfect," a woman lawyer had said wistfully.

"I bet your wife is beautiful," said a psychiatrist who had never met her. "She's a stewardess."

But students concentrated on much more than appearance. I walked in on a class in a mock-up of a 727 cabin. A dozen students clustered around a serving cart as a classmate breathed into the mouth of a baby doll, practicing CPR.

In another room, life-sized resuscitation dolls lay scattered all over the floor like bodies after a crash. The dolls had names. "Resuscitation Anne." "Resuscitation Junior." As usual, every job, including lifesaving, was broken down into step-by-step procedures.

"Heart Attack. Cardiac Arrest," read the instructional list. "Begin a primary survey. Ask 'Are you okay?' "

"Does victim respond?" the board said.

If yes, "Monitor ABCs if there are signs and symptoms of a heart attack. Have the victim stop activity. Have the victim rest in comfort. Position. Loosen restrictive clothing."

If no, "Call for help. Open airway. Is breathing present?"

Debi Hamby had led me from the resuscitation room into a room filled with fire extinguishers, oxygen bottles, smoke hoods to be worn while fighting fires, loudspeakers, and other emergency equipment.

We visited another mock-up, this time of emergency doors. Students practiced opening different doors while the rest of a class looked on.

"Who goes next?" the instructor said. A shy-looking blond woman in a pleated skirt faced the class, beside the freestanding and heavy-looking sliding door of a B-757. Suddenly the room filled with the taped sounds of an airliner going down.

The class yelled, "Grab ankles! Get down! Stay low!"

I recognized the words. I remembered walking into my New York apartment years before, hearing my wife upstairs, practicing for an update test, yelling the same thing at her cats. I'd sneaked upstairs to see the cats staring at her from the bed.

In the mock-up room, the screaming nose-dive noises stopped.

"Evacuate!" the class yelled. "Release seat belts! Get out! Get out!"

The student at the door worked levers. The door slid open.

"Come this way! Jump and slide!" she shouted.

The class clapped. Good job.

It seemed like fun at times in the mock-up room, the mood reminding me of one of those make-money-quick seminars, where motivational speakers pump up real-estate salesmen. Even students couldn't always take the scenarios seriously. One flight attendant told me about antiterrorism training. Suddenly one day, in a mock-up, a man in a ski mask had "hijacked" it.

"He had a machine gun. He was yelling, 'Get your head down!' All I could think of was, Why would someone hijack a mock-up?" she said.

Nevertheless, even mock emergencies could get scary. Especially in simulators, actual fuselage sections mounted on hydraulic stilts designed to pitch the cabin around as if there were a crash landing, midair collision, runway crash, gear collapsing, fire.

I went through one emergency evacuation class in a mock-up. Inside, it looked exactly like a plane. Same seats. Same aisles. Blacked out windows, as if we were flying at night. The whole cabin rocking gently, as if, up at 33,000 feet, we were sailing on the jet stream.

About thirty beautiful woman sat inside, in neat jeans, sweaters, new white socks. Like some kind of models' convention.

The only out-of-place sight was a man in a glassed-in control booth where the forward bathroom would be. Pushing buttons, he would make the plane "crash."

And what lent even more seriousness to the scene was the fact that two days earlier a US Air plane had pitched into New York harbor after a missed takeoff from LaGuardia Airport. The flight attendants inside had had to cope with the real thing.

While we waited for the scenario to begin, I chatted with the girl beside me, Florence, from Chicago, a raven-haired student with a faint whiff of cigarette odor coming off her clothes as if she smoked off-duty or knew somebody who did. She was breadwinner for her family, she said, after her husband had lost his job as a Midway Airlines pilot when the airline folded. He was home, taking care of their sixteen-month-old son. "Playing Mr. Mom."

"What would you do if a passenger got stuck in the door?" instructor Frances Scianrone called out as we waited for the scenario to begin. "How would you send a blind passenger down?"

Suddenly the plane pitched right as a landing gear "collapsed." In real life at this point, we would be skidding across the ground, wing filled with jet fuel dipping toward the runway as the pilot tried to keep it from touching, and blowing up or catching fire.

The lights went off.

We had to get out. Fast.

The girls yelled, "Release the seat belt! Go to the back! Hustle! Move it! Let's go!"

They shouted, "Keep moving! Arms out! Don't take anything with you!"

With the red fire light pulsating, I moved with other passengers toward the back door. The slide looked awfully high from up here, even though it terminated on a carpet. I must have hesitated too long. I was supposed to cross my arms over my chest and step out into space. The way all those cartoon passengers did on warning cards in the seat pockets of 714.

"*Move it!*" yelled Frances behind me. I jumped.

Ten minutes later I was attending swimming-pool class. Ditching-in-the-ocean class. What-if-714-goes-down-in-the-Pacific class. This time the girls thrashed around in the Olympic-sized pool, trying to climb into a big yellow raft, the kind 714 carried. The first two made it easily, pulling themselves up, slim calves and feet disappearing over the top. An Oriental girl had trouble, fell back in the water, tried again, fell back.

They hauled her in, sopping.

Soon the raft was filled with flight attendants. It held up to fifty people, the instructor said. I saw lots of little extras that came with the raft. Like stubby foot-high protuberances on the pontoons, to support a tarp that would protect survivors from the sun and catch rainwater for drinking. And red blinking lights powered by a water-activated battery. An emergency locater transmitter radio, to help rescue planes find the raft. A survival kit with red flares for daytime and white ones for night. A sea marker to turn ocean water yellow around the raft, making it easier to spot. Desalting tablets. A pint of potable water, which did not seem like much. A whistle to call to boats in fog. Dramamine tablets against seasickness. A flashlight. A hand pump to pump out water. Another to pump in air. Ammonia inhalents. Repair clamps against rips. Charms candies to supply moisture.

My favorite was the package with six vitamin C pills.

"Six vitamins?" I said. "For fifty people? What can you do with six vitamins?"

Pilot instructor Bob Stallings, looking on, laughed. "Eat a lot of fish," he said.

After the pool, I sat in on a class in customer service, which comprises a third of the curriculum at flight attendant school. Again, a class of about twenty-five women attended, sitting at tables of six as instructor/attendants Jill Jackson and Jennifer Gamblin gave them scenarios to solve.

Troublesome passenger scenarios.

Without uniforms, lacking the Delta image at the moment, the students seemed to have grouped themselves by personality type. Public relations escort Betty Moore and I gave the groups names. There was a sorority table, where the girls had frosted hair, painted fingernails, soft twill type skirts. Pony tails. Lots of makeup.

The eclectic table, where no two students dressed alike. One wore a leather jacket. Another a sweatshirt.

The Revenge of the Nerds table. The Natural Beauty table, where five of the girls looked as if they were walking out of a *Redbook* fall issue.

In high school, I would have committed murder to get into a room like this.

"Saying 'I'm sorry' is a pretty good tool with customers," Jill was telling the class. She was a current flight attendant with twelve years on the line, sitting on a stool, legs crossed like a lounge singer. "But some problems call for action." She stood up, going rigid, hands balled at her sides, chin straight ahead. "What kind of customer is this?" she said.

The students chanted, "Combative!"

"Where's this passenger most likely to sit?"

"The aisle!"

Gee, I thought. I sit by the aisle. Charts on the walls listed other types of passengers, all to be handled differently, all part of the great revenue-producing masses.

There was the "I win, you lose" passenger, the combative kind

Jill had just acted out. The "I win, you win" passenger, everybody's favorite, someone who would let attendants know their needs without being obnoxious about it. The passive customer, a trickier type since they keep wants to themselves but feel hurt if flight attendants don't guess them.

"What's the passive customer's best weapon?" Jill asked.

"Writing a letter of complaint?" someone at the sorority table said.

"Writing a letter? Maybe. But *he won't come back!*" Jill said. And there it was. The threat. That passive passenger would take his money and give it to TWA. Or United. As she spoke, I saw all those smiling flight attendants I'd watched on 714, serving drinks, answering questions, only now, in my mind's eye, they surveyed the aisles as they worked, thinking, 'Ah ha! 25D! Passive passenger!'

"Watch yourself and your body language," Jill said. "Some of us roll our eyes. We have real expressive faces. Watch out for yourself."

I thought, infected by the boosterism, I hope I'm an "I win, you win" passenger.

Class was interrupted as a delivery man brought in two dozen red roses from somebody's boyfriend. "I love you. I miss you," the note said. "Oooooooh," the women said. Jill smelled the roses. "Mmmmmmmm," she said.

Then we moved on to a class exercise. Jill would pose a problem the girls might encounter on planes. They would suggest the proper course of action to solve it. First one: A businesswoman on a flight is furious over a delay. What do we tell her?

"How about, I understand the importance of your meeting. However, in a delay the captain's priority is to ensure we reach our destination safely," someone said from the Natural Beauty table. Boooo, I thought. That answer wouldn't make me too happy.

"Anybody else?" Jill said.

The Revenge of the Nerds table suggested, "I could say, Can I get you a cup of coffee *now*?"

"Good. Immediate gratification," Jill said.

"You may not always be the right person to deal with a customer," Jill said. "You may look like his ex-wife."

When the scenarios were over, it was time for the closed-circuit television session. The girls stood in pairs in the center of the room,

acting out the part of flight attendants greeting passengers. Instructor Jennifer Gamblin played the passengers, all of it taped so
afterward students could see how they stood, used their hands,
their speech, their expressions.

Jennifer walked shyly up to the first pair and handed them a
note. She was a lean blond wearing black tights and a yellow and
black pullover. And she was a pretty good actress. The first "flight
attendant" took one look at the note and giggled. It said, "I only
speak Russian."

The flight attendant gently led her to her seat.

Next Jennifer played someone trying to sneak a gigantic picture
of Elvis Presley into a plane. "They *always* let me take Elvis," she
protested when the attendant said she'd have to check the poster.

"Passengers always say, 'They always let me do it,'" Jennifer said.

She became a loving wife—well, at least she *told* the next two
flight attendants she was a loving wife. "Is Edgar aboard?" she
asked kindly, holding out her palm. "He left his keys."

Jill warned the class: "When a person buys a ticket, he enters
into a legal contract with our company. We protect his identity.
We're not supposed to release it, not supposed to say, 'I remember
that name!' And if you choose to go in and make a PA announcement, and he's there, but he tells you, 'Wait a minute, I don't want
my wife to know I'm here,' you'd better be prepared to walk out,
lie through your teeth, and never give away that you've conversed
with our customer."

Jennifer cried to the next two students, pretending to hold on to
a struggling four-year-old, "I told Billy he could *go in the cockpit!*"

She became a mother handing two young children, who would
be flying without her, to the flight attendants. "Make sure Aunt
May picks them up. Under no circumstances let them go with Aunt
Bea!"

Jill advised, "Let the gate agent deal with this. Unfortunately we
get a lot of kids going back and forth between Mom and Dad. And
situations being abused. You never want to reveal to anyone who is
or isn't on a flight."

"I'm going to the Mardi Gras!" cried Jill Jackson, taking over the
passenger role, grabbing at the next two students, trying to pull
them toward her. "You go too! It'll be good!"

The student said, "Uh—are you hungry? Do you want something to eat?"

Jill screamed back, "Are you trying to tell me I'm drunk?"

"Don't give a drunk coffee. There's nothing worse than a wide-awake drunk," she told the class.

When the class took a break, I chatted with Susan Fadal, a lean, poised, raven-haired woman who had handled her mock unruly passenger with aplomb. She looked about twenty-four. She said she was thirty-six.

"Becoming a flight attendant will be fulfilling a dream," she said. "To travel. Go places. See what life is like on the other side. A lot of us have limited vision."

Susan said she had sold her jewelry store in Lexington, Kentucky, All That Glitters, after what she characterized as a bitter divorce. "I needed a change." She'd been told that when she graduated in a week, she'd be assigned to Cincinnati, her first choice.

Tammy Duffy, who had also handled her passenger well, was a twenty-nine-year-old ex-director of advertising and corporate relations for Hitachi in Houston, Texas.

"I met my husband, transferred to Chicago, took a position in marketing. I became stressed out," she said. "My husband was making good money. He offered me the opportunity to do whatever I wanted. I said, This is kind of crazy, but I'd like to be a flight attendant. I always wanted it. I'm thrilled. It's an opportunity for me to be home a lot, because I'm family oriented. It fits into our travel plans. The Delta benefits are good. I got an offer from every airline I interviewed with, but my heart was always with Delta. I'm a southern girl."

The way they both talked made me remember what my wife had said about being a little girl, seeing stewardesses in advertisements, going to exotic places, places she might otherwise never go. It also reminded me of something flight attendant Wendy McCrabb had told me the week before on a flight from Kennedy Airport to Salt Lake City.

"Little girls on planes idolize us."

Five percent of Delta flight attendants are male, but Marvin Scott hadn't even known men could get that kind of job when he entered

Georgia State University to study journalism in 1974. He figured he'd end up as a news broadcaster on TV. He worked hard to put himself through school, as a salesman at Sears, in a car dealership, and in a record store. But three and a half years later he had to quit to get a full-time job because he needed money. Now he said he would never go back.

"I met someone who was a flight attendant for Eastern. He was talking about the job, the time off that enabled you to do other things. I applied and was taken almost immediately, which was a little embarrassing because everybody in flight attendant school said they'd been applying for years."

Remembering the way Jill and Jennifer had acted out unruly passengers in flight attendant class, I asked Marvin if he ever got them. He said recently a man had gone berserk on a flight.

"The passenger clutched his leg, screaming he was having a stroke," he said. "I asked if I could help him. Then he started yelling, 'Kill the crew.' We immobilized him. He started beating his head against the wall. He screamed the second officer was a spy. He screamed that he was ruler of the world.

"There was a Secret Service man on board who helped restrain him," Scott said. "He was tied up for about an hour and a half. Later the man got sent back to a mental institution. Which was good, because I might have had to go to court."

I asked Scott and other attendants if they had more passenger stories. They said:

- We were going to show the movie *Mermaids* on one flight. A woman on board with her child said, "That movie is risqué. If you show it, I will stand up in front of the screen." I said, "Ma'am, that will be a problem." The captain had to tell her, "If you so much as move, I will land the plane and put you out of it."
- I was on my very first flight, overseas. A woman came up to me and said two men were following her, trying to kill her. She said they'd tapped her phones. I said, "Ma'am, I don't want to know the details. But I'll do everything I can to protect you." I could see the two men she was talking about, in the back. So I moved her up in Coach. But the two men got up and moved up too. So we moved her into First Class, and alerted the authorities on the

other end. When the plane landed, police took all of them away.

- An off-duty Delta pilot and his wife locked themselves in the bathroom. They were in there a long time. Mile-high club.

- During fare wars, you get different kinds of passengers, people who have never flown before. One man was fidgeting more and more as we flew. He kept asking when we would land. Finally I asked him why he was in such a rush. He said, "I have to go to the bathroom." He didn't know we had bathrooms on planes.

- After one flight a passenger wrote Delta complaining that the pilot had announced, "Put your life vest on! We're having an emergency landing!" But he'd never said that. The passenger had misheard the announcement about where the life vest is. We all had to write up affidavits.

- A guy walked on a plane with basil all over his hair. He said, "I love the smell of basil."

- A passenger started yelling, "Woo Woo! Gotta Gotta!"

They laughed at the funny ones, but there could be scary times too. Scott said, "Like when you're on takeoff, and you're going fast, and you feel the brakes go on, which means something's in the way. Or when the plane dives suddenly. There's only one reason for that—something in the way. All of a sudden the plane's at a different level, the captain's gunned the engines. The flight attendants look at each other. I get a knot in my stomach. The passengers are totally unaware, and we're standing there in horror. It lasts fifteen seconds. If you don't hear a big boom, you know it's okay."

Marvin Scott laughed.

"That only happens once every couple of years," he said. "Ninety-nine percent of the flights are routine."

But even "routine" meant hard work. I'd tried being a flight attendant on 714 on one leg from Honolulu to Los Angeles. I'd put on the blue apron. Brushed up my smile. I'd wheeled out a cart to serve beverages.

"You may notice that one of our attendants isn't exactly in uniform," the coordinator announced jovially over the intercom as I started serving drinks. "He's a writer. Doing a book on this plane."

Book, hell. Where's my drink? The instant I started serving, the world reduced itself to a tunnel filled with reaching hands. Like in

Night of the Living Dead. Did I have tomato juice? Beer? Coffee? My flight attendant partner smiled impatiently. I was slowing up service.

I'd never seen so many hands in my life.

Seven-fourteen was in the air now, heading north through a starry, black night. Scott had already checked the number of meals against the number of passengers. He'd made sure, before we took off, that all the emergency equipment—fire extinguishers, megaphones, oxygen bottles—worked.

He'd direct the in-flight service. Make announcements to passengers instructing them on what to do during landing. And when we landed, since this was his last flight today, he'd go home to the three-bedroom suburban home where he lived alone, in Sandersville, Georgia, where he'd grown up.

Tomorrow, on a day off, he'd work in his commercial photography studio, taking advertising pictures for banks and other businesses. He also taught aerobics at the YMCA. One reason he loved being a flight attendant was that it gave him time to pursue these other interests. He tended to work long flight-attendant stints, bunching up his free time so he could do other things.

"I like things the way they are," he said.

Like a surprising number of people I met at Delta, he didn't use his free passes much to travel overseas. He was too busy at home.

"I don't like traveling by myself," he said. "If I was married, it might be different."

"Any marriage in the works?"

"I wish," he said.

As long as we were talking about marriage, I figured I might as well bring up sex, although the two aren't always connected. Flight attendants, the popular notion went, got lots of sex. I remembered as a boy seeing paperback books in candy stores showing an airplane on the front, against a pink racy background, a half naked stewardess draped over the fuselage, one shoe dangling, long leg extended, sated but ready to start up again at a moment's notice.

Even in 1992, when I told people I'd been flying around on 714, many had said, with knowing smiles, "With stewardesses?"

Just a week ago I'd turned on the television, tuning by chance into *Airport*, at a scene where Pilot Dean Martin says to the flight attendant, "Honey, you keep revving my engines up and putting them in reverse." Which sounded at first like she was fighting him off, until I learned he'd made her pregnant.

I had also been divorced since I'd started the book, which was no fun, and I hoped all these sex stories were true.

"I've heard the sex stories. But I've never witnessed anything," he said.

I told him the story my now-ex-wife had told me when we'd first started dating, about sex on L-1011s. And another story I'd heard a few years ago when we'd gone out to dinner in a Virginia restaurant with a Pan Am flight attendant and her boyfriend. Over steaks and pasta, I'd asked them how they'd met. They'd blushed.

"Well, there's this plane that has a downstairs galley and an elevator," the flight attendant began.

"Wait a minute," I interrupted. "You took a passenger down to the galley and had sex with him?"

They nodded.

At Delta, I'd met one copilot who admitted to having sex in the galley with a flight attendant, but whenever I'd taken one of those cramped one-person elevators down there, instead of finding some bacchanalian orgy going on between the ovens, I'd seen sweating flight attendants pulling meal trays out, or struggling to wedge the heavy carts into the elevators, or cramming a one-minute meal into their mouths in a corner, by a porthole, during a five-minute break.

Marvin Scott smiled. "Nothing's ever happened to me, but if someone were flying with a mate on a long flight, I could see them getting frisky down there," he said.

Nobody got frisky on tonight's late flight. After a while the beverage service was over, and the lights of Atlanta grew visible below. The seat-belt sign lit up on the baggage rack. Marvin Scott checked with Captain Gordon and advised the passengers that we would be on the ground before twenty minutes were out.

My rotation was over. It was hard to believe I'd only been in 714 for three days, not three weeks. Hard to believe the plane had traveled so much in a mere seventy-two hours.

From the ground we would be just one more bright globule of light floating down toward the airport. One more anonymous machine coming in at the end of the day. In a month, when I'd ask

Marvin Scott for his memories of the flight, there would be nothing special to recall. Man and machine coming together for two hours, taking care of each other, departing strangers, the way they had come.

Seven-fourteen touched down and rolled to the terminal. Marvin went back to the doorway, hands folded, smile in place. Seven-fourteen's big engines were cooling. No new flight crew waited outside to take Fred Gordon's place. From the cockpit, I could see that outside in the terminal wives stood expectantly, watching for husbands. A boy held roses in his hand, smiling, shifting foot to foot. Twin girls pressed against the glass, waving at the crew in the lighted-up cockpit.

Back in the cabin, passengers filed out, heading home on Friday night.

"Thanks for coming. Come again," said their host, Marvin Scott.

NEAR DISASTER

The passengers were gone. The cockpit empty. At 11 P.M., 714 was home—that is, if a machine that spends eight hours a day flying, parks in a different city every night, and traverses half the planet between rests can have a home.

Alone, I wandered down the port aisle, past a crumpled blanket on seat 2C and discarded ticket stub for Wright. As if Orville or Wilbur had sat in First Class and marveled over how far aviation had come since they'd been gone.

From the cover of a *People* magazine on 6E, actor Nick Nolte looked up at the baggage bin.

A half-empty Chivas Regal miniature nestled against 12A.

Engines off. Heat off. Seven-fourteen reminded me of a theater when the show is over, and wrappers and programs litter the aisles. Or a stadium after a game, the empty seats unreal beside the life they had contained. My frosting breath seemed illusory against the coffee steam I remembered. The silence less tangible than the memory of announcements, rumbling carts, flight attendant laughter, engines.

Friday night in Atlanta. I went outside. On the ramp, the rows of gleaming planes and floodlights made the 34-degree temperature seem colder. Mechanics Jim Ganopulos and Rich Steer peered up at 714, their only movement the rising vapor of their breath. Two men in hooded thermal sweatshirts and peaked hats. On the late shift. Workmen in the universal stance of humans concentrating on a problem. Hands in pockets. Heads cocked as they eyed the engine on the tail.

Elsewhere, mechanics attending the parked fleet looked aphidsized alongside the 767s and L-1011s. And when I reached the ground, 714 loomed huger, the nacelles the size of baby elephants, the landing gear as far apart as the corners of a house.

Rich was more serious, with his wire glasses and neat mustache. He watched public television programs like "Skyscraper," he had told me when we met, because they showed the way something complicated was put together. Each week a different segment, describing a different part of the building. The frame. The beams. The flooring. The skin of the skyscraper; windows and bricks and panels, fastened to that.

"A great show. You should watch it," he'd said.

Jim was more outgoing. He liked harmless jokes. He'd asked me to help "freak out" another mechanic. I was to stomp up to the man, demand to see his identification, turn to Jim and say, "*This* is the guy!"

"Ha Ha. He'll think you're FAA," he'd said.

Now a thoughtful, piercing smile appeared on Jim's face.

"Can I ask you something?" he said. "Why'd you pick 714, *this specific plane*, to write about?"

Delta people always asked that. I gave the usual answer. I'd wanted a long-haul plane. A plane with history. That went to sexy destinations. That epitomized the way the company had grown. Which meant I'd write about a TriStar in general, and as for 714 specifically, I said, wondering why Jim was looking skeptical, I'd looked over the L-1011s on Delta's computer, and 714 had been going to Hawaii that day.

I laughed. "It's like in kindergarten when you take a seat on your first day, any seat, but the minute you sit in it, it becomes your seat for the year." I smiled at the randomness of it. "When I saw 'Honolulu' beside '714,' I picked that plane."

Jim's weird smile widened. "What's the *real* reason you picked it?" he said.

Rich stared at me too.

"Oh, come on," Jim said. "You picked it because of that *thing* that happened in 1986. Right?"

"What *thing*?"

"When the wing cracked."

I figured he was making another joke. "Right," I said. "It was just flying, and the wing cracked."

"Look," Rich said, beckoning me under the wing. It looked huge above us, a triangular expanse of gleaming aluminum skin. He pointed up at a long thin strip of metal running diagonally over the original surface. Clearly not part of it.

"See that patch? That's where the crack was. Fuel was pouring on the hot wheels as the plane landed," Jim said. "They thought they had a brake fire. It was smoking like crazy."

Rich said, "The crack was 8 or 9 feet long. You could put your fist through it."

I felt a chill. "Wait a minute," I said. "I just flew almost 16,000 miles on this plane. You're telling me it's been traveling around for seven years with a cracked wing?"

"It was the wing spar that broke," Jim said. "That's the rear supporting structure. It happened at LaGuardia, as the plane landed. Delta had to fly a crew up there, put a tent over the plane, and work on it for weeks before bringing it to Atlanta to finish the job."

"What caused the crack?" I said.

Jim shrugged.

"Could the plane have crashed from it?" I was still unsure whether to believe them.

They didn't know.

"But it's safe now, right?" I said.

They were lean, young, both about thirty. Before the night was out, they would have to sign their names on a card promising the company, government, and 200 passengers booked on the 9:30 A.M. to Las Vegas that 714 would fly. To ensure that, they had to determine why one of those warning lights on the engineer's panel, an "overheat loop" in the number 2 engine, had been going on all day. And to do *that*, they would have to sift through about 10,000 parts in the next few hours and isolate the problem.

If they didn't fix it by morning, their company would lose money and manpower, and maybe have to assign a whole flight crew to bring in another L-1011 to assume 714's job, distracting scheduling people, equipment control people, ramp tower people, flight control people. If Rich and Jim failed to find the cause of the light coming on, at 9 A.M., at that daily briefing senior management went to Chairman Ron Allen would hear someone report, "Ship 714 is still on the ground in Atlanta."

Rich said, strolling back toward the mechanics' field office to start the job. "It's *very* safe."

Very comforting. Or maybe they'd been joking. Trying to fool the guest, like the mechanic Jim had asked me to trick.

I would get the maintenance records on 714.

But if the story were true, I wondered, how could such a big crack have developed without anyone finding it long before the plane took off that day, especially after all the checking and rechecking 714 had gone through when it had been certified. All the Lockheed, Delta, and FAA inspectors poring over the plane. All the fatigue tests scientists had conducted in laboratories.

And *after* the plane had started carrying passengers, all the nightly layover checks, the walkarounds by mechanics and engineers, the months-long heavy maintenance visits in Delta hangers.

A 10-foot crack?

Right now Jim and Rich were part of a standard "layover check" Delta requires for every plane on the ground more than four hours. Back in the mechanics' field office, one of several scattered around the airport, the lead mechanic had assigned them the repair job on two items pilots had recorded in the flight log since last night. The overheat loop. And the audio system was broken on seat 25A.

Neither item had been serious enough to stop 714 from flying, but they had to be fixed now.

Simultaneously, four other men would do the standard part of the check.

Jim and Rich went to the back corner of the station—a big room filled with long tables, food machines, a TV, and lots of mechanics—and pulled up blueprints for L-1011s on a microfilm machine. As they studied engine diagrams, they were looking at the same drawings Milt McKnight had pored over in a motel room in Palmdale, California, eighteen years before, reviewing Lockheed Tri-Star manuals, making sure each description was precise enough for Delta before the airline would accept them.

Now the accuracy of McKnight's theories, two decades later, would enable Rich and Jim, who had been fifteen years old then, to put 714 in shape for tomorrow's takeoff.

"There. The loop," Rick said.

We walked out to the plane. The four other mechanics were already doing the standard check, working from a Lockheed maintenance list of ninety-four items to be inspected on layovers. They checked off each one as they completed it, nothing left to chance.

They went over emergency equipment, lights, windshield-washer fluid, galley sinks and drains, spare fuses, circuit-breaker panels, hydraulic system for leaks, bearings for cracks, tires and brakes, fuel sumps, baggage compartments, engine oil, gearbox, emergency lights, smoke detectors, exhaust ducts, engines, and more.

They read over the ship's log in case one of the cockpit crews today had forgotten to report a problem. They hadn't.

Meanwhile, two Hispanic men in civilian clothes dragged vacuum cleaners around the ramp, disappearing into planes, cleaning them.

At 2 A.M., with the standard check long finished, Rich, Jim, and I stood 30 feet up on a hydraulic lift, inches away from the white expanse of tail assembly. They had not yet figured out the problem. Close up, I felt like a fly on the side of an elephant. I touched the cold tail, saw my fingerprint, drew eyes. A mouth. A button nose.

When Jim opened a plate on the assembly, I peered inside with a flashlight. The "loop" curved into the darkness of the engine, an intestine-shaped copper wire about half an inch thick. Doctor Jim. Doctor Rich.

Engine number 2 seemed surprisingly vulnerable without the skin of the plane protecting it. The view demystified flight, broke it into understandable pieces; wires, ducts, parts that, arrayed differently, might be in a car, air-conditioning system, refrigerator, locomotive.

"Were you telling me the truth about the wing?" I said.

"Yep."

At 2:30 A.M. the overheat problem still puzzled Jim and Rich.

At 3 A.M. we were in the cockpit, opening the floor escape hatch and descending into the hellhole, the kind of room engineer Don Repo had disappeared into the night Eastern Airlines flight 401 smashed into the Everglades. It looked like the hold of a ship down here, with rows of black boxes the size of automobile batteries— the electronics controls of the ship—lining shelves.

It was freezing. We lay on the metal floor. Jim and Rich replaced boxes.

"Cracked," I said. "You're telling me the wing was *cracked?*"

They gave me a job. While Rich and Jim went back to the tail section, I would stay in the cockpit alone and watch the light. They would try the old home fixit man's method. When in doubt, jiggle wires. If I saw the light come on, it would mean they'd found a short. I would alert them immediately, over headphones.

I sat back in the engineer's chair, never taking my eyes off the light. The stark cockpit made the instrument board grayer. "Hey! You asleep?" I heard in my earphones. I made snoring noises and heard laughter back.

Fifteen minutes later they returned, stared at the engineer's panel as if that might trigger an answer. Five hours to flight time.

"We'll start it up," Jim said. "Set the emergency brake. Pilots don't do it sometimes because that helps the plane cool down faster. Then if mechanics forget and start it up, the plane rolls forward. Usually it smashes the radar dome into the terminal before you can stop it."

"I'm not touching the brakes," I said. I envisioned tomorrow's morning briefing again, only this time a Delta vice president would report, "And then he screwed up the controls, and the plane rolled into the terminal."

Jim set the brakes. "A plane got away from me one time," he said. "I'd towed a 727 out of a hanger after it had been repaired. I figured I didn't need the rubber chocks we wedge under the wheels to keep it from rolling. I drove off to bring the next plane into the hanger and suddenly saw everyone pointing. The 727 was rolling toward the hanger.

"I leaped off the tug. I ran along with the plane, trying to stop it by putting chocks in the path of the wheels. It just rolled over them. Finally I grabbed the tow bar, still running, and turned the wheels right."

He looked relieved.

"The plane stopped."

Rich and Jim said some nights, while mechanics work on planes, police or FBI hold antiterrorist exercises. "They crawl up the L-1011s, through the S duct, across the back of the fuselage, and drop a rope over both sides. Then they pull the emergency escape on the outside of the doors, and it pops the doors up."

Finally at 5 A.M., with darkness dissipating into gray light, they found the problem in the hellhole, in a faulty "logic card," an electronic conduit that routes signals between the loop and its warning light.

They replaced the card but still had to fix the audio on seat 25A. By 6:30 they finished the paperwork.

"When I get in tomorrow, I'll check the way 714 performed today," Rich said.

"Delta makes you follow up on repairs?" I said.

He shook his head. "We don't have to. But I want to know what happens to a plane I work on. You get concerned with the job you're doing. I want the job to be good."

By 7 A.M., with the rest of Atlanta starting to head for work, the mechanics were on their way home. Rich drove I-85 south to Peachtree City, a planned community where many Delta people live, had coffee with his wife, a computer expert at Metropolitan Life. Then he played with six-month-old Ritchie Jr. and was sound asleep by the time ship 714 took off for Las Vegas.

So was I.

I waited for clearance to visit Delta's records office and met Dave Columbus, Lockheed's liaison with Delta for the L-1011 fleet. Even though the California company didn't build or sell TriStars anymore, they still took part in planning and monitoring repairs and modifications. Both Delta and Lockheed were legally liable for the fleet.

Columbus was a middle-aged man, bulky in a brown suit, and legendary among the mechanics when it came to TriStars, Jim had said. "He knows everything about them." When I told him I was concentrating on ship 714, his mouth twitched a little, and he asked, as if he suspected an answer, "Why that ship?"

"No particular reason," I said. "Why? Did something special happen to 714?"

Dave Columbus paused a little too long.

"No," he said.

I phoned Kathleen Bergen at the FAA and asked if the agency had records of problems with ship 714. She found an FAA "service difficulty report" on the plane. It listed incidents Delta had reported to the FAA, involving 714, between January 1986 and May 1992.

In July of '86, for instance, a 2-inch crack had been found in a panel strengthening one of the passenger doors, the two-page printout said. It seemed like Delta had anticipated the crack and repaired it per Lockheed recommendations. No big deal.

In October '86, corrosion damage had been discovered on a cylinder strut in the landing gear. The gear had been replaced. No big deal.

Newark, read the name of the airport on the next incident. And there it was. Not at LaGuardia, as Jim had said. But close enough.

The report said:

> After landing in Newark, Tower advised ship 714 that fuel was leaking from the airplane. Subsequent inspection revealed that right rear wing spar was broken approximately three feet inboard of the gear. Cause of spar failure was a fatigue crack in the rear spar web . . . final cracking was caused by . . . a hard landing.

Of the remaining sixteen items on the list, twelve were cracks.

I went to Oklahoma City where I met Dr. Aldridge Gillespie, an articulate, soft-spoken ex-academic in charge of the FAA's accident investigation and antiterrorism programs. He'd gotten his Ph.D. at the University of Arizona by applying "principles of fracture" to airplane fuselages, which meant he'd studied the way airplanes crack.

"We were trying to determine not just the rate of crack propagation but the way pressurization affects cracking," he said. In experiments he'd worked on, researchers would pump pressure into a fuselage, he said.

"Then we'd drop a weight—a chisel or knife—into the skin, to break it. We'd increase the weight and watch the size of the cracks. We knew that once a crack existed, it would grow eventually to a critical point and go rampant. We needed to know how long it would take to reach that point. Six inches long? Eight? Up to a certain point, if you punctured the skin the air would go out, nothing more. But at that point, when the chisel dropped, the fuselage would explode."

I asked him about ship 714. He said, in his quiet way, "Pressurization wouldn't have affected that wing spar. Wing spars would be vulnerable to cracks from metal fatigue."

"What *is* metal fatigue?" I said.

"Metal crystalline structure changes because of the environment," he said. He picked a paperclip off his desk and twisted it back and forth. The clip turned black at the juncture where he was moving it. The clip broke.

"Chemicals affect metal. So does atmosphere. Oscillation. Environment," he said. "When you saw the clip change color, you were actually watching the crystalline structure appear on the surface. As I bent it back and forth, something happened called 'work hardening.' I found it harder to bend the metal. But when I kept doing it, I was repeating the load, on and off, on and off, so many times, it failed. That's metal fatigue."

Watching the paperclip move made me remember all those times I'd looked out 714's window, any plane's windows, and seen the wings gently undulate up and down as the plane flew. I held up a spiral memo book to approximate an extended wing. I moved the book up and down so the end swished.

"So if this is a wing, the fatigue occurs here?" I said, touching the middle of the memo book, where the movement started.

"Yes, but metal fatigue occurs not just where the oscillation is taking place, but where there is some sort of an impurity, a little flaw in the metal. A hole. A crack. A sharp corner," he said. "Something that will elevate the stress. Then you apply a standard load. Because of the flaw, the fatigue crack will grow."

"*After* an accident, investigators can figure out where fatigue occurred," I said. "But when Lockheed is building a plane, and it doesn't even exist yet, hasn't been subjected to flying, how do they know how much stress a wing can take, and where the wing will experience the stress?"

"They build it in a lab and subject it literally to millions of cycles of tests," he said. "Cold. Bouncing. Rapid changes in loads. A computer-controlled hydraulic jack can simulate loads and stresses caused by landings, takeoffs, or even random stress."

Gillespie added that some pretty surprising reasons for failure could pop up. "Recently researchers looked into landing-gear mechanisms that had seemingly failed for no reason. It turned out the hydrogen ion-based cleaning solvent airlines used acted against the alloy that made up the gear. The solvent was weakening the steel."

Gillespie looked pleased with the state of crack-propagation research in general.

"If it's so thorough, why did 714's wing spar crack anyway?" I said.

Gillespie said, You can't anticipate everything.

To check 714's records I drove to Delta's massive Technological Operations Center, one of the largest airplane overhaul facilities in the world—forty-two acres of hanger, maintenance shop, and office space, twenty-three acres of more buildings under construction. All a few miles from Delta's main headquarters outside Hartsfield Airport.

Entering the employees' parking lot, eyeing the red "Fly Delta Jets" sign, I envisioned a wing half-severed from a plane. Smoke billowing from the hot wheels. I told myself maybe I was overdramatizing. What did "cracked wing spar" really mean? Bridge engineers I knew said cracks in bridges weren't necessarily dangerous, at least right away. Were cracks on planes common? Anticipated? Dealt with regularly with standard operating procedure?

Also, if Delta's inspection program was as terrific as I'd been led to believe, how had a plane with a cracked wing spar been allowed to take off in the first place? And after the near accident, how could it have been repaired so well it was still flying seven years later.

The records office turned out to be surprisingly small for all the information it contained, the size of a private law firm library. Clerks at desks updated reports on every plane in the fleet. Three

FAA inspectors sat at a table in the center of the room, randomly poring over reports. The year before, men like these had charged Delta with thirty-one category 1—or more serious—violations in maintenance, an average number for a big airline, FAA spokesmen said. Category 1 includes items like missed deadlines for inspections or overhauling potentially flawed components in planes.

In 1991, most of the Delta violations involved errors in records keeping. Among the worst, the FAA charged, were waiting too long to replace engine blades on one L-1011, incorrectly classifying major repairs, which would have required FAA approval, as minor ones. And missing deadlines for component inspections on two Boeing 727s and one rudder-control unit on a DC-9.

None of the alleged violations placed the flying public in danger, an FAA spokesman told reporters.

And after the inquiry, Delta revamped its computer program to prevent missed deadlines on part replacement and inspection, and revised maintenance manuals to prevent mistakes, said spokesman Neil Monroe.

In the records room 714's history was on microfilm.

Here was the birth notice: "I have inspected this aircraft and issued a certificate of airworthiness, FAA 9/26/74 . . . Signed, William R. Huber."

Here, dated October 9, 1974, the record of the delivery flight from Palmdale to Atlanta. And soon after, 714's first passenger run, from Atlanta to San Francisco.

And then the parade of maintenance documentation began, recording the incessant whine of 4 million parts clamoring for attention, and not letting up for eighteen years.

- "Cockpit door hard to latch." FIXED.
- "Right wing anti-ice light on with switch off." FIXED.
- "Weather radar number 2 drops off one third of the sweep on both Captain's and First Officer's screens." FIXED.
- "Number 4 lead tire has deep cut." REPLACED WHEEL ASSEMBLY.

On one flight in 1975, reading lights had flashed on and off. On another, windshield wipers didn't work on the copilot's side.

Thousands of routine maintenance items completed, and only thirty-one missed in a year a remarkably small number beside that. A nervous flier would have been soothed by the record. Part broken. Part fixed. Each job described on index cards on microfilm. Each job initialed, step by step. First by mechanics. Then by Delta inspectors. The Delta inspectors followed by FAA inspectors.

For all the heavy work 714 did, it was babied from the second it touched earth to the instant it took off again.

I remembered all those times I'd landed in 714's cockpit, watching the line maintenance man waiting for us as we rolled to the terminal, hearing him on my headphones asking how the plane was, listening to the captain tell him, "She's a good plane," or "Light acting up," and within minutes a gray-jacketed mechanic would be with us in the cockpit to look at the problem.

I set the microfilm on a slow roll, and the years went by. "Fuel cargo bin fixed . . . aft cargo bin . . . loose light . . . flight recorder light . . . galley lift . . . carpet in galley . . . coffee maker broken . . ."

I stopped scrolling at November 16, 1986, the day the wing spar had cracked. I whistled to myself. If the amount of paperwork given a problem indicated its seriousness, the crack had been dangerous all right.

I winced, reading, "Fuel was leaking under the right wing." "Rear wing spar cracked." "Brace aft of spar bent." "Rib torn loose. Clips to stringers broken . . . rib twisted . . . web torn."

The bones of the ship, the metal braces and support structure keeping it together, had been tearing themselves off the fuselage when the plane landed. It was clear 714 had narrowly missed disaster, averted by a hair becoming to the L-1011 fleet what Turkish Airlines ship 29 had been to the rival Douglas DC-10—the plane that crashed before a structural problem was identified.

The fact was, until November 15, 1986, no L-1011 had ever suffered the kind of damage 714 did that day. And afterward, when other airlines initiated special inspections, after being alerted of the Delta incident, they found cracks in the wing spars on other planes. After a decade in the air, TriStars had begun showing a kind of wear never anticipated by Lockheed tests at Palmdale.

Lockheed and the airlines beefed up the spars. The TriStars flew on. And none ever crashed because of wing spar separation.

And as for 714, the paperwork confirmed what Jim Ganopulos had said. The repair, remodeling, and test flights had taken months, first at Newark, then in Atlanta. And after that 714 had gotten the most complete kind of overhaul Delta gives a plane. A heavy maintenance check, normally given every 48,000 miles, had taken another two months.

My last shred of uneasiness over flying on the plane disappeared. But I still wanted to meet the people who had worked on it in 1986, to make sure their version matched the paperwork.

Back at my Atlanta apartment I turned on the television to see TWA Chairman Carl Icahn interviewed about older planes. TWA's fleet was the oldest among the big airlines, the announcer said. He asked Icahn if that meant the planes were less safe. No, Icahn said. Planes are rebuilt constantly.

At Delta too, management told me planes were "rebuilt" when the subject of age came up. What did that mean? I wondered. Did workers actually replace fuselages? Wings? Rudders? Was 714 like television's Six Million Dollar Man, looking on the surface like the same airplane that had rolled off the assembly line two decades earlier, in reality a marvel of improved valves, alloys, circuits, skin?

To find out and meet the men who'd fixed 714, I went back to the Tech Ops Center, to the big maintenance hangers, where on the day I visited a newly acquired Air Canada TriStar was getting its heavy maintenance check, so crucial to the healthy operation of any airliner. Seven-fourteen's next visit was scheduled a month from now.

Inside the cold hanger at noon, mechanics in zipped-up sweatshirts and jackets swarmed over ship 767, which—surrounded by scaffolding and jacked up on a hydraulic lift, landing gear gone, engine cowlings off, fuselage cradled on wooden braces like a whale being transported—looked like it was in traction. The radar dome was off, giving the tip a blunt, vulnerable aspect. The doors were open.

Seven-six-seven's flaps and slats were extended full length, as if the plane were landing, because with power off they could not be moved so mechanics could get at them. From the rear, considering the hawkish profile of the plane in flight, 767 resembled a taxidermized bird.

Mechanics, fifty-five of them at the moment, went in and out, peered into engines and trapdoors on ladders, carried electrical components back to separate shops in the center, crawled on the girders in the baggage compartments, where floors had been removed, looking for corrosion.

Sheet metal experts in protective plastic glasses cut aluminum with high-speed drills. The patches would be used to reinforce areas susceptible to cracks. Mechanics pounded brand-new rivets into the fuselage with electric hammers. They stood around drafting tables like architects, peering at electrical connection charts. They rode by on bicycles, headed for other jobs in the massive center.

The heavy maintenance would continue around the clock, three shifts, twenty-four hours a day, for weeks, my escort, Erwin Gettys, added. He said much of the work is preventive. Structure is beefed up. Areas susceptible to wear are strengthened. Sections of wing and fuselage are x-rayed to determine if cracks are beginning to form, to see if the molecular structure of the plane is changing in ways not yet visible to the eye.

We walked around the plane.

TriStar 767 looked more like it was being built than repaired.

Loudspeaker announcements boomed and echoed over the grinding of drills and hammering of rivet guns, summoning mechanics to one job or another or to the foreman's office.

The floor around the plane was a clutter of mechanics' portable rolling tool boxes, orange work stations for each man's personally owned tools, the boxes showboards for bumper stickers or patches: "Keep Out of My Drawers!" "CREW CHIEF MILITARY AIRLIFT COMMAND." "Alice's Donuts." "97 ROCK!" I saw a photo of a ski slope, the bright blue of the sky unreal in the glare of the hanger. A magazine cutout of Arnold Schwarzenegger.

I mounted the scaffolding steps like a 1940s passenger walking up to a plane in a big city airport. Passengers still use them in smaller airports today. On a steel platform outside the forward passenger door, veteran sheet-metal mechanic Nelson Camillo riveted a "doubler," or sheet of reinforcement, onto a foot-wide space adjacent to the doorway where, on another L-1011, a hairline crack had appeared. Lockheed and Delta had determined that the reinforcers would keep the planes strong. The FAA had approved it.

"A crack is like throwing a stone in the water," said Nelson Camillo. "The waves go out from it. But doublers keep them small."

I remembered the FAA report that had accused Delta of committing thirty-one maintenance violations in one year. Yet just at this second, on this one plane, mechanics were performing hundreds of coordinated maintenance acts. And what kept this concentrated activity from degenerating into anarchy was a small board 3 feet away from Nelson, where, arranged in rows, on long index cards, each job to be performed was listed, and assigned to a specific worker, who would have to sign off on it before an inspector could sign off on *his* job, and 767 could be closed up again, and wheeled outside, and test flown, and finally, after any last kinks were worked out, put back on line to carry passengers.

I stepped into the plane and gasped. It looked nothing like any airplane I'd ever seen. I was in a tube-shaped cave. No seats. No bulkheads. No carpets. No aisles. No galley elevator. Ceiling and wall gone, replaced by plastic sheets. I glanced into the cockpit. The instrument panels were gone, stripped. In pieces, they'd been sent to special labs so each component could be checked.

To the whine of drills and staccato pounding of rivet guns, I walked down what had, days before, been an aisle of a plane. Now, with the electricity off, glowing, freestanding fluorescent lamps lined the floor at regular intervals. Like camping lamps. There was no engine power to provide light. Plywood boards covered gaps in the floor. Blueprints lay on a drafting table where the First Class section had been.

Mechanics crawled across a grid of beams beneath the floor, checking for corrosion. One man hung into a hole, using a long-handled mirror, curved at the end like a dentist's, to peer at hard-to-see areas. He kept a paper cup filled with rivets nearby to replace any that were worn down.

He inspected every single rivet. Rivet by rivet. Every stringer between beams. Every inch of metal.

"Looks strenuous," I said.

"I have to put my name on this job," he said.

The lavatory doors were gone. So were the toilets. Down below, on the baggage and galley level, more men and women lay on beams, vacuuming up dust, dirt, rivet shavings.

Erwin Gettys explained that the worry was that somehow, over the last forty-eight months, as 767 flew through rain, heat, and cold, moisture had gotten into the guts of the plane. Seeped through hairline fractures. Eaten like acid into the metal. Weakened stringers and beams and the outer skin of the plane. Corroded the spars keeping the wings in place. Daily layover checks and periodic less comprehensive overhauls had kept any damage from becoming dangerous. Now it was time to make sure corrosion wasn't eating away at hard-to-reach areas.

"TriStars have several areas that need constant inspection," Erwin Gettys said. "One is around the passenger doors. And we always inspect the wing spars. But every plane in its life has cracks. There's nothing automatically dangerous about cracks, but you take care of them."

"Are they rebuilding the whole plane?" I said.

Gettys smiled. He was a lean man with a flattop haircut, very polite, but I had the feeling he'd rather be working in his office than giving a tour.

"We don't rebuild everything," he said. "When Carl Icahn said that on TV, he probably meant that planes are inspected continuously. On 714, of the structure, probably 95 percent is original material. But the seats and all the components have been changed many times."

In fact, at the Tech Ops Center, we'd already walked through what seemed like acre after acre of specialized work shops—sixty of them—administering to the needs of the fleet. In the tire shop, reeking of rubber, I'd stared at a tubeless 50-inch-high tire for an L-1011. "Fill to 185 pounds," lettering on the side said. I'd looked over a 400-pound brake assembly. In the sheet-metal shop, workers had rebuilt larger parts, spoilers or flaps, off the planes. In the plastics shop they'd used wooden molds to make plastic armrests and toilet seats and latch handles. In the carpet shop, computerized carpet cutters had unrolled endless streams of carpet, and cut them for planes. Workers in the electric shop had stretched whole wiring systems off planes onto long boards, where they looked like ganglia, testing each connection, each circuit before the systems went back into the jets. Black boxes went to the electrical accessory shop during big layovers. There was a landing gear shop. An engine shop. A buffet shop for galley components. A cabin interior shop.

In a month, when 714 came in for its heavy maintenance check, mechanics would strip the plane and distribute parts to appropriate shops; good parts to be checked and returned, faulty ones to be discarded before the ship took off again. In fact upstairs at the center, computer printouts already listed mandatory modifications slated for 714, all part of keeping the plane safe eighteen years after its first revenue flight.

In a month, the printouts said, 714's wing spars would be further strengthened, and the upper surfaces of the wings as well. Doublers would be placed around fuselage doors. A wheelchair would be installed on the plane, according to new federal regulations. Lavatory smoke detectors would be replaced. So would electronic guidance system components.

It would be 714's first heavy maintenance visit since May 1988, four years ago.

Erwin Gettys admired the TriStars in the fleet. "They're great aircraft," he said.

We walked away from 767 and into a small, glassed-in mechanics office off the main hanger. Jimmy Martin, lead mechanic today, told me he'd also been the lead mechanic back in 1986 on the 714 job. He'd flown up to Newark with an emergency crew that day.

Martin was a rough-looking man who showed the kind of visible pride in his work I'd come to associate with Delta employees. "When a plane comes out of here, it's hopefully good as new," he said. "We're the foundation for the airline. If we don't do a good job, our ships can't make better time. And then the line can't make flights. Everything starts for Delta right here."

I asked Martin about the 714 job in 1986, about the wing spar separating when the plane landed. Uncertainly, he glanced at Erwin Gettys, who was listening from a chair by the doorway.

"Are we allowed to talk about this?" he said.

"Tell him whatever he wants to know."

"The wing spar didn't separate when the plane landed. That's what we thought at first. It happened in the air," he said.

A chill came over me.

"When I saw the crack, it had separated this much," Martin said, holding his palms a foot and a half apart. "I could stick my head through it. I was up there thirty days working on it."

"Well, how dangerous was it?" I asked. "To me, it sounds like it was dangerous."

"You sure this is authorized?" Jimmy Martin asked Erwin Gettys.

"Say what you think."

"In my opinion, there are very few things I've ever seen that would cause an airplane to crash right away," Martin said. "This was one of 'em."

I thought of how far away the earth looks from 33,000 feet. "Then the passengers were lucky that the damage occurred when the plane was coming in for a landing, instead of while they were cruising?" I said.

"My opinion is, yes."

"But how did it get to that point?" I said. "Could the crack have happened quickly, while the plane was in the air? Or did it happen over a long period of time? Was it a fluke?"

Martin shook his head, not liking the subject at all. "It must have happened over a long period of time," he said. "Within a day we were inspecting all the other airplanes in our fleet. There were cracks generated at the same point in other 1011s. Look," he said, defending any craft he worked on, "the L-1011 is a great plane. And every aluminum plane has corrosion. You can give a very wrong impression to people if you say this wrong."

"We ride on these things too," Gettys said.

"Structural damage is not unusual," Martin said. "Once an airplane gets six, seven, eight years old, you find this deterioration. As a result of 714, we put heavier spar webs and spar caps on all our TriStars."

Outside the glass office, in the bright hanger light, mechanics worked on the underbelly of ship 767, removing rivets and hammering wooden wedges between flaps where sections of the undercarriage came together, peering at the space between, determining if any corrosion had occurred there since the last heavy letter check. Examining the craft inch by inch. Sawdust-colored clay lay in piles on the floor to keep oil spills from getting slippery. Workers pedaled by on bicycles. A tour of Japanese businessmen went past, led by a Delta guide whose presentation was written down, to the last word, in a little green book the company gave him.

"Airplanes are built with a 10 percent fail factor," Martin said. "It's got 10 percent more of everything than it needs. You think of the worst possible thing that can happen and build 10 percent more."

Erwin Gettys nodded. Seven-fourteen was flying an East Coast route that day. Atlanta to Boston. Boston back home. It would have an overnight check this evening, perhaps from Rich and Jim. Tomorrow it would go to Portland, Oregon, with a stop in Salt Lake City.

Seven years after Jimmy Martin's crew put 714 in shape after the near-miss at Newark, it was still carrying passengers.

"It was a pretty tough machine to go through that and survive," Erwin Gettys said.

I would not be flying in 714 anymore, not in the cockpit. As I left Erwin Gettys and walked back to the Tech Ops parking lot, I thought back to the night I'd spent with mechanics Jim Ganopulos and Rich Steer.

When I'd left them before dawn, the long terminal corridors had been empty. The restaurants closed. The newstands locked for the night. A lone janitor had mopped C Concourse, not bothering to look up.

Hartsfield Airport had been so quiet I'd heard my heels echo as I walked.

I'd wandered awhile through the halls, past the newspaper machines, yogurt stand, bookstore, all the familiar sights of landfall to a modern air traveler. The conveniences and generic services that suck individuality from a place.

I guess I'd been saying good-bye.

In a few hours, I knew, the access roads to Hartsfield Airport would be clogged. And in the month of April 1992, ship 714 would make 107 revenue flights for Delta Air Lines. Carry over 20,000 passengers. Fly roughly 7.9 hours a day and suffer only a single delay of fifty-five minutes in Honolulu, due to a faulty fuel valve.

Queen of the fleet.

• • •

In June, I loaded my clothes back into my Honda, and headed back to New York State. A three-day trip 714 could have completed in two and a half hours. I went back to being an average passenger again. I flew on a Delta 767 to Los Angeles to give a lecture. I flew on an Air France Airbus to Cairo, on assignment for a magazine. I took a TWA 747 to Tel Aviv. On vacation. And a Twin Otter prop plane to Syracuse, to give a speech.

And each time I entered any plane I thought about the hundreds of people who took care of it: the pilots and flight attendants, the schedulers, the weather staff, the cooks in chef's hats, the cleaning men, the mechanics on the tarmac at 3 A.M., the lawyers negotiating contracts, the marketing people wooing passengers, the president of the company at the morning briefing sessions, the dispatchers planning routes, the controllers watching blips on radar screens, the FAA inspectors blending into crowds at gates, the manufacturers keeping tabs on planes they'd built, the engineers testing wing spars for cracking, the public relations people trying to make the airplanes glamorous, the revenue control analysts following millions of fare changes a week.

All of them concentrating on the flying machines. Working to keep 714 in the air.

Each time I arrived at an airport, walked through a terminal, saw a jumbo jet tail gliding by, I strained to see the number on it, hoping to see 714.

In the fall I flew to Utah to hike in the desert. A friend picked me up at the airport, and we drove south to a remote area near Canyonlands National Park. We arrived after dark. The desert night was splendid. We parked by a dirt road, unrolled bedrolls, and lay on the ground. It was a warm October evening, with a promise of good climbing tomorrow. From our sleeping bags, we looked up at bright stars.

After a while I realized some stars were moving. They were planes. I was watching one of those invisible highways in the sky. From the east, every few moments, a blinking aircraft would appear. Droning faintly, it would traverse the sky and disappear over the horizon.

At times, as many as three or four aircraft followed each other along the night.

Inside those planes passengers ate, slept, watched movies. Captains checked guidance systems. Flight attendants served drinks.

I wondered if any of those lights belonged to 714. I thought it would be funny if it was overhead at this very moment. Headed for Honolulu, maybe. Or Portland or Los Angeles. That would be a private joke between us. Both of us being here. On the ground and in the air. Up at 33,000 feet sailing along by the jet stream. Down on earth nestled against the still-warm floor of the desert. Passenger and machine. As if 714 had a consciousness and in its computer brain would get a kick out of my presence. The way I smiled, imagining it within view. We shared some kind of secret communication. Its circuits and my synapses. Its fuel and my blood.

In the desert sound carries.

"Hey 714," I said softly. "Is that you?"

ASIA

arita International Airport, serving Tokyo, lies two hours by ground from that city. Its taxiways bulge with brand-new jumbo jets, so many that a traveler feels like Gulliver in the land of the giants. Boeing 747-200s from Air Singapore and Air Malaysia and Air Iran, rolling toward takeoff, past a tiny farmer's field in the middle of the airport. Just a mound of wet earth with a few rows of scrabby trees poking from it. The man had refused to sell his land.

In the terminal, crowds of Japanese quietly gaze up at headline boards announcing news of the day: JAPANESE TEENAGE GIRL SLAIN IN AUSTRALIA. Spanking new trams whisk riders between gates and terminals as recorded voices warn in English and Japanese, "The tram will be stopping soon," so they can brace.

Several months after my last flight on 714, I stood at a gate at Narita looking out at Delta's newest acquisition, a model that will replace the L-1011s over the next decade and a half. New queen of the fleet. And a plane that, as much as 714 ever did, epitomizes the aviation advances, dangers, and controversies of its time.

Inside and out, the MD-11 was beautiful, streamlined where 714 was hawkish in landing, dolphin-shaped at the gate. The nacelles closer to the body, the hull more gently rounded, like a torpedo. The end of each wing angled sharply upward, as if retractable, which they are not. "Winglets" improve air flow and fuel efficiency.

The third engine, on the tail, lacked the thick bulge of the S-shaped intake duct on the Lockheed models. The intake worked straightaway here, as on the MD-11's predecessor, the DC-10.

Truth was, I felt a little guilty admiring the plane. Delta was replacing the L-1011s with the next generation of their old enemy.

Outside, dusk had fallen, and a light rain gave the plane a sheen. The illusion of compactness was so profound that it was a surprise to remember that the MD-11 could carry 248 passengers for Delta up to 6,900 miles without refueling.

In one hour it was scheduled to take 150 American and Japanese passengers, including myself, 4,343 miles to Portland, Oregon, a projected eight-and-a-half-hour trip. Takeoff weight, 504,000 pounds. Fuel needed just for this trip, 167,000 pounds. Cloudy skies and possible turbulence predicted as we headed northeast out of Narita at 37,000 feet, crossed the International Date Line near the western tip of the Aleutian Islands, flew over the Bering Sea, the Alaskan peninsula, and the Gulf of Alaska. Then we would turn southeast and descend over the north Pacific, making landfall at Olympia National Park.

A Delta gate agent escorted me into the plane. Inside, male and female Japanese workers in lavender jump suits, black peaked caps, and cotton cloth booties polished and cleaned. The New World Symphony pumped from the intercom. The video screens showed American wilderness scenes to rows of empty seats. The great Pacific Northwest forest. The desert of the Southwest.

Unlike 714, with its brighter gold and aquamarine colors, the MD-11s were done in soothing grays and blues, "nonagitation hues," a consultant at McDonnell Douglas had explained. Unlike 714, the ship lacked an elevator, so flight attendants didn't have to lug food up from a galley below. (No sex either. Rats.) Unlike 714, the First Class section looked extra spacious, more like a luxury movie screening room, with wide leather "sleeperettes," and electronically controlled recline, lumbar support, and leg rest.

"Voice recorder!"

"Checked!"

"Hydraulic panel!"

But the big change was the cockpit. It required only two pilots, not three. Capt. Nick Gentile, whom I'd met out in the terminal, was a thirty-year Delta veteran and would be line check airman on today's flight, just as OJ Greene had been the first time I flew in 714. Once again I'd be watching someone learn to fly a plane.

Capt. Dick Seals, making his second supervised trip as pilot on an MD-11, would be at the controls. Gentile was a fifty-eight-year-old ex-native of Staten Island, a blocky, good-natured man who'd flown everything from DC-6s to Convair 880s to ship 714 during his time with the company. Seals was a white-haired, youthful looking Coloradan with weather lines on his face and a Harley-Davidson sticker on his briefcase. He'd come to MD-11s from flying Boeing 727s, a much older plane.

I remained quiet while they prepared. The instruments they worked on looked nothing like 714's. Gone were the dials, gauges, and meters. Six video screens lined the console instead, glowing with easy-to-read information in electric blues, purples, and whites, information duplicated in front of each pilot.

Looking over their shoulders, I read "hydraulics," "electric," "air," "engines" on one screen. The computers could simultaneously and automatically monitor these systems. On another screen I saw diagrams of the fuel tanks, and the amount of fuel inside. The flight master, the little blue basketball floating behind glass, the cross hairs pilots used to keep the plane on track, the instrument that had driven me crazy when I'd tried to fly the L-1011 simulator, was a video depiction here, not a real ball.

"In the MD-11," a McDonnell Douglas PR release I'd read had bragged, "pilots have become aircraft flight managers."

The flight engineer and his instrument panel were gone, their functions computerized now. There was still an instrument pedestal between the two pilots, for navigation, but there was also a lot more empty space on the walls.

"Pac Man pilots," was the way McDonnell Douglas engineer Joe Ornelias, a designer of the cockpit, described its crews.

Now flight attendant coordinator Michele Gorman stuck her head in the cockpit. "Everybody's down," she said. Gentile told Air Traffic Control in English, the international language of aviation, "Delta five two. We have our engines running. We're clear to push."

We proceeded down the taxiway in light fog. The amber and crimson ground lights glowed with an intensity I'd only seen in simulators. I was strapped into a jump seat behind Dick Seals's left shoulder, the same place I'd be in 714, but lower down. Seals needed seven supervised crossings and four takeoffs and landings before he could command a ship.

To my right, in a fourth seat, sat relief pilot Roy Gustaveson. Relief pilots are required on any flight over eight hours long for a two-person cockpit. All three men scanned the sky and instruments as we sped down the runway, and there was that exhilarating instant of liftoff, and the ground fell away, and we were climbing.

At 4,000 feet we hit turbulence. I found myself yearning for 714, never mind how it was eighteen years older. I remembered reading about problems a few early MD-11s had had. Like the one the FAA had found in December 1991 when it ordered airlines to inspect their MD-11s for cracking and wing-flap peeling that had appeared on several aircraft.

"This condition, if not corrected, could result in fatigue cracking and possible structural failure of the outboard flap," the FAA's airworthiness directive had said.

And the directive the agency had released before that, saying an "uncontained fuel leak" had been detected in an aft fuselage compartment on one MD-11, which had been improperly sealed.

"This condition, if not corrected, could result in a fuel leak and the possibility of an in-flight or ground fire," the directive had said.

Or how about the fact that several MD-11s had developed software problems in flight?

We rose to 8,000 feet, the lights of Japan below, blinking in and out from clouds. Delta hadn't found any cracking or peeling on its MD-11s. It hadn't found any fuel leaks either. "Teething problems," was how Delta's Bill Berry had described the early glitches to the press. Nothing dangerous. "When you put a new airplane in the air, you expect these types of teething problems."

At 10,000 feet I asked Nick Gentile about it. "The Lockheed 1011s had a lot more kinks than this one did when they came on line," he said, making me feel better. "There was never any danger," he said. "These things are normal on a new plane."

Gentile turned off the seat-belt sign. In the cabin the flight attendants would be starting service. We rose above the clouds, and I saw the early stars. The flight grew smooth. Steadily, we climbed toward our assigned cruising altitude.

"Is it hard to learn to fly this thing?" I asked Dick Seals.

He turned sideways and grinned like a cowpoke. He seemed glad class was over. "Hardest thing I ever did in my life."

In the future, some aviation writers predict, cockpits may only hold one pilot. Cockpits may be built without forward views. Instead of looking out, pilots may use "virtual reality"—three-dimensional simulations re-creating sight, touch, and sound.

I remembered, looking out the window, how in *Scientific American* I'd seen a picture of an Air Force pilot with a gargoylelike helmet over his head, making him look like something from the movie *The Fly*. A picture beside that showed what the man was looking at inside the helmet, which was a landscape like a cross between a cartoon and a video game. The caption had read, "A more advanced version of this helmet might one day let a pilot fly an actual fighter aircraft while watching a scene that resembles a video arcade game."

At McDonnell Douglas, in Long Beach, I'd told Engineer Joe Ornelias that even the two-man cockpit reminded me of the joke I'd heard often in 714, about the cockpit of the future holding a pilot and a dog. The pilot to watch the controls. The dog to bite him if he touches them.

"I'm glad you said it, not me," Joe said.

Ornelias had explained how the MD-11's two-man cockpit had been designed. "Three of us worked on it," he said. "A pilot. A flight engineer. And me. The airlines told us they wanted to go to two pilots for cost reduction. But the workload for the two pilots would never exceed the workload on a DC-10. We looked at the instruments. We asked ourselves, how do we get rid of the flight engineer tasks? We ended up with a couple of new philosophies. First, if we can tell a pilot or flight engineer to do something, we can automate it. Second, if a flight engineer has a lever or button he moves, we can automate those. We can create aircraft systems controllers. And automate the way pilots scan their instruments."

The upshot, Delta pilot Jerry Battenhouse had told me on the flight to Japan yesterday, was "less work for us. Less chance for miscommunication with two pilots. The pictorial navigation system means you don't have to stop and figure out where you are.

There's less chance of error. It's safer. This plane is probably more reliable than the old L-1011. The automation is a little more difficult to learn, but once you do it—and automation has reached such a stage of reliability that all the glitches are out—well, it's a great plane to fly."

Still, automation can be a controversial subject. Is it possible to put *too much* automation in a cockpit? some scientists ask. To reach a critical threshold where so much control is taken away from a pilot that a plane becomes *less* safe?

Take the "stick pusher." A stick pusher is an automated device in some planes, not in an MD-11, that automatically pushes the throttle up if it senses that a plane is about to stall. That's a pretty good idea when a plane is up at 30,000 feet, but a couple of years ago during an air show in France, an Airbus 320 was coming in for a landing, slowed a little too much, approached stall, and the stick pusher drove the throttle up and shot the plane into a forest, where it crashed, and killed all aboard.

Critics also worry that too much automation may produce overconfidence in crews, and dangerous complacency. They point to an Air China 747 which fell 30,000 feet on the way to San Francisco in 1986, after it rolled over in the air. The crew, preoccupied with restoring engine power to a failed number 4 engine, and figuring that the plane would keep itself steady, failed to notice the roll starting. Miraculously the pilot got the plane under control, and landed.

And shortly before that, a DC-10 ran off the runway at Kennedy Airport when the autothrottle failed, and the crew, unaware of it, failed to realize the plane was moving too fast.

After the DC-10 incident, the National Transportation Safety Board ordered the FAA to begin research on possible problems relating to "degradation of pilot performance as a result of automation."

Back when I'd visited McDonnell Douglas, Joe Ornelias had been acutely aware of the line between automating a pilot into nothing more than a passive monitor of computers, and keeping him or her an active participant in flying.

"You walk the line," he said. "You give him information. You allow him to selectively process data. You allow the pilot at any time to selectively override the system. But more and more the environment is becoming structured. The old flight engineers were mechanics. They could take apart an engine. The Eddie Rickenbackers are gone now, the guys with scarfs on their heads."

On the down side of automation, finally and ironically, came the charge from critics that while automation decreases pilot workload during quieter times in flight, it can actually *increase* it during critical landing and takeoff.

"You get into a situation with a computerized plane, where, say, you're coming into Atlanta, or Dallas," one pilot of 714 had told me, over the Pacific one day. He'd asked me not to use his name. "Then Air Traffic Control suddenly wants you to change to a different runway. In an automated plane the tendency is to program your computer for the new runway, instead of just flying it in. You get occupied trying to reprogram the computer. You're flying heads down, looking at the computer, not scanning the sky."

"Does that happen a lot?" I'd asked.

"Too much. And quite frankly, it can be very . . ."

"Harrowing?"

"Yes," said the pilot, who had flown automated 767s for Delta. "I didn't want to say dangerous. You have two people. The copilot's on the radio. The captain's flying, or vice versa. But they're both preoccupied, heads down looking at the computer when they ought to be looking out. You get so tied up with automation you're not flying the airplane anymore. You're programming it."

"What would you say to a passenger worried about flying in planes with two-man cockpits?" I said. "Because it sounds like you're saying they're less safe."

The pilot had grown a little uncomfortable. "We have classes on this subject," he said. "They let us know it's a problem. Anyway, when you're coming in, you shouldn't be changed to another runway."

"But you just said Air Traffic Control *does* change you."

The pilot had sighed. "Yeah, they do it. And then they say, 'Wanna go around?' And to go around would take another fifteen minutes. The company says safety first. They'll never criticize a crew for taking a conservative approach to safety," he said.

"Then what are you complaining about?"

"There's a lot of subtle pressure to do the job."

"Let's get to the bottom line," I said. "Because it sounds like you're going back and forth on this. Are you saying it's just a matter of time before an automated plane gets in trouble?"

"No. You come through it, but you've been pushed to the limit of what you can do safely because of those changes in runways," the pilot said. "But it's safe."

So I'd figured it was one more case of "what if?" The old "what if" question, continuing into the twenty-first century. Aviation people obsessing about what can go wrong to keep it from happening. What if the runway gets changed? What if the pilot gets bored? What if the computer breaks?

The machines kept changing but the fundamental question remained the same.

Even Earl Wiener—the University of Miami professor famous in aviation for his research on automation and "vigilance monitoring," human factors related to automation, a man who regularly brings up all the concerns about automation in flight in his writings— wrote in one paper, "Overall, the movement toward cockpit automation has undoubtedly enhanced safety." And when I'd had lunch with him in Miami, he'd told me, over burgers at a dockside restaurant, "Nobody knows how many accidents have been prevented by automation."

So now, up at 37,000 feet, I asked Nick Gentile and Dick Seals and Roy Gustaveson if they thought there would ever come a point where only one pilot flew an airliner.

"Not in my cockpit," Gentile said.

Or if they thought there would ever be airliners built without a forward view.

"Uh uh," Gentile said.

"They couldn't build a plane for only one pilot," Dick Seals said. "What if the computer goes down. Do you realize how much work that would be if there was only one pilot in the cockpit?"

"Has that ever happened to you? A computer going down?" I said.

Nick Gentile grinned. "I'm sifting through the myriad of times," he said.

"Here's another reason there'll never be only one pilot in the cockpit," Roy Gustaveson said, getting up and heading for the door. "I'm going to the bathroom. How do you do that if there's only one person at the controls?"

I left the cockpit when the pilots began taking breaks, since they needed both of the jump seats to do it. One by one they'd stretch out between the seats, close their eyes, maybe throw a blanket on.

In First Class I leaned back in the leather sleeperette, feeling like I was in that luxury screening room again. There was only one other passenger in First today, but we had up to three flight attendants taking care of us. On the seat beside me was my First Class overnight kit, zippered, in burgundy leather, containing backless slippers, Scope, Wilkinson shave cream, an emery board, Lubriderm lotion, blinders for sleeping, a razor, a toothbrush and toothpaste.

Michele Gorman brought a cart with a sushi selection on it. I looked longingly at the next offering, iced Stolichnaya vodka and silver trays of caviar. I left the liquor alone. No drinking allowed for anyone in a cockpit.

Today's movies would be *Sneakers*, with Robert Redford, and the original *Grand Hotel*. I ate fresh garden salad. Herb-encrusted rack of lamb with rosemary and grain mustard sauce, served with braised leeks, carrots with pear brandy, and a potato-and-turnip puree flavored with roasted coriander. A selection of red and white wines I passed up. A fruit and cheese tray. Ice cream sundaes or tarts for dessert. Hot coffee. Chocolate mints.

What a life. These transoceanic flights had to be the apex of luxury for a First Class airline passenger. It made me think back to Long Beach, where when I'd visited McDonnell Douglas I'd spent a night on the *Queen Mary*, once an ocean liner, then a hotel. Before turning in I'd strolled through the mansion-sized hallways, the promenades, the bars. From the prow I'd looked out at the lights of Long Beach. In my cabin, I'd savored the deep bed and fine wooden walls. At one time this had been the way people crossed oceans. A far cry from being seat-belted into a leather chair, plugged into a video outlet, watching Robert Redford run down a street.

Of course the *Queen Mary* had needed a bit more than eight hours to cross an ocean. In the time the ship could get from New

York to London, an MD-11 could go Tokyo to Portland over twenty times. Just yesterday I'd overheard Flight Attendant Coordinator Michele Gorman complaining to Relief Pilot Jim Fox that she'd be working on her birthday, in Japan, two days from now. Then I'd been surprised to realize she wasn't even talking about this trip, but the next one. That meant three trips across the ocean for her in as many days, including a day or two off. No big deal in 1993. Like taking a bus. The discussion was about where to get a drink, not how fantastic it was for planes to make the trip.

I also knew that the luxury of the cabin as well as the Asian route we were flying and the $100 million plane itself were all part of Delta's long-range gamble, in 1993, to survive the carnage in the U.S. airline industry, to grow into a global megacarrier, to emerge, in the twenty-first century, as one of the two or three premier airlines in the world.

The principle is, experts say, that as the global air market becomes more deregulated in the new century, airlines will be less protected by their governments, they will be permitted to expand to markets where they were barred before, will be able to take passengers away from other airlines that were protected before, and had better grow into these new markets or they will be closed out of them, shrink, and die.

But instituting this growth theory had turned bloody for Delta in the year since I'd started work on this book. It's reputation, bright and untarnished a year ago, was hurting. To read why, I picked the *Barron's* financial newspaper off the seat beside me. Concerned flight attendants had lent it to me.

The cover drawing showed a Delta jet with a hot water bottle on its head and a thermometer in its mouth. "Delta Air Lines, once the premier company in its industry, runs into stiff financial headwinds that have cratered earnings and threaten credit ratings," read the summary.

Delta's working capital had dropped to a $1.84 billion deficit from $263.1 million the year before, the piece said. Senior debt had been downgraded on the financial market to triple B, and some of Delta's debt was on Standard & Poor Corporation's credit watch.

"Until recently Delta was the envy of the airline industry but . . . Tara is no more," *Barron's* said. . . . "The company's management

is in a panic." . . . "Delta has fared even worse than its main rivals."
. . . "The carrier is currently just a few notches above junkland."

The Pan Am sale had hurt. So had the fare war. And the recession. Over the last few months Delta had tried to slow the hemorrhaging with some unprecedented changes. A 5 percent management pay cut. Medical plan deductibles up, not by much, but up. Pilots reducing their maximum flying hours for a month to keep seventy-five pilots from being furloughed. A layoff of temporary employees. Within months, pilots would be furloughed.

"We're going to do everything possible to avoid permanent employee layoffs, but we can't rule them out," Chief Financial Officer Tom Roeck had told *Barron's*. Roeck, I remembered, had been the man with all those little glass paperweights on his office shelves, commemorating debt.

Barron's was tough on Delta. The Pan Am deal had been a "blunder." The company had been slow to get into the European market, and had been shut out of Heathrow Airport as a result, *Barron's* charged. Delta had further fallen behind its rivals by being slow in instituting a computerized reservation system. Not to mention that it paid its employees more than any other U.S. airline, an average of $56,816 in 1991.

And yet to reduce the compensation package could invite unpleasant repercussions. Damage to traditionally warm management/employee relations could give "a jolt to employee morale that could cost Delta its vaunted service reputation with the high-margin business customer," *Barron's* said. "The choices are likely to be agonizing for a company that puts such stock in family spirit."

I knew that, considering how fast the airline industry changes, by the time this book came out, Delta could be triple A again. Riding high again. Back to profitability again. Or for all I knew, it could be broke.

But at the moment how humiliating this all must be for management accustomed to high praise from the industry.

I asked Chairman Ron Allen about it a few weeks later on a warm January Atlanta day. Delta's financial situation hadn't gotten any better in the interim, according to news reports. Allen was a tall, cordial man, soft-spoken in a deep-voiced way, bald on top, with a slightly hooded, avuncular look, deceptive in the sense that he got down to the bottom line right away.

The fiscal situation *was* serious, he said. Serious enough that Delta's survival was at stake—not as a company, necessarily, but as its traditional, southern, paternalistic, service-oriented, family-style self. Cross-legged in an easy chair in a corner of his office, gesturing with his big hands as he made points, Allen said that working in the airline industry in the early 1990s was like playing football in a game where the rules kept changing.

"You need ten yards to get a first down," Allen said. "Suddenly, you find out you need twenty."

"Which rules have changed in the last year?" I asked.

The fare wars were one example, he said. "That four-tier fare structure and the half-fare war cost us an estimated $800 million in 1993.

"Fare wars hurt everybody," he said, meaning airlines. But Delta had to go along with them because once you lose customers, it's hard to get them back.

"If fare wars are destructive why do smart people start them?" I said.

"Many people take the short-term view." And anyway, the problem was bigger than just fare wars, he said. A major problem was that healthy airlines had to compete with bankrupt ones. Healthy airlines, like any healthy business, had to pay their creditors, and needed to generate enough revenue to do that. Bankrupt ones, "propped up by subsidies from the bankruptcy court," were protected from their creditors. This meant they could keep operating if they charged enough to pay their workers and meet daily operating costs. And *that* meant they could charge lower prices than airlines that were healthy.

By keeping bankrupt airlines operating, Allen was saying, bankruptcy courts may be saving jobs, but they also fundamentally weaken healthy carriers.

"Another change, in the last five to seven years . . . ," Allen said, "we've had a lot of financiers come in to the business with very self-centered interests. Some of 'em have gotten their personal cash out of the business and basically to hell with the rest of the business, including the people in their own companies. You have individuals focused on taking all the value out of a company. That's what some of these leveraged buyouts have done in America. And then you have a very sick airline, and they start doing irrational things from the standpoint of long-term health. But we have to compete with them."

"But what about your problems caused by the Pan Am buyout?" I asked. "That wasn't a rule change but a choice on your part." Allen nodded grimly when I brought up the *Barron's* article and *USA Today* piece. They'd hurt personally, he said, grimacing.

"*USA Today* said we're an airline in a tailspin. Yeah, I mean, it's in a *dive*, but I'd call it a controlled dive," he said. "And we're unhappy with the fact that revenue's going south on us. But Pan Am. That deal was still right. It was a crunch up there. You're basically at an auction of the bankruptcy court. That final day, on a Sunday afternoon, you're bidding against all the other airlines to get pieces of Pan Am. We'd done as good an analysis as we could on the potential of all the routes, back in the spring, and our data was pretty good. What we didn't have was data on the condition of some of the Pan Am facilities and equipment. We knew they were bad. We knew the JFK terminal would need some help. And we got the best airplanes they had. But the cabins were shoddy in some cases. Not laid out properly for the kind of internal service we provide.

"The other factor is, Pan Am had a proud old name, but we didn't realize how much that name had deteriorated. So the passenger mix was weak," he said, meaning in part that the people who flew Pan Am at the end were not necessarily fiercely loyal passengers guaranteed to return.

"We probably should have jumped on the transition quicker and more drastically," Allen said. But he said, unwaveringly, "I feel like Pan Am is one of the most important things we've ever done. Despite the problems, I feel better today having that competitive transatlantic feed and the ability to compete. What if we hadn't done it? We'd have a little bit more cash reserves but we'd also have less ability to generate revenue. It would be very difficult for us to go out and develop things at the same costs we got the Pan Am routes for.

"We would have lost the opportunity of a lifetime."

Allen leaned forward. His wall units were filled with souvenirs garnered over decades. A plaque of mounted wings off an Aeroflot crew he'd flown with in the cockpit during a visit to the old Soviet Union. A baseball commemorating the airline's sponsorship of the Braves in 1987. A little Rolls-Royce engine on a plaque in memory of an engine that lasted longer than any other without needing repair. Lots of hardhats from Delta construction projects. A weird homemade screwdriver on a plaque, a joke from the mechanics to Allen after, on one flight, he helped pry free a passenger locked in a bathroom because the crew was flying the plane. "Toolkit in Flight Repair," said the caption.

Allen still did an occasional shift with cabin services people. "It shows them management's not some ivory tower executives sitting up here making decisions about our people's future without relating to them." He still answered his own phone sometimes. "Someone'll call saying, 'I got a complaint. I'd like to talk to Ron Allen.' I say, 'I'm Ron Allen. What's the complaint?' "

Allen said, "Three years ago Delta was criticized for being conservative. *Not* growing. *Not* being competitive. We *were* growing, but we wanted to pay attention to what was going on around us. Now the same people say Delta's grown too much. I don't agree with that. You could not predict these losses. We were extremely well prepared going into the summer of 1992.

"If we'd just tried to stay put and not grow and protect our routes, we would have been taken over by someone else by now."

Allen laughed when I brought up the line from *USA Today* that his effort to make Delta prosper again was "the fight of his life." But more somberly he agreed that the airline would have to make more changes to make up for the mammoth losses.

"We must do what we must do," he said, meaning that when further cuts must be made, everything would be on the table. "The pay cuts? We agonized over it. We didn't just say, take that out of our people's hides. We tried for a balance. A conglomeration of capital expenditures reduction, cost reduction, and reduction of individual salaries," said Allen, who'd cut his own salary 20 percent.

"Our people are still paid well. I want to protect their jobs, but they're not guaranteed." And even the dreaded furloughs wouldn't "violate the trust we have with our people if they understand the tough choices and agonizing decisions we have to make," he hoped.

"Furloughs are a last resort," I said.

"Yes."

"Are you closer to doing that?"

"Yes. We've used up a lot of our options. We've got to turn this situation around." And we've got to do it, Allen said, without damaging the fundamental cooperative mood that existed throughout the company—which I had seen over and over during my time there.

Within two weeks, Delta would furlough some newer pilots.

"I had a *USA Today* reporter in here," Allen said, "and he asked me, 'Why do you think Delta is going to come out of this?' And I told him a story about his own publisher, who I was riding with in a car some years back, and she started telling me about the uniqueness of Delta, the spirit, the environment of approval and caring for the company. His own publisher, and she spent time studying these things. Hell, we got to build on that. Not tear up the formula. We got to protect it. You know what kind of response we got after the pay cut? Approval. Letters from people.

"But I worry about it.

"Maybe someone from the outside could come in and really tear our costs down and get great reviews from Wall Street. I think that would be the wrong decision. We're gonna make the decisions but we're gonna keep Delta's uniqueness in mind."

"You sound confident," I said. "But bottom line, could Delta be broke in five years?"

He didn't hesitate. "Any company can. Sure."

Which brought us back to furloughs. Allen told me a story about years before when, as head of personnel, he'd have to fire people.

"It was always wrenching. I finally had to come up with the conviction that I was protecting Delta Air Lines, our core strength. If you allow someone to go on and on working, you lose the respect of everyone working around that person. Rules are being eroded. You're doing no good, and the majority of people no good. And that's what I'm doing right now.

"I remember one mechanic. He and his wife came to see me when I was in personnel. He was irresponsible. I counseled him and his wife, thought I'd gotten through to him. They were financially overcommitted, and he'd get distracted from his job. Then two months later he'd be back. Finally I had to cut the tie on someone like that." But Allen's voice softened when he said it. Then his voice hardened.

"You have to do it," he said.

"This is such a tradition-minded company, and you've come up through the ranks," I said. "Do you ever carry on conversations in your mind with Mr. Woolman about problems?"

"I don't carry on conversations with anyone in my mind," Allen said. "But sometimes I wonder what Mr. Woolman would think about how we've done." He half turned in his seat to indicate three chairs halfway across the room, facing his desk.

"I sat in that middle chair right there," he said, "and Mr. Woolman gave me fatherly advice. I'd travel with him. I felt a kinship with him because I really liked what he said about people. That's one of the reasons I came to Delta. The people aspect of the business, working to bring out the best in them.

"Mr. Woolman was a wonderful, wonderful man. But he was just a man. We like to immortalize people and put 'em on a pedestal. We forget their faults and flaws, and Mr. Woolman had his share. I don't mean to be degrading him. He was a unique individual. But the fact is, after Mr. Woolman died, Delta started expanding some of those traditions."

Allen laughed in a private way that made me wonder if people often brought up Mr. Woolman in his presence. "Mr. Woolman knew everybody. Shook their hand. Well, I'd love to do that. If we were still operating with two hangers out there. A couple thousand people. Instead of 75,000. I still get around as much as I can. I've gone over and worked cabin service with a Delta ramp uniform. I don't think Mr. Woolman did that.

"I think Mr. Woolman would be proud of us," he said. "How far we've come. I remember the day Mr. Woolman's body was flown in here, September 1966, in an old C-130 cargo plane. A windy afternoon. I remember standing out there. I'd been with the company three years, some of it part-time. I'd had a chance to travel with Mr. Woolman . . . I think he'd be proud."

Meanwhile, there was business to complete, as usual. So far, on the day we met, Allen had been catching up on work after five days lost to the flu and a week on jury duty. He'd started work at 6:30, read reports, talked on the phone with American Airlines Chairman Robert Crandall as airlines looked for a new head for the Air Transport Association. He'd gone to lunch with a reporter from the Atlanta paper. He'd conducted meetings to prepare for scheduling and financial-analysis meetings scheduled two weeks later. He'd also gotten a letter from a man complaining about mechanical problems on an L-1011.

"A passenger?"

"Yes. He and his wife had been delayed. I sent it over to Russ Heil so he could check it over and call the man back."

I was surprised. Russ Heil was the vice president of technical operations, rumored heir apparent to the chairmanship, a powerful man within the company with thousands of workers under him. I figured the letter had come from someone notable.

"Who wrote the letter?" I asked.

Allen didn't understand why I was asking the question. "I don't know who he was," he said. "He was a passenger."

What if? What if? Long into the twenty-first century, for as long as commercial jets continue to fly, long after space travel begins for commercial passengers, the keepers of flying machines will undoubtedly keep asking themselves, "What if?"

What if, in the middle of the Pacific Ocean, 2,000 miles from land, the computers go down? No more picture. No more navigation system. How does the pilot get the plane home?

"I'll show you how, now," Nick Gentile told Dick Seals.

Back in the cockpit rest period was long over. We approached the West Coast. It was standard procedure to show the new guy how to operate if the nav system goes out.

"We don't do this over the middle of the ocean because there's a chance we might not get the system back," Gentile said. "But we're close enough to land now."

Gentile switched off the dual nav systems and brought one back on line immediately, so after the demonstration, if the first one stayed off, he would still have automatic navigation.

We flew through a soup of colorless clouds 37,000 feet up, the sky outside not even gray, not even white, just bleached and thick and nameless. Screens glowing. Engines throbbing. No sense of movement in the cockpit, above the North Pacific.

"If you lose the FMS [navigation] system, the basic computation system, you lose the ability to hook it into your autopilot," Nick said. "You lose your power computation for the throttle. The autopilot will no longer be navigating, but it won't tell you that."

"Out over the ocean, you'll have to go to dead reckoning," Nick said. What he meant was, during a system outage, a pilot should go to his charts and maps to compute position and route. He pulled out the flight map of today's route, with its little checkpoints along the way. Gentile located the last checkpoint we'd passed. He stabbed his finger into the next one on the route.

"Okay, the average true course between these two points is 107 degrees," he said. It was like being back in high school math. What he meant was, if you picture a circle, that circle is 360 degrees all the way around. If a plane is sitting in the middle of it, zero degrees is straight north, 180 degrees straight south, 107 degrees somewhere between that, in the southeast.

"But you figure at least a 25-degree magnetic variation," he said. "And a drift correction of 6 percent because of wind. So the average magnetic reading becomes 76 degrees, more or less. When you computed our heading after that last turn, what was it?"

Seals looked impressed. "Seventy-six degrees," he said.

Gentile didn't look surprised. "So you put it on 76 degrees," he said. "You wait for the plane to steady out. Then you do time/distance. And you'll come down close. Or if you can find that airplane out there, follow him. There are a lot of days you can see contrails. One night I flew all the way, side by side with a Cathay Pacific 747, and we could have followed each other across. That happens a lot. Don't forget that."

We were just about home. This would be my last flight in the cockpit of a Delta jet. I asked Nick Gentile, in all his years of flying Delta airplanes, if he had a favorite model.

He smiled. "The L-1011. Best flying airplane I've ever known."

"Better than this?" I said, looking at the cockpit filled with technological marvels around us.

"Yes." His smile broadened. "The L-1011 didn't have the magic, didn't have the automation. But it had the best engineering; engineering that in 1966 exceeded the engineering of 1990. It flew great. It handled weather better'n any plane I ever flew. Crosswinds. Thunderstorms. Ice. Snow. It has greater capability than this airplane. It was the best."

We were down to 18,000 feet. We'd reach 10,000 feet soon and go to silent cockpit. "Do you miss the TriStars?" I asked.

"Yep."

"You could be flying them still."

"Well," he said, "I developed this training program for the MD-11, and I'm still here."

Delta Senior Vice-President Russ Heil had told me ship 714 might fly for Delta until 1996. Which meant it would outlast Nick Gentile, who was scheduled for retirement a year before that. Afterward, he said, he might fly for a foreign airline, but he'd miss Delta. And there was always the hope that magically, the retirement age would change. In the meantime, as more MD-11s came on line, there were lots of new MD-11 pilots to train.

And at the moment there was the landing to take care of. "Landings are harder than takeoffs on this plane," he said. "Because it's got a computerized tail. The computer operates the horizontal stabilizer. It gives the plane a certain feel down to 100 feet, then it quits, and the pilot has to take over. Suddenly the plane has a different feel."

So much of a different feel, he said, that a few times, during landings, he'd had to take over control from his students.

"At a hundred feet?" I said, thinking, That's pretty close to the ground.

"No. At a hundred feet I can still talk to him. Generally it happens right down by the runway."

"Do the pilots get angry and humiliated when that happens?"

"Yep."

"What's the—uh, most memorable time you had to take over?" I asked, unsure if I really wanted to hear this before landing.

Nick roared with laughter. "I don't remember," he said, and laughed again.

I pulled both shoulder straps down and snapped them in, and brought two side straps over my thighs. This would be Dick Seals's second landing as supervised pilot of an MD-11. Portland, coming into view below and fading out regularly through clouds, was dusted with snow. All three pilots leaned forward intently, scanning the sky. Dick worked the yoke. Nick, in the right seat, had his hands on his lap but within grabbing distance of the controls.

The gears went down with a rumble. "Landing gear down and four green," Nick called out, meaning the system was working. The plane was buffeted by wind so violently that later I would find out the flight attendants in back were joking that I was landing it.

As we approached the runway, a Northwest 747 touched down ahead of us, smoke puffing up by the wheels, rolled forward, began to turn out of the way.

More wind buffeted us.

"Don't hesitate to blast out like any other airplane if you have a problem," Nick said calmly.

"Two hundred fifty feet," he said.

"A hundred fifty!"

At a hundred feet, when the computer would stop controlling the horizontal stabilizer, Nick's hand slid closer to his yoke but still didn't touch it. The move was so subtle you had to be watching to see it.

We hit the runway hard, and Dick reversed thrust on the engines and the MD-11 slowed. "Good landing," Nick said. Back in the cabin, the passengers clapped.

One hour later I boarded a Delta 757 for my flight to Salt Lake City and home to New York. I was a regular passenger again now. No more cockpit flights. I sat in First Class and sipped a Manhattan and the man beside me introduced himself as Max, and said he owned an employment agency in New York.

"Look at that one! *That's* a beautiful plane," he said, eyeing one of the MD-11s out his window. "Delta's buying lots of those. And *that's* an L-1011, it was pretty advanced for its time," he said, spotting tail number 712 going by. "Last week I was at an air show in St. Louis. Wow. Those fighter jets," Max said.

He whistled admiringly. "You barely see them in the distance, and suddenly they're overhead."

Max and I chatted about aviation. He was an aviation enthusiast, he said, although not technologically knowledgeable about planes.

After a while he grew a little quiet and lowered his voice.

"I have to say one thing though, one thing I've never been able to figure out," he said. He leaned closer. He grinned shyly. Suddenly he looked like a ten-year-old.

I knew that look. I knew what he was going to say.

"Well," he said. "Um," he said.

Max looked around and his grin broadened.

"How does this thing really stay in the air?"

INDEX